Follow the
Shaman's Call

## About the Author

Mike Williams, Ph.D., (United Kingdom) is a shamanic practitioner and teacher trained in soul retrieval, spirit extraction, divination, and assisting the dead and dying. A founding member of the South Wales Shamanic Group, Williams studied with indigenous shamanic teachers in Siberia and Lapland and attended teaching sessions with Native American elders.

Mike Williams, Ph.D.

Follow the
Shaman's Call

An Ancient Path for
Modern Lives

Llewellyn Publications
Woodbury, Minnesota

First Edition
Fourth Printing, 2014

Cover art © Ron Dahlquist/SuperStock
Cover design by Lisa Novak
Editing by Rosemary Wallner
Llewellyn is a registered trademark of Llewellyn Worldwide Ltd.

**Library of Congress Cataloging-in-Publication Data**

Williams, Mike, 1968–
 Follow the shaman's call : an ancient path for modern lives / Mike Williams. — 1st ed.
     p.    cm.
 Includes bibliographical references.
 ISBN 978-0-7387-1984-9
 1. Shamanism. I. Title.
 BF1611.W76 2010
 201'.44—dc22

                                                                2009041698

Llewellyn Publications
A Division of Llewellyn Worldwide Ltd.
2143 Wooddale Drive
Woodbury, Minnesota 55125-2989
www.llewellyn.com

Printed in the United States of America

## Forthcoming Books by This Author

*Prehistoric Belief: Shamans, Trance and the Afterlife*
(Stroud: The History Press)

*For Vanessa*

# Contents

# Acknowledgements

Throughout the writing of this book, I have been thinking of you, my reader. I am both humbled and privileged that you are considering drawing my words into your life, and I hope that we shall enjoy our time in each other's company. With you so much in my thoughts as I wrote the book, it is to you that I offer my first thanks of acknowledgement. I sincerely hope I have lived up to the words I wanted to offer you.

I would also like to offer my deepest thanks to those I have met on my spiritual quest this far and to acknowledge the help that they have given me in writing this book. I have liberally drawn on their wisdom and experiences but, in every case, have changed both names and identifying characteristics to preserve anonymity. Despite this, you still shine brightly from the pages of the book.

To all those involved in the production of this book, particularly Carrie Obry, Nanette Stearns, and Rosemary Wallner at Llewellyn, and Matt Botwood for making the author photograph session painless (for me). I feel privileged that we will always be connected through the book.

To my agents, Susan Mears and Julian Robbins, for their faith. Your help, encouragement, and warmth towards a new author reveals the soul in what you do. Denise Ward was also wonderfully helpful in the early stages of the book's development.

To Sarah Howcroft-Lane for organising and running our shamanic journey circle and especially to Barbie, Kath, and David for trying out some of the exercises included in the book. Your company means a lot to me.

To Professor Richard Bradley, who was my supervisor when I took my Ph.D. at Reading University. Although your interest in shamanism might be strictly academic, I think you would have been recognised in the past as one of the truly great shamans.

To Simon Buxton who, through his Sacred Trust, has arranged and organised so many teachers and guides from around the world to share their knowledge with so many of us. Your work is, indeed, sacred.

To Nick Breeze Wood from *Sacred Hoop*, and Timothy White from *Shaman's Drum*, two of the best shamanic magazines on the planet, for printing some of my words and thoughts. Encouragement to a developing writer is worth more than gold.

To my wonderful, wonderful tutees in the Order of Bards, Ovates, and Druids. All of you are in my heart but Al, Anna, Brian, Nadia, and Vicki touched the book in ways that were special. I would also like to thank Susan, Gladys, and Sara for making the tutee system work so amazingly well for both tutor and tutee, and Mary, for being everything a tutor should be.

To my Russian friends, Balgze, Damba, Dolgor, Luba, Marina, Nadya, and the families that allowed me into their homes and shared their lives with me. As you said at the time, our ancestors are the same and I will never forget your kindness.

To my Sámi friends and, in particular, Nillas and Mardoeke for their enthusiasm for the book. What you shared, I still treasure.

To all of those who have sat with me in a circle and shared something of the incredible power of shamanism, but especially to Christina, Deirdre, Elizabeth, Jenny, Jude, and Rowen. You all have a place in my heart.

To those who, over the years, have touched me so deeply that you are now my Tribe of Family. To David, Debbie, Francesca, Gudron, and my new Godson, Edward, Helen, Katie, Kirsti, Paul, Phillipa, Richard, and Sachiko, you make me who I am.

To my grandparents, Auntie Marion, and Uncle Bob. You never gave up, and you were right. I do not have a heart big enough to hold the love and gratitude that I feel.

To my power animals and spirit guides. You walk with me always. I hope that this book contains the words that you wanted heard.

To Mabon, Megan, and Chester. You are a part of me and you lead where I follow.

To my wife, Vanessa. This book is for you since you brought it into being. I truly do not know where I end and you begin; my life is only possible because you are at the centre of it. Your love contains me and I can only offer all of mine in return.

# Introduction:
## The Bison That Roars

The sound was what the people heard first: the low note of a bison roaring. It was a call full of danger, and of death. Then, barely discernable through the smoke of a fire, people caught sight of the animal itself. Its horns scuffed the dry ground with a violence that was palpable and, momentarily rearing on its rear legs, its sharp hooves scythed the air with a sound like a spear in flight. Then, it charged. The people sat quite still, as if mesmerised by the power of the creature. At the last moment, just before its first victims should have been ground into dust, the beast reared and shook with rage. The creature's head was a mass of wet fur, thick with mucus and foamy blood, which dripped, still hot, on those who were nearest the animal. Even now, the people sat in silence, watching as the horror unfolded before them. Then, quite suddenly, the bison fell to the ground writhing, as if in great pain. The head and pelt rolled back slightly so that the people caught a glimpse of the woman inside, wearing the newly butchered skin of the bison. By this time, however, the woman had already left them far behind, her body lying prone whilst her soul journeyed to places only she knew; for she was a shaman and her role was to serve her people.

*Shamanism*, the ability to journey beyond this world and into the supernatural otherworld, is a technique as old as the first human who walked upon the earth. Throughout history, shamans have been the most powerful among the community, the most respected, the most feared. They had the guidance of the spirits and did wonderful things: healed the sick, tended the dying, and foretold the future. Shamans were people who had reached their highest potential and who used the power that this gave them, not for themselves, but for the good of their communities. Today, shamanism is still a hugely empowering path to follow, and it is as relevant to people today as it was to those who lived so long ago.

Since each shaman has to find his or her own way of working with the unseen forces of the world, there can be no easy definition of *shamanism*. Academics argue long and hard when they try to define what they mean when they use the term *shaman* and yet, in so doing, they miss the fundamental point of any shamanic work. Shamanism is about a personal relationship with the spirits. The spirits decide how you practice your shamanism, and they determine what is expected of you. Shamanism is as rich and as varied as there are people following its path. When you begin your own explorations, you add your thread to countless others; only together is the tapestry of shamanism defined.

Despite the myriad forms shamanism can assume, some fundamentals are common to most who practice it. Shamans walk between the worlds and can journey beyond our limited reality to enter an alternative realm. This otherworld is the domain of the spirits: animal; human; and, sometimes, something else entirely. Shamans work to befriend these entities and allow the energy of the spirits to channel through their bodies so that they might become a conduit for the power contained in the otherworld. Once they feel this power coursing through their very being, one final undertaking is crucial if the practitioner is to be a shaman rather than just a tourist to these realms: the power that the shaman assumes must find its outlet for the good of others. The shaman has always been contained, held, and situated at the heart of his or her community. It is only through service to that community that the shaman can exist.

To journey to the otherworld, shamans induce trance. This sounds daunting, even frightening, until you realise that trance is every bit as natural as anything else you do. Dreaming, for example, is just another form of trance and yet is something you accept might happen every time you sleep. Shamanic journeying is similar and just as natural. Unlike dreaming, however, the shamanic journey is about intention and control. You might enter trance in order to initiate your journey but from then on you are very firmly in control and you must observe and listen to all that unfolds. Of course, the spirits might take you on adventures of epic proportions but, at their very core, the intention you hold, the reason you are there, determines what you will find.

Since trance is a natural part of being human, it follows that all those who have gone before, back to our most ancient ancestors, must have also had the capability to access the otherworld and interact with the spirits. In fact, humans probably evolved because of their use of trance; it may have given them the edge they needed to survive. In this book, you will meet some of the earliest humans, people just like you and me, with the same capacity to dream, enter trance, and visit the otherworld. In prehistoric times, it is likely that all people were shamanic; it was not a separate skill that people learnt and practiced, it was just always there: a part of everyday life. A few might have been exceptionally gifted, and these people were singled out as shamans, serving their communities as doctors, councillors, wisdom-keepers, and leaders. As populations grew and people organised themselves into larger and larger groups, institutionalised priests replaced the community shamans and what had once started as a common and shared set of beliefs formed the kernel of new religions. These grew and developed until their shamanic origins were left far behind.

Today, most Westernised people have completely forgotten their roots. Trance is now something strange, even deranged, and we shy away from the experiences it might hold. To leave this world and to journey to others is considered childish, fanciful, even a sign of madness. How much we have lost as a result. Not all people became Westernised, however; and it is in these communities that shamanism still flourishes. Moreover, like the people themselves, the ancient traditions have not stagnated and, much to the chagrin of academics, shamanism has developed and grown into the rich and varied confetti that we have today. From the tundra of Siberia to the rainforests of Brazil, and from the ice sheets of Greenland to the deserts of Australia, the ancient traditions of shamanism have survived and found a new and wonderful flowering.

I cannot recall my first experience of the mysteries that underlie shamanism; they have just always been there. The inner realms that only I could access were as real to me as anything else in the world. All children are born like this; it is only later that our innate abilities are squashed and we forget what was once quite natural. When I was young, I was obsessed with the past and ever since I can remember, the ancient world filled me with wonder. Here were people who lived thousands of years ago but left remains that I could visit, literally walking in their footsteps. As I got older, I wanted to know more: I wanted to know what these people talked about, what they thought, and, most of all, what they believed in. I was a child for whom the supernatural was near enough to touch and, at some level, I knew that those who had lived in the past felt the same.

My childlike enthusiasm for the past never waned, and I spent much of my time seeking out stone circles, burial mounds, and all the other wonders that punctuate our land. Eventually, my love of these mysteries overtook me and I resigned from my job and returned to University to study full time. I first took an M.A. and then a Ph.D., studying the ancient beliefs of our European past: the shamanic practice of our ancestors. This book is fruit of that time.

Whilst studying, I did not neglect my spiritual practice and, after a lot of searching for a place I could call home, I found the Order of

Bards, Ovates, and Druids, the largest Druidic training organisation in the world. As I followed their training through all three grades, I felt as if it had been written just for me, so close did it mould around my being. Perhaps it was natural that I have now become a tutor for the Bardic grade, helping others find their feet on a path that still means so much to me.

I researched many modern shamanic communities from around the world to set the shamanism of our ancestors into context. This research provided essential background for my degree but also allowed me to explore many different shamanic traditions. Those that called to me strongest were, perhaps unsurprisingly, those of northern Eurasia: the Sámi of Lapland and the many groups that populate the Siberian plateau. These are the people whose traditions stretch back, almost unbroken, to the time I was studying. All of a sudden, the mute remains of the past found a voice. I had the good fortune to travel through Lapland and Siberia and to work under some of those who still practice the ancient arts. I also studied core shamanism and attended myriad training courses and workshops wherever and whenever I could. Eventually, my own practice formed. None of this really matters, however. I relate it here only to introduce myself. The only thing that matters in any shamanic practice is to listen to the spirits. Anyone can do that and therefore anyone can have a shamanic practice. I have merely indulged myself a little on the way.

For our ancestors, shamanism was meshed so tightly into their lives that it would have been impossible for them to conceive of a reality without it. Nobody needed an explanation of how to journey to the otherworld and interact with the spirits; it just formed part of who they were. Today, we have lost this intimacy with shamanism and, even if we feel the call to become a shaman ourselves, there is often little indication of where and how we should start. Since you are reading these words, perhaps you have heard the call of the spirits yourself. Will you now answer that summons and follow your ancestors in walking the ancient path of the shaman? If you decide to do so, this book will show you the way.

Whilst shamanism has many and varied forms, I have never found a tradition from any part of the world that speaks to me as clearly as that which arises from the earth beneath my feet. However, this book does not provide an explanation of a living tradition of shamanism; plenty of others admirably do that. What this book offers is a tradition that has been pieced together over many years of research into the shamanic practices of the earliest Europeans. Since these were the same people who had only just divided and fanned out to all five continents, much of what I have discovered may well underpin shamanic traditions from other parts, maybe all parts, of the world. These are ancestors who belong to us all. Drawing on the remains that they left behind, you can follow in their footsteps to meet your own spirit allies. You can learn how to empower yourself to be all that you are capable of becoming and discover how to channel this power for the welfare of others and for the good of the planet. Shamanism, as you will see, is an ancient path for modern lives.

All journeys to the otherworld begin with trance. There are many ways of inducing trance but the safest, gentlest, and easiest to control is to listen to deep, repetitive drumming. Many shamans the world over use a drum and, once you have tried it yourself, you will understand why. Whilst journeying to a live drum is a wonderful experience, it is a luxury, not a necessity. If you can find a partner to drum for you whilst you undertake your journeys to the otherworld, then you are very lucky. Most people rely on a recorded drumming source and, fortunately, this does the job perfectly. Many excellent recordings are on the market and, as your practice develops, you will probably find your favourite. To start with, however, and to make things easy, I have put a drumming track on my Web site, which you can access at www.prehistoricshamanism.com. Download the track for free and use it straight away. I hope it helps.

Almost all the exercises in the book begin with the drum and, should you eventually feel drawn to buy your own, it will rapidly become a much loved and trusted friend. You also will have your spirit allies to call upon so that, in following your shamanic path, you will never be alone. At first, however, you may find trance a little daunting; so throughout the book, I have shared experiences from those who have walked the path ahead of you. Think of them as leaving a trail you can follow or leave as you wish. I have kept their identities hidden and changed personal details where necessary but the hearts of the individuals still shine through. In a way, these are the real teachers in the book. I met most of these wonderful individuals on my travels, either through my Druidic responsibilities, at drumming circles, on courses, through training sessions, or by making friends with those who have sat in a circle with me. Perhaps most humbling of all are those who have come to me for teaching or healing and, in so doing, have put their trust in what I do. I stand on their shoulders in writing this book.

Shamanism is not a belief system or a religion; it asks us to take nothing on faith. What you discover, you will do so through your experiences and through direct contact with the spirits. If shamanism is to live, it must work and be useful; only take those things from the book that you find satisfy both requirements. The following pages introduce the shamanism of our ancestors and impart some of its most fundamental tenets. They show how our ancestors experienced their world and explore the signs they left behind of their own shamanic practices.[1] Many things today claim they will change our lives; only shamanism has the potential to change our world.

*As the shaman in the bison skin returned from her journey to the spirits, she walked deep into a fissure in the earth. On the cave walls she drew herself, dressed as a bison and then, all around her, she drew the spirits that she had seen. Although she could not have known it then, her painting was to survive, to be discovered thousands of years later in southern France, providing those who came after her a glimpse of the power wielded by the ancient shamans. But that is all in the future. For now, you find yourself back in time, during the height of the Ice Age. It is cold and you pull your furs tight around you. Ahead lies the dark entrance that you know leads to the painted caves of the shamans; it is time that you entered them. Bending stiffly, you crawl into the tiny passage, your guide leading, just ahead, with a guttering lamp. The passage is long and narrow and you begin to get anxious; who knows what you will find at its end. For now, you can do nothing but continue to crawl, deeper and deeper, into the earth . . .*

# 1
# Deep in the Painted Caves:
## First Steps in Shamanism

**Y**ou are crawling down a narrow, damp passage into the depths of the earth. You feel the ground beneath you and it is worn smooth, as if many people have come this way before. Ahead, you can just make out a burning lamp, the light showing the route you must follow. The air gets thicker here and the walls about you begin to intrude. You feel your breath becoming laboured and wonder how much farther you will have to endure the darkness of the tunnel. Your mind wanders and waves of dizziness come over you. It is only the nudge from another who is following you into the darkness that gives you the will to move forward. Suddenly, and with no warning, you emerge into a large cavern. The brightness of the lamp blinds you momentarily but, as your sight returns, you notice animals painted onto the rock walls all around you. There are antelope, horses, a mammoth, and herds of deer charging around your head, seemingly floating in and out of the cave walls as the flickering light of the lamp picks out each detail. Moving closer to the surface of the rock, you notice that each animal has been outlined in black pigment but in a furious style, as if the artist wanted, above all, to capture the movement and grace of the creatures depicted. Not all are complete, as if they are emerging from the wall of the cave itself. In one scene, the animals are drawn one on *top of another, so that it feels like you are at the centre of a charging herd, kicking up the dust of the floor and making the cavern echo to the sound of their hooves. For a moment you are with them, your feet flying over the earth, your head lifted in a primeval roar of power. Blinking hard against your vision, you see other shapes among the animal forms: several hashed lines, a zigzag pattern, and two hand prints spaced so far apart that, by placing your hands on each print, your face is now only inches from the rock. You can smell its mustiness and yet, in the faint light of the lamp, it is as if the surface is permeable and, with only the slightest pressure, you would disappear into its confines. This is not the world you are used to; this is some other place and the rules are different here. You step back and stare again at the animal maelstrom about you. This time, as the dizziness strikes, you no longer fight it but let your mind merge with the thundering herd, following their forms to places you have never dared to imagine. Welcome to the otherworld: the ancient realm of the shaman.*

## Primeval Visions

Some of the oldest remains of modern human beings, people just like you or me, are found deep underground in the painted caves of southern France and northern Spain.[1] They date from around thirty thousand years ago, when thick sheets of ice covered much of the land to the north, until around ten thousand years ago, when almost all the ice had gone. The wondrous animals depicted on their walls have enthralled explorers and archaeologists for generations; and yet, the reason why they were painted remained elusive; nobody really knew what our ancient ancestors were doing. Although Ice Age people could certainly draw, and some of the images remain unsurpassed in their drama even today, they did not use written words and, therefore, almost everything we know about them comes from the images they painted in the caves and the odd belongings they left behind. At first, it was thought the pictures were art as we might know it in the modern world: painted for pleasure alone. However, the location of the images argues against this; if the pictures were painted to be seen, surely they would not have been so difficult to reach. Later, it was thought the images may have been used in some sort of hunting magic but, in the absence of any further evidence, this idea is difficult to prove. In short, nobody really knew what the paintings were for and so they were just recorded, admired, and left for someone else to think about.

A few years ago, during the mid-1980s, two South African archaeologists took up the challenge of solving the mystery of the Ice Age cave art. They had worked with images painted onto rocks when they had studied the Bushman paintings of their native country. Although the tribes that painted those images were extinct, other Bushmen remained in Africa, and the archaeologists asked the tribal elders what they thought the art might mean. They were unequivocal in their answer: the images depicted shamans in trance and the visions of the otherworld to which they journeyed. The archaeologists were invited to attend a shamanic ceremony performed by the modern Bushmen and, with growing excitement, realised that what they were seeing was the same as the images they studied on the rocks. The images were quite definitely shamanic.[2]

What the South African archaeologists had discovered inadvertently is one of the most glaring limitations of Western thought and understanding. Our entire way of life presupposes that only one reality exists: the rational, scientific world. What we have forgotten is that this world is a modern invention. For the countless thousands of years before the Industrial Revolution (and for the vast majority of people living a traditional way of life today) there were two realities: this world and an otherworld that can only be entered through trance. This otherworld is the realm that the African Bushmen described to the archaeologists and is what they paint onto the rocks. The images represent the visions of the otherworld as witnessed by the shamans on their trance journeys to this strange and powerful realm.

The archaeologists then had a thought: given the apparent similarities between the southern African rock art and the painted caves of Europe, could the latter also depict what shamans saw in their trance journeys to the otherworld? Unlike in Africa, however, no surviving tribes could verify this hypothesis, so the archaeologists did the next best thing: they looked into their own minds to see what was there.

It is a strange quirk of evolution that the way we are today is no different from the way people were thirty thousand years ago: both our bodies and our minds are the same. So the archaeologists looked at modern research into trance states, and what they found amazed them: anyone entering trance follows a similar pattern. First, shapes appear before the eyes. Anyone who has had a migraine headache is familiar with what these are: hashed lines, zigzags, and the like.[3] These shapes are found on the Ice Age cave walls; in fact, almost every shape that is witnessed in trance was painted somewhere on the walls. The next stage of trance is for these shapes to coalesce into a spiral (sometimes this happens so quickly that the shapes are hardly present at all). All those who enter trance agree that this looks just like a long tunnel stretching before them. This is also exactly how people had to enter the caves to see the art: they had to crawl down a long tunnel. Finally, people in trance come to the end of the tunnel and step out into another realm. At this stage, one of the most common images is of animals; sometimes hundreds of animals, running and flying in great herds that make one dizzy to look at them.

Finally, the archaeologists had the solution to the cave paintings: they were drawn by shamans to show people exactly what they saw in the otherworld. From the journey down the long tunnel, to the shapes and images that arise before the eyes, to the sensation of stepping out into another world to be surrounded by a maelstrom of animal forms. This is what the Ice Age otherworld looked like.[4]

To the Ice Age people entering the painted caves, however, the images probably did not merely represent the otherworld but rather they *were* the otherworld: the actual spirits of the animals, thundering around the cave walls. At a cave near Altamira in northern Spain (the place where cave art was rediscovered in 1879), some of the images were painted to incorporate aspects of the cave structure so that the animals appear to be floating in and out of the wall itself. Perhaps the wall was seen as a membrane between the worlds, and the spirits of the animals were able to float through it before returning once more into their realm. If so, then it might explain why some of the Ice Age visitors to the cave scraped away a little of the walls and took it back with them to their world. At Cosquer Cave in France, there are many scrape marks on the soft clay of the walls, making a small indent through the membrane of the worlds.[5] For the painters too, the animals may have seemed like spirits. The paint they used contained manganese oxides, and since some of the art was painted by spraying the paint from the mouth, it is likely that manganese poisoning gave rise to visions.[6] For those painting the animals, these were indeed visions of the otherworld.

## Crossing the Portal

Although the people of the Ice Age had their own means of entering a trance state (crawling into the confines of the cave and poisoning themselves with manganese, for example), there is a much easier way. Repetitive drumming induces trance, and it is through listening to the beat of a drum that you can make your first journey to the otherworld. You will not see the same images as our Ice Age ancestors; you will see your unique vision of this extraordinary realm.

---

### Exercise: Crossing the Portal

*Although you can undertake shamanic journeys anywhere, for this first journey find a time and a place where you will not be disturbed. Different people like to prepare themselves and their surroundings in different ways: some like to darken the room if they are indoors; others wear a* scarf over their eyes. Some people like to lie down when they journey, whereas others like to sit. You will find your preferences over time, but for now, lie on the floor with some support for your head. Do not get too comfortable, though, as you do not want to fall asleep.

Still your mind and let the pressure and demands of everyday life fall away. When you are ready to start, state the intention of your journey; in this case: I am journeying to the otherworld to connect and to look around. Repeat your intention a couple of times so that it lodges in your mind. You might want to say the words out loud; like most things in life, if you have a clear goal as to what you want to achieve, it will be easier to obtain. When you are ready, begin your drumming recording or, if you are working with a partner and have a drum available, ask them to drum for you, using a steady, repetitive rhythm (all of the journeys to the otherworld in this book will be to the sound of the drum). Most drumming recordings last ten to fifteen minutes before they stop, usually with a series of loud beats. There is then a pause before the drumming starts again at a much faster beat. This is your signal to return; you must always make your way back at this time. The fast rhythm will again end with a series of loud beats, at which time you should be back in your body. Get your partner to practice first if they have not drummed before. You can then do the same for them when you return.

Now, imagine a place in nature where you feel calm and untroubled. It might be a garden, a wood, a park, or anywhere else where you feel safe and comfortable. Then, find a hole in the ground. This might be a cave entrance, an animal burrow, an upended tree-root hollow, or even a rainwater drain; it really does not matter (and do not worry if it is a small hole: just imagine yourself being small enough to fit inside it). Step into the hole and you will find a long tunnel before you. Move along the tunnel in whatever way suits you best. If you find yourself stuck, repeat your intention again and push farther through the tunnel. After a while, you will discern a light at its end: this is what you are aiming for. As the light gets brighter, a landscape

*begins to emerge. Keep going. Eventually, you will find yourself at the*
*end of the tunnel and will be able to step out into this strange new*
*world. This is the otherworld, the realm our ancestors have visited for*
*thousands of years.*

*Do not worry about what it looks like; everyone sees something*
*entirely unique to him or her. Some people might not even "see" the*
*otherworld at all but sense that they have reached it in other ways.*
*Take time to look around, walking a little distance into this new*
*place. Do not do anything on this first journey: just look around and*
*marvel at what you witness. When you hear the drumming stop and*
*the faster call-back rhythm begin (and you will definitely notice, how-*
*ever engrossed you are in your otherworld experience), finish your ex-*
*ploration and retrace your steps back to the mouth of the tunnel. Go*
*along it again and emerge at the other end, exactly where you started.*
*As you return, become aware of being back in your physical body and,*
*when you are ready, sit up. Congratulations: you have just taken your*
*first journey to the otherworld.*

---

Although every journey to the otherworld is different, and what
you saw will almost certainly be unique, Joan's experience is typical
of what may be found there. She told me: "I chose to enter the otherworld via a large tree in my garden. I imagined sitting against it and
just spent some time feeling the bark against my back and the ground
beneath me. Then, I entered a hole beneath its roots. A tunnel appeared before me, dark with rough edges, but not in the least restric-
tive or threatening. I travelled along the tunnel until I could see light
at its end. As the light got closer, I began to see shapes and eventually
stepped out into woodland. It seemed dark overhead but I could see
clearly, as if things were lit by an internal glow. I walked through the
trees to a meadow and then down to a river. It was beautiful. I saw
a deer flit through the trees and then a hawk hover above me, but
neither seemed to notice I was there. My surroundings felt familiar

but also very different. I felt very relaxed and peaceful there. When I heard the recall drumming, I retraced my steps back to the tunnel and returned."

## Was It Real?

Whatever your experience, it is natural to wonder what actually happened: was it real? The answer is a resounding "Yes!" You have seen how trance states are perfectly routine to people living a traditional life today; in fact, more than 90 percent experience trance on a regular basis and this was likely true throughout the past.[7] Moreover, we all experience a type of trance every night through the dreams we have whilst we sleep. Trance is a normal and perfectly natural state for humans to experience and the reason for this lies in the way in which our brains are wired.

When you are awake, the neurons within your brain pulsate at a regular rhythm and this is called a *beta* state. By relaxing, you can slow this rhythm to enter an *alpha* state, when you feel more grounded and aware but also relaxed and open. This is the state you can reach through meditation or when you are so engrossed in an activity, you have no recollection of the passing of time. Slowing the rhythm still further, you enter a *theta* state and this is equivalent to a deep shamanic trance.[8] When you work with the drum, you probably achieve a state midway between an *alpha* and *theta* state. Ann, for example, describes her trance states as deeply relaxing: "I feel calm very quickly. My skin tingles and I can feel warmth rising throughout my body. Each part of me feels almost like liquid, as if they have joined to interrelate in a more fluid, flowing way. I feel larger and time falls away. I have no idea how long I have been in trance." Interestingly, the very oldest part of your brain begins to take over when you enter trance and, again, this hints at the huge amount of time that humans have been having these experiences.

As you slow your brain rhythm, you may begin to see the geometric shapes our Ice Age ancestors painted on the cave walls: hatched lines, dots or flecks, zigzags, nested curves, and filigrees. These are called *phosphenes* and they are formed within the eye itself with no outside stimuli.[9] A study of children's doodles often throws up these shapes, suggesting that they are a very early part of our human experience.[10] In prehistoric times, the shapes are not only found on cave walls during the Ice Age but also several thousand years later on Iron Age metal items such as mirrors and coins (see chapter 7 for more discussion about these items).

Although these geometric shapes are not seen by everyone in every trance, the next stage, of visualising the tunnel, is universally experienced. The reason for this is that the neurons that fire as you enter trance have a spiralling tendency and the brain interprets this as a tunnel.[11] The same part of the brain creates near-death experiences, which almost always involve going along a long tunnel. Eventually, the tunnel gives way to very vivid images and you find yourself stepping out into another realm: the otherworld.[12]

What you see there is unique but depends upon your experiences in this world. The brain tries to make sense of the myriad of visual stimuli coming its way by interpreting things in the form it is most used to. So something tall and brown with green bits at the top becomes a tree, and something flat and blue that gently moves becomes the sea.[13] Of course, individual life experiences today are varied, and you have many references to draw upon when you interpret your otherworld experiences, but this was not so in prehistoric times. During the Ice Age, people lived very similar lives and therefore the image-store within their brain was far more limited when it came to interpreting their experiences of trance. It is very likely that, at this time, people *did* see the same things in the otherworld and perhaps this increased the bonds between them (something that was essential to our survival as a species). Even today, we still seem to hold knowledge about things in discrete chunks of information. "Having breakfast," for example, is understood all at once without needing to think about each individual item independently.[14] Some of these chunks of knowledge, such as the wise teacher, the trickster, or the wounded healer, appear again and again across many cultures. These common images may relate to the archetypes identified by Carl Jung and popularised in the writings of Joseph Campbell.[15] Moreover, these patterns of thinking are wired into those ancient parts of our brains that are especially active during trance. They draw upon very old sources of human wisdom and you can tap into them through your shamanic journeys to the otherworld. This is not a case of learning anew, but more a case of remembering what you have forgotten.

Not everyone is visually predominant, and this is reflected in how each person experiences the otherworld. Rose, for example, finds that although she can see objects very clearly in the otherworld, people, and particularly faces, are very hard to make out. However, the people she meets speak with an intense clarity and it is likely that her brain is distorting her visual stimulus to help her concentrate harder on what she is being told. If you have journeys where you do not see much, or if what you experience comes mostly through sound, or even sense and touch, then you must accept that this is perfectly right for you: your brain is giving you exactly what you need. However, if you find that one sense is unduly dominating and you want to start developing the others, journey to the otherworld with the express intention: *I am journeying to see/smell/hear/touch* (or even) *taste the otherworld.*

All this scientific explanation may appear to reduce your experiences to no more than a coincidental firing of a few cells in some obscure part of your brain, causing you to see things that are not really there. Perhaps. But then, perhaps it is because your brain has actually evolved to accommodate two realities, this world and the otherworld, and you are merely rediscovering a realm that you were always meant to reach. What is beyond dispute is that shamanism is one of the oldest and most longstanding human behaviours to exist. If it were all make-believe, then why would this be so, and why, as you will learn throughout this book, is it so useful to our everyday lives? Shamanism and journeying to the otherworld is as natural and important to human beings as eating and sleeping, whatever our rational minds might think.

## Moving Farther and Faster

Now that you have journeyed to the otherworld and taken time to explore its reaches, it is time to see what else you can do whilst you are there. On your next journey, run from place to place, and then run very fast. In the otherworld, you are no longer constrained by the laws of physics. On another journey: fly. This may come naturally or it may take a bit of practice, but feelings of flying are a common part of trance experiences. You might find that your body grows so that you become very large or perhaps everything else expands so that you become very small.[16] Experience these sensations when you journey by holding one of them as your intention when you start.

Swimming is another activity to try. In trance, people often report hearing a rushing noise in their ears, which the brain interprets to be water, so water has always been connected with the otherworld.[17] When humans first started burying their dead in cemeteries during the middle Stone Age, they often chose places close to water.[18] Whilst some people think that this was to stop the dead from haunting the living (since the dead spirits are said to be unable to cross the water), it is more likely that people were buried in these places precisely because they *could* cross the water and thereby enter the otherworld of death. The living were using their own experience of trance states to determine how they should treat their dead. In a much later period, the Bronze Age in Scandinavia, people even buried their dead in graves shaped like a boat.[19] The tradition was so strong and so natural that it was able to continue for almost ten thousand years.

Exploring the otherworld is an important first step to learning how to master its power. People probably did the same in prehistoric times and perhaps their inner explorations eventually led to outer explorations.

Modern humans originated in Africa, but we spread rapidly from there to colonise the rest of the world. Exactly why we did this remains a mystery; since populations were small, there was no real impetus to expand. Perhaps people were already used to exploring the otherworld of their minds and it therefore seemed only natural to extend this exploration to the everyday world. If so, then shamanism really did make us what we are today.

## Why Journey?

Life during the Ice Age was tough. The weather was harsh and unpredictable; prey was scattered and took skill to hunt; and everything that people needed for living had to be gathered, processed, and made by their own efforts.[20] With all of these pressures, how did people find the time and resources necessary to paint the caves with their experiences of the otherworld? Whatever they gained from visiting this extraordinary realm had to be worth a great deal.

There is evidence that trance expands the mind as it joins areas of the brain that are usually kept apart—like our right and left hemispheres, often associated with contrasting analytical and emotional faculties.[21] Joining these areas causes instability, which often leads to brain cells making new connections. In other words, trance makes your brain grow and develop in ways that would not be possible otherwise.[22] New brain cell connections lead to new understanding and realisations and make trance a good basis for problem solving and decision making. (Have you ever said you wanted to sleep on a problem? If so, you were quite literally hoping that the trance of sleep might help in finding a solution.) For our Ice Age ancestors, the otherworld was a place where they could seek answers to problems. This also holds true for us today; visiting the otherworld is a good place to think and meditate upon issues and challenges that affect us.

Looking for answers to problems, however, is probably not the full explanation as to why people visit the otherworld. In trance, the changes in your mode of thinking often divorce you from your usual way of being. You feel open and in tune with the ebb and flow of the greater existence all around you. This flow of energy in the universe has been recognised throughout history and is acknowledged as being a great source of power. Our Ice Age ancestors probably entered the otherworld to feel this connection, perhaps to influence the habits of their prey to ensure a good hunt, or to shape the weather and lessen the frigidity of winter. Situating and aligning yourself with this perpetual flow of energy is empowering: it can be at once healing, energising, and deeply relaxing. Steve describes this sensation in a most appropriate poetic manner: "I can almost hear the energy about me, like a sound on the wind. I can feel it in my heart and in my blood, beating with the rhythm of nature. My mind expands to blend with the universe; I can feel its presence like an ancient being." No wonder the shamanic journey is often called a flight of ecstasy.[23]

Did our ancestors think the otherworld was real? Almost certainly the answer is yes. Although no written records exist for much of prehistory, right at the end of the Iron Age, a Roman historian recorded a few facts about the Iron Age Celts. In particular, he noted that if gambling debts could not be settled immediately (a common occurrence in the competitive world of the Celts), they could be repaid in the otherworld of death. This seemed to be acceptable to all parties and shows their complete faith in the existence and reality of the otherworld.[24] But then, if they had been journeying to that place all their lives, why would they not believe it to be real?

## Control

Mary told me that she is always journeying to the otherworld: "The tunnel appears and I just have to go down it." I asked her if this was at a time she had decided to journey. "Oh no, it just happens and I can't seem to stop it." Although Mary felt that her connection to the otherworld was strong, it was also unhealthy; Mary needed to accept that she had to control when she journeyed. In traditional societies, shamanism is sometimes considered only a short step from madness and, perhaps, this is true. It is only our control that keeps apart the two. Setting an intention before you journey is a very important step since that intention keeps your mind focussed on what you want to achieve whilst you are in the otherworld. Going without an intention is the shamanic equivalent of channel-hopping: it might be fun but is a little pointless.

When and where you journey, however, is up to you. Whilst sitting in a darkened room with incense and candles burning, where you can drum beforehand and call in your guides, is nice, that setup is not really necessary. For example, I mostly journey outside, near a bubbling stream, when I take my dog for his afternoon walk. Gary journeys to the sound of the drum on his MP3 player on his commute into work, and Katie journeys on the beach, carried to the otherworld on the beautiful rhythm of the breaking waves. The key is to find a time to journey that fits into your life and your daily routine; by doing so, you make journeying a habit rather than an activity for a special occasion. Of course, distractions are more of a hazard when you journey in busy places, but once in the otherworld your mind generally becomes absorbed in whatever you are doing and most distractions fall away. If your mind is causing the distraction itself, however, with niggling issues at the edge of your thoughts, don't fight it. Instead, thank that part of yourself that is holding the distraction for bringing it to your attention, promise to deal with it on your return, and then let the distraction float away. If the distraction persists, then perhaps the subject is one you *should* be thinking about in the otherworld.

The only real rule of journeying is that, when you hear the call-back drumming, you return from wherever you are in exactly the same way that you got there. If you ever have to leave a journey unfinished (perhaps due to an interruption), remember to begin again where you left off and return as usual. Vikki, for example, found that she often fell asleep when she was journeying last thing at night. This did not worry her because falling asleep while in trance usually meant a really good night's sleep. The following morning, however, she felt terrible, drained of energy, and exhausted all day. I suggested that, when she fell asleep during a journey, she return to the otherworld in the morning and then come back in the usual manner. She did and the results were instantaneous: "I now feel so much more alert, alive, and active!" Meanwhile, Rachel suffered a different problem: when she returned from the otherworld, she often felt disorientated and dizzy. I told her to take her time after she returned to her physical body and, if the feeling continued, to eat some fruit. Eating grounds our bodies and Rachel's dizziness quickly went away.

Keep a note of your journeys to the otherworld, either on your computer or in a journal. Sometimes, the messages you receive are not immediately relevant, or themes can continue in future journeys, and only by recording them can you get the full benefit. Writing down your experiences is also a good way to fulfil one of the most sacred duties of the shaman: to remember all that you experience whilst you are in the otherworld.

You now know how and why our ancient ancestors journeyed to the otherworld, and you have explored some of the earliest visions of this realm on the walls of the Ice Age caves. Most of the cave paintings were of animals and there is a particular reason for this. Animals are among the most important guides you will find in the otherworld, and every individual has at least one animal guide that is theirs and theirs alone. Your animal has been there from the moment you were born (whether you knew it or not) and perhaps now would be a good time to meet it.

# 2
## Dancing the Animal Powers:
### Finding Your Power Animal

*Y*ou take the skull of the deer in your hands. It has been expertly butchered so that the antlers and cranium are hollow and clean but the heavy pelt has been left attached to the back of the skull so that it falls to the earth in dense folds. Others stand around you on this moonlit night, each with their own skull and pelt, and you watch as they place the skull over their heads and loosely secure the furred skin of the deer around them. You do the same and notice that two holes have been drilled at the front of the cranium, just at the level of your eyes. It is difficult to see through the mass of bone but even this small amount of vision allows you to observe your surroundings and the undulating ground beneath your feet. As soon as the skin of the deer encompasses your form, you begin to feel strange. It is as if the spirit of the deer is running through you and, momentarily, it makes you afraid. You swallow back your apprehension and let the spirit of the deer carry you. Your limbs grow long and your hands and feet turn inwards to form hooves. Your neck muscles bulge and you slice the air with a murderous sweep of your antlers. The wind carries scent and you raise your mammalian nose to take it in: water, reeds . . . and humans. They are close and you roar a note of alarm to your companions. There is panic, a tearing of bodies as hunter and prey *begin their terrible dance. You turn, but it is too late. A hunter is close, with an arrow aimed for the kill. You sweep your antlers and leap. The bow is taut. As you sail into the air, freedom just a short grasp away, the bow lets fly and you know that you must have been hit. The ground slams into your form and you accept that you are lost. You writhe in the embrace of death; your head wrenched backwards so that your cries can better escape. The hunter falls upon you, flint dagger raised. You are spent and submit; your head rolling languidly as you await the blow that will end your life. But the hunter retreats and you find ready arms to carry you to your feet. The dance of the deer is completed. The hunters have won; there will be meat tomorrow when the herds arrive at daybreak.*

## Finding Your Power Animal

In prehistory, animals were good to hunt but they were also good to think with. Our hunter-gatherer kin used dances to enter the minds of their prey and ensure that their hunt was successful. The hunters emulated the red deer, their favoured prey, but others emulated different animals. In the Ice Age caves, we witnessed many animals: most of them prey species. However, if we look again at the maelstrom of animals painted on the walls, we see that, in amongst the herds of thundering deer, or stalking at the edges of some grazing horses, there are other animals: lions, leopards, and the mighty cave bear. These were the top predators of the Ice Age and, if I were a hunter trying to make my way across the desolate expanse of a frozen Europe, these are exactly the animals I would want to emulate and have on my side. Perhaps the reason that our Ice Age ancestors were journeying to the otherworld at all was to get in touch with these predators, to take on something of their strength and power, and to learn what made them supreme in the hunt. Some of these animals even seem to have been adopted as personal totems and we find skulls of the cave bear and other predators placed in the caves as if they are watching over and protecting their human brethren. What these animals became were the *power animals* of the hunters: animal spirits that are incredible sources of strength for those who seek their aid.

Whilst the Ice Age hunters probably chose those animals that they thought were best suited to helping them with the hunt, in modern times, it is far more likely that our power animal will choose us. In fact, our power animal has probably been with us throughout our lives, joining us at birth to walk through life as our ally and guide. This is why many children have "imaginary" animal friends. I know a small girl who has two tigers that follow her everywhere; when she grows up, she will have powerful allies indeed. For others, certain animals make their presence known, but without a shamanic reference, they can often be overlooked. Ruth, for example, always had a huge attraction for wolves: she read about them, collected books about them and, when on holiday, even got the opportunity to go hiking with one. She felt enormously connected to wolves and yet had no idea why. Of course, as soon as she learnt shamanic journeying, there was Wolf waiting for her, and she has now deepened her relationship with this wonderful animal to the extent that she can call on Wolf's power wherever and whenever she needs it. Tim, in contrast, had forgotten his childhood experiences with animals, but as soon as Horse identified itself as Tim's power animal, Tim remembered a horse from when he was a child: "I loved that horse so much as a kid and now he has returned to me." Incidentally, when we speak of power animals, we usually call the animal by its name: *Wolf, Horse,* or *Tiger,* rather than *a* horse, *a* wolf, or *a* tiger. A power animal is not *one* of these animals; rather, it represents the spirit of *all* these animals: the entire species. So, the spirit of Horse represents all horses and the spirit of Wolf represents all wolves. Of course, many people can have the same animal as their power animal and the relationship will be different in each case, but they will all be relating to the same animal spirit, representing all of the animals of its type.

To find your power animal, the animal that has been your ally and companion since your birth, journey to the otherworld with this as your intention. A power animal, in almost every case, is as keen to renew its acquaintance with you as you are to renew it with them.

---

## Exercise: Finding Your Power Animal

*Begin this journey in exactly the same way as your last journey to the otherworld except, this time, set your intention as: I am journeying to the otherworld to find my power animal. Go down the tunnel, step out into the otherworld, and then look around you. It may be that an animal is already waiting for you, or you may have to move around and look. When you do see an animal, it might only be for a moment before it moves away. Do not follow in pursuit but just carry on with your search; if that was your power animal, then it will return. When you have seen the same animal a number of times (four is thought to be significant) or if an animal makes it clear that it is waiting for you to initiate contact (this is especially the case if an animal approaches you or if there is an animal waiting for you as soon as you arrive in the otherworld), then go over to it and ask "Are you my power animal?" If it says "No," then carry on looking and wait until another animal approaches you or until you see a new animal several times. However, if it says "Yes," then you have found your power animal. Do not worry about what type of animal it is; just trust that it is entirely right for you. What you do next depends on what your power animal advises. Take your cue from him or her. Just remember that, whatever else is happening, you must return in the normal way as soon as you hear the call-back drumming. Explain to your animal that you now have to return, thank him or her for being there for you, and then retrace your steps.*

---

Finding, meeting, and getting to know your power animal is one of the most important things you ever do. Your power animal is the source of enormous shamanic power and, from now on, you always will have an animal ally by your side. After I had learnt to journey and found my power animal, one of my first shamanic teachers said to me: "Mike, that is all you will ever need from me; your power animal will teach you the rest." In a way, he was right, my power animal has taught me so much and I would be bereft without his support and guidance. Although I still learn as much as I can from indigenous shamans and other teachers, I discuss everything with my power animal and obtain his views on all that I am taught. Your power animal always will be your wisest and most dependable counsel. In my house, for virtually any problem, we always ask: "What did your power animal say?"

Although you might be surprised by the animal that comes to you, trust that it is exactly right. Brian, for example, met Bear when he searched for his power animal, but did not immediately feel worthy of such a magnificent creature: "I came upon a huge male bear. I hardly dared face him but he said that, yes, he was my power animal. I asked why something as powerful as a bear had come to me as I hardly felt up to it. Bear replied that he had come because I needed him. I sat opposite Bear, hand against paw. I then saw through his eyes. 'We' were running through a field, and then down to a lake. After our run together, I sat with him until I heard the call-back drumming."

Wendy found her power animal by sound rather than sight. Although a very visual person in this world (she works as an artist), in the otherworld, her sense of hearing is dominant: "I heard what sounded like hoof beats and the neighing of a horse. I waited and heard Horse come closer and closer until I asked 'Are you my power animal?' She replied that she was and invited me to mount her back. I did so and we raced around the landscape: the wind in my face and the sound of her hooves drumming the ground."

Tom was having difficulty getting down the tunnel to reach the otherworld when Rabbit first approached him. There was almost no need to ask if Rabbit was his power animal as he had already come to Tom's aid. After that, Rabbit always waited in the tunnel for Tom to arrive, ready to lead him the last bit of the way.

In prehistoric times, people also seemed to rely on their power animals to lead the way to the otherworld. You can get an impression of what these animals were by looking at the animal symbols buried with the dead. The journey to the otherworld of death was the last a human would take; a journey that was clearly deemed so important that their power animal accompanied them. At a hunter-gatherer cemetery in Denmark, for example, a small child was placed on a swan's wing that had been carefully laid in the grave.[1] We can perhaps imagine the grieving relatives taking comfort that the small child would not have to embark onto the great journey into death without his ally and protector by his side. Water birds are also prevalent in graves of a later time: the Bronze Age of central Europe. Small models of water birds were placed with the cremated remains of bodies for the same reason that the swan's wing was left with the child.[2] People at this time, however, were a little more worldly, and they also placed drinking vessels in the grave. On occasion, water birds were even fixed to the rim of these vessels: no doubt to ensure that they would not be forgotten.[3] At a Stone Age tomb in Orkney, up to twenty sea eagles were left at its entrance.[4] Again, these were power animals left with the deceased to watch over them and make sure they had an easy passage into the otherworld of death.

## What Is a Power Animal?

Seeing images of animals is one of the most common experiences of trance.[5] If humans are to interact with anything in the otherworld, our minds are biased towards animals. Why should this be so? Is it merely a fluke of evolution that made our minds this way or were we always meant to connect with the spirits of animals? Perhaps this question can never be answered, but from the very first records of human activity, people have shown an affinity and a connection to animals that defies anything other than a straightforward explanation: this is what we are meant to do. Like journeying to the otherworld, your relationship with your power animal is a natural and normal part of being a human being.

Your power animal has one aim and one aim alone: to make you all that you are capable of becoming. It has no artifice, no jealousy, and no ulterior motives: it helps you and this is its sole purpose and aim. If you journey to your power animal with a problem, it always will help you to search for a solution. Your power animal is an inexhaustible source of wisdom, help, and assistance. Your power animal also protects you; helps you to heal your pain; and looks out for your well-being. I know an extremely competent shaman who went skydiving and got into trouble, his strings getting twisted as he deployed his parachute. Undaunted, he calmly called on his power animals to help. They did so; the strings untwisted and he performed a perfect landing.

Always use a degree of discernment when listening to your power animal, however. Like all sources of wisdom, apply the advice to your life in the best and most appropriate way. Jennie, for example, had a fear of losing all her money and possessions and living on the street. This was her darkest dread and yet, when she discussed it with her power animal, the response was: "How exciting; we should certainly give that a go!" It made Jennie laugh and, in a way, diminished the fear a little. Her power animal had found a way to help, even if its advice, on this occasion, was respectfully ignored.

Power animals differ for every person and, whatever their pecking order in this world, they all have the same degree of power in the otherworld. I have known people who work with mice and squirrels and, in the otherworld, these are just as powerful as lions and tigers. Whatever animal appears, trust that it is exactly right for you and can provide all the help that you need. (By the way, power animals never,

ever *eat* each other in the otherworld.) The only animals that are un-usual to have as power animals are insects, and some traditional peo-ples believe that no one should accept insects as power animals. The Iron Age Druids, however, worked with Bee, and Spider and Butterfly are common power animals (even if Spider is not strictly an insect), so make your own judgment. Similarly, some believe that reptiles should not be power animals but Snake can be found in hunter-gatherer cem-eteries in Finland, where small effigies were left with the bodies of the dead.[6] Snake has particularly powerful associations with the oth-erworld since its skin is shed periodically and this is likened to a form of death and rebirth: something a shaman does every time he or she visits the otherworld.

Other types of animals that rarely become power animals are do-mesticated animals and the reason can be traced back to the Iron Age. In northern France, there are several places where enormous quan-tities of animal bones were accumulated.[7] The arrangement of the bones suggests that this was not random but that species and catego-ries of bones were kept together. What is particularly striking, how-ever, is that not a single bone out of thousands and thousands came from a wild animal; all the bones were from domestic animals. The reason is due to the relationship people held to their livestock. Hu-mans controlled domestic animals and hence humans were the mas-ters of these animals: people cared for them rather than the other way around. Wild animals, however, had never been under the control of humans and they had another master: the Master of the Animals.[8] People could develop relations with wild animals. Therefore, that would be unthinkable for domestic stock.

You can see the form of the Master of the Animals on a silver caul-dron, called the Gundestrup Cauldron, which was found in a peat bog of the same name in Denmark in 1891.[9] Among the many designs on the vessel, one stands out. It is of a man sitting cross-legged with ant-lers rising from his head. In his right hand he holds a torc, a neck or-nament associated with chiefs, and in his left hand he holds a snake, a powerful symbol of the otherworld. All around him are animals, and a design of leaves suggests that he sits at the base of a tree. Perhaps, in his features, we can get close to how the Master of the Animals actually appeared to those who knew him in the past.

There are exceptions, however, to domestic animals acting as power animals. Marjorie, for example, who had had two beloved dogs recently pass away, found that they returned as her power animals. She was surprised and a little concerned by what she had read about pets not being power animals, so she went to see a shamanic practitioner for a second opinion. Without knowing beforehand, he confirmed that she did indeed have her two dogs as power animals. She was ecstatic.

## Making Your Power Animal Feel at Home

After you have met your power animal in the otherworld, you may find that similar animals in this world seek you out. I once obtained a power animal for a friend who suddenly had been taken seriously ill (chapter 9 explains how to obtain power animals for others). I knew that Stephen would probably not be receptive to shamanic ideas but he welcomed any help I could offer him. As he lived in the far west of America, I could not visit him in person but, upon journeying, I found that Bobcat was his power animal and I sent it to him remotely. Wondering about its effect, I spoke to Stephen a week later and asked if he had seen any animals over the past few days. "I've not seen any animals," Stephen told me, and I feared that my help had not worked. "But we did have a bobcat walk around the house a few nights ago, and it left its tracks in the snow." So it *had* worked, and I am happy to say his condition stabilised and the crisis passed.

Of course, if your animal does not naturally live by you, you are unlikely to see it in this world (and if it is a dragon or a gryphon then you are unlikely to see it anywhere), but you should keep a look-out for pictures, sounds, and other signs that your animal is making contact.

Kerrie, for example, found that Lion was her power animal. Once he had come to her, she saw lions everywhere: on the television, in magazines, and even on an advertising billboard outside her office. Eventually, when taking her children to the local zoo, she paused outside the lion enclosure and the solitary male lifted his head from his sleep and met her eyes: "He looked at me for minutes and he definitely knew who I was; it was as if something passed between us."

Journey to your power animal regularly, taking your problems with you and letting your power animal help you. Your power animal may talk things through with you, show you images that shed light on an issue, or take you on a journey through the otherworld where everything that happens is somehow relevant to you. If you do not have any burning issue to take to the otherworld, then just go and hang out with your animal: go for a walk, a swim, or even a flight; take some food and have a picnic; or ask your animal to share something of its life.

Even when you are not journeying, gather reminders of your animal that you can keep with you. Find an image of your animal to keep on your desk, in your locker, or by your bed. If you cannot find an image, paint or draw one—which is exactly what our Ice Age ancestors did on the walls of their caves. If you have a computer, find images to use as wallpaper on your desktop or download some sounds of your animal. My computer starts every morning with the sound of my power animal, and that sound is a marvellous way of connecting with his power.

Keeping small models of your animal is another good way of reminding yourself of its presence, and these models are easy to find in local stores or on the Internet. In the Ice Age, people made models of the animals they painted and several striking examples have been found in Germany.[10] Mostly carved from mammoth ivory, they include lions, bears, and horses. Both the lions and the bears are modelled in aggressive poses and one particular lion has his ears cocked back as if it were stalking prey. If these animals were required to help with the hunt, this is exactly the sort of pose you would expect to see. One of the horses is different, however, and is most likely a stallion impressing his harem of mares. Whoever owned this model was not calling upon the power of Horse for the hunt but for a rather different activity altogether. Interestingly, each of these model animals has marks carved onto them and these are exactly the same as the phosphenes that were painted on the cave walls. Since phosphenes are usually only seen in trance, it further confirms that these models represented spirits of the otherworld: people's power animals.

## Animal Tokens

Collecting actual parts of your power animal is a good way of keeping its power with you. However, not everyone feels comfortable collecting animal parts so use your judgment as to what is acceptable. If a claw seems too invasive, then find a piece of fur or a feather. Sometimes, though, you might find that you have little choice in the matter. When I first met Tiff, for example, I had no idea that she was interested in shamanism. On our third meeting, she looked slightly embarrassed and handed me a small package, saying: "I think this is yours." I carefully unwrapped the tissue paper, and there lay a tooth from my power animal. I was flabbergasted; how did she know? Of course, she did not, but my power animal did and he sent his tooth through her so that it would find me. Needless to say, Tiff and I had a great deal to talk about afterwards. Marcie had a similar experience: she works with Buzzard and asked her farmer partner if he would look out for any buzzard feathers that he might find on the land. The next day he brought home an entire buzzard carcass: "In all my years farming," he said, "I've never seen a dead buzzard before." The carcass was more than she wanted but, knowing it was a tremendous gift from her power animal, Marcie kept and used every piece of the bird, honouring the gift she had been given.

People in prehistory also collected teeth and wore them around their necks. Fox, wolf, and hyena teeth were all popular and, again, all come from successful predators.[11] However, deer teeth were also worn, perhaps because deer were a favourite prey and it was good to understand the mind of your prey. Some traditional hunters talk of an animal willingly giving its life to the hunter, providing it is asked properly and its body is treated with respect.[12] Perhaps the deer tooth pendants show that these attitudes have very ancient roots.

In addition to teeth, prehistoric people kept other items of significance. In Denmark for example, a Bronze Age body has been discovered that is thought to be that of a shaman.[13] As if to mirror the shaman's role of straddling two worlds, the grave also seems to straddle two burial traditions. The body was cremated, which was an entirely new tradition (this body was one of the first to be burnt) but the ashes were then placed in the usual stone-lined grave. However, it was what he was buried with that is really exciting. Attached to his belt was a small pouch and within the pouch was a cornucopia of shamanic items, including an amber bead, some red chalk, a shell (which had come all the way from the Mediterranean), a conifer-wood cube, dried roots and bark (and bronze tweezers for sorting them), and, especially relevant to us, the tail of a grass snake, the claw of a falcon, and the jaw and teeth of a weasel. This shaman was taking symbols of his power animals with him on his final journey to the otherworld of death. From the pouch's worn condition, it is also clear that this shaman carried the pouch around with him when he was alive, perhaps so that he had symbols of his power sources close by his side: a touchstone of energy he could call upon whenever he needed it. Making a similar pouch is easy and is a perfect way of carrying items that are meaningful to you and especially those items you might have collected that represent your power animal.

## Exercise: Animal Tokens

*Gather together some fabric to make a small bag or, if you feel comfortable with it, some leather or buckskin; some thread to sew the bag; and a cord or thong to hang around your neck.*

*Journey to your power animal and ask if there is anything you should do before commencing work, such as passing your materials over a candle flame, blowing scented smoke across them, or singing a power song while you work. Remember, you are undertaking a sacred task.*

*When you return, cut a long rectangle of fabric, the same width you want your pouch to be. Fold the fabric in half and sew down the sides. Then turn the pouch inside out. Cut a few small holes around the open edges and pass your cord or thong through. Pull tight and your bag is complete. Decorate your bag by sewing some objects to it or by beading its surface. Use the bag to keep items you gather with you at all times as a reminder of your connection with your power animal and with the otherworld.*

When you next journey, you may find that a pouch appears in the otherworld and you can fill this with items you gather on your journeys and travels in this realm. Occasionally, an item you receive in the otherworld may even find its way to you in this world. I was once working with the spirit of Horse in the otherworld, for example, and, as a symbol of our work together, I was given some horse teeth to wear around my neck. Two days later, whilst I was out walking my dog across the moors, I came across a small animal hole and, just to its side, were two horse teeth, just like those I had been given in the otherworld. I thanked Horse for the incredible gift and now keep the teeth with me in my neck pouch.

# Shapeshifting

The best way of connecting with your power animal is to dance. Dancing is as old as the first human beings and, even now, it is almost impossible to watch a fire burning outside without wanting to get up and move to its noise and rhythm. The Stone Age hunter-gatherer people who lived on the banks of the Rhine in Germany in decorated slate plaques with images of people dancing, along with the animals that they hunted.[14] Imagine the community, sitting around a fire and dancing the dance of their animal allies, perhaps honouring those who were to give themselves in the hunt, and showing that they would be honoured after their deaths.

The dance described at the beginning of this chapter took place at Star Carr in Yorkshire, more than 10,000 years ago.[15] When these people danced, they wore the masks of their main prey species: the red deer. Wearing a mask is a good way to get in touch with your animal, as a mask breaks down your identity and allows your animal to take over. This practice is called *shapeshifting*, as you shift your shape into that of your animal and learn what it is like to live in their skin. Shapeshifting is not possession, but a controlled merging of human and animal characteristics to bring through the power of your animal. The people who painted the Ice Age caves certainly knew how to shapeshift as some of their models have both human and animal characteristics. Particularly striking is one model that shows a lion's torso and head standing on the legs of a human.[16] Clearly, whoever this represents knew how to shapeshift. Similarly, from Georgia comes a fine silver goblet dating to the end of the Stone Age.[17] Engraved upon it are a number of people who walk purposefully around its surface. However, each of these people has the head and tail of a wolf and, intriguingly, each walks towards a central figure seated under a tree. Could this be another depiction of the Master of the Animals, this time overseeing shapeshifting shamans?

When you feel ready, you can also shapeshift into your power animal; all you need is the space to dance.

---

## Exercise: Shapeshifting

*Begin the journey as normal but set your intention as: I am journeying to the otherworld to shapeshift into my power animal. When you arrive in the otherworld, find your power animal and ask if you can shapeshift into its form. If the answer is yes (and it almost certainly will be, as power animals love to dance), come back from the otherworld but, when you feel yourself returning to your physical body, do not stop the regular drumming beat but let it continue.*

*Stand up into a relaxed posture, half-open your eyes and begin to feel your animal within you. What you have done is invited your power animal to cross over into this world and, for a short time, merge with your body. Feel your power animal's arms or wings, its legs or flippers; feel its head, its face, and its teeth. As you are doing this, let the awareness of your body fall away: you now have claws for fingers, a beak for a mouth, and feathers or scales instead of skin; you are slowly taking on the form of your animal. Feel how your animal might breathe, how it might move its limbs. Finally, begin to move. Do not think about what you are doing: just do it! Move as your animal would move; breathe as your animal would breathe. You are now dancing your animal; you are now shapeshifting. Do you feel the power of your animal coursing through you? This is now your power and it is within you always. You might want to cry out with the voice of your animal; you might want to chant its name to the beat of the drum; do whatever feels right. Carry on for as long as you wish, delving deeper and deeper into your animal's power.*

*When you want to stop (you do not need to wait for the call-back drumming this time), become aware again of your own body and go through the stages of changing back into your human form. Take as much time as you need until you feel fully human again. Send thanks to your power animal who will now be finding its own way home to the otherworld. Finally, look around you; does the world look slightly different now that you have seen it through an animal's eyes?*

---

Shapeshifting dances are so powerful that they have survived through many centuries of change. In Italy, the tarantella is a dance brought on by the bite of a spider, where the dancer must dance with a fury until the spirit of Spider has left the body. Similarly, the Abbots Bromley horn dance from Staffordshire, where dancers wear the antlers of the deer, has a strange resonance with the ancient dance of our hunter-gatherer kin. In fact, it is difficult to think of many occasions where dance is not an integral part of the activities.

Shapeshifting through dance is intense and powerful and draws the energy of the otherworld to course through your very being. Kerrie, for example, found that drawing on Lion gave her added strength to face the challenges of her working day: "I merge with Lion so that I can be a lion on the outside but still feel like me underneath. I can have a tough exterior but still allow myself to be open on the inside. I always feel much better as a result." But dancing is not always the most practical way of drawing on your animal power; sometimes, all you want is a bit of discreet help. One time, for example, as I was heading to the library, desperately needing to check something in a particular book for a talk I was giving at the weekend, a red kite swooped low over me. Of course, I greeted it warmly and kept its presence in mind when I went for my book. Unfortunately, the book was not on the shelf and I thought my talk doomed until I remembered Kite. These birds have exceptional sight and are scavengers, good at seeking out the tiniest morsel. In the middle of the library I quietly (and as unobtrusively as was possible) shapeshifted into Kite and began my search. I found the book almost immediately; it had been placed in the wrong section. I returned to my body and thanked Kite for its help; my weekend talk had been saved.

In prehistoric times, people sought food, not books, and at Lepenski Vir, a Stone Age fishing village next to the River Danube in Serbia, people used shapeshifting in order to obtain it.[18] The inhabitants of the village were dependant on the annual run of beluga fish that swam up the river in the spring. Clubs and fish bones took pride of place in their houses where we would keep ornaments in ours. When people died, they were buried between the houses, with their heads facing downstream. As spirits, their job was to journey down the river. Once there, they had to persuade the fish to swim back with them so that they could feed the inhabitants of the village. To enable them to journey down the river, the spirits of the dead shapeshifted into fish themselves and stone-carved images, which were half-human and half-fish, were given pride of place on special platforms within the houses. The shapeshifting dead must have done their job well, as the village lasted through many generations of fishers. Intriguingly, henbane, which was a common weed at the time, causes trance and convulsions when ingested. These convulsions have long been compared to someone turning into a fish.[19] Henbane is found on other prehistoric sites, and if it was taken at Lepenski Vir, it adds yet another element to the inhabitants' strange shapeshifting relationship with the fish.

Your power animal is an enormous source of power and wisdom and, as my old teacher said to me, you do not really need anything more. However, other teachers wait for you in the otherworld if you want to find them. To meet these teachers, you need to journey to another realm: the upperworld.

# 3

# Between Earth and Sky:
## Portals to the Three Worlds

Υou are on a boat, riding the swell of the sea off a jagged coastline of soaring peaks and hidden fjords. Above you, the sky is a deep grey and the surface of the sea trembles, as if it feels the approach of a storm. Around you, others are sitting, some holding drums and others looking out over the water as if they can see something that is hidden from normal sight. The front of the boat is a huge curved prow, like the head of a sea-beast rearing up from the waves. All at once, your companions start to drum. It is a fast, regular beat that you have heard before and you quickly settle into its rhythm. Some of the others rise to their feet and begin to dance a slow, sensuous dance that tells of the sea and the approaching storm. You watch their movements and feel drawn to the swaying of so many arms. Their rhythm increases and you notice that many look towards the sky, their faces impassive, as if their spirits have already broken free. The drumbeat gathers you to it and you submit to its lead. You are used to leaving your body, and you gently rise from the confines of your skin. The boat seems more distant now and you realise that you are moving above it. Your body still sits with the dancers but you are now leaving it far behind. You fly above the boat, noticing how the craft seems suddenly insignificant in the enormity of the world. You fly higher still,

43

*until the boat becomes a speck upon the glass of the sea. Rising yet*
*farther you see the curve of the earth and the continents beneath you.*
*It is now darker ahead but you carry on rising, leaving the globe of*
*the earth behind. Stars begin to shine and yet still you rise. Will there*
*be no end to this journey?*

## The Three Worlds

In northern Norway, at a place called Alta, high above the Arctic
Circle, the ancient inhabitants of the land decorated the rocks with
images of reindeer, bears, and people in boats.[1] When I went to this
place, one image stood out. It was of a boat filled with many people,
some drumming whilst others danced. Above the boat was another
person who was clearly flying. This image was at the bottom of a huge
sloping rock and, halfway up the rock, were footprints, pointing upwards. Following their lead, and going higher still, the flying figure
reappeared, as if confirming that this was indeed the correct direction
to take. Moving to the very top of the sloping rock, the vista opened
out across the adjoining fjord and through a narrow gap in the hills out
to the open sea. It seemed to me that here, engraved onto the rock,
was an almost perfect instruction manual for would-be shamans: this
is the direction to the otherworld and this is how you get there. When
you have visited the otherworld, however, you have always journeyed
down, into the earth. The engraving suggests that you can also go up,
into the sky. In fact, you can do both, and the location of the images
shows why this is so.

The engravings, and there are thousands of them from several millennia, were positioned right on the rocky shoreline, on the interface
of earth, sea, and sky.[2] This was very deliberate and reflects people's
wider understanding of the composition of this world and of the otherworld or rather, *otherworlds*, as the otherworld is actually divided
into three vast realms: the lowerworld, the middleworld, and the up-

perworld. The shoreline position of the images reflects this division since the water corresponds to the lowerworld, a place with which you are already familiar (and you have seen in previous chapters how water has often been associated with this realm). The land corresponds to the middleworld, a place you will visit later in this chapter. Finally, the sky corresponds to the upperworld, a place you will visit next.

Interestingly, the images were engraved by the ancestors of the modern Sámi people, who still live in the area today, and who were historically a shamanic people. Every Sámi shaman had a drum patterned with various images, many replicating the same subjects that were engraved on the rocks.[3] Many of the patterns on the drums were divided by three horizontal lines, and these also reflect the division of the otherworld into three. Similarly, at a place near Kivik in Sweden, there is a stone-lined Bronze Age burial tomb and, on the surface of the stone slabs facing into the tomb, various images were engraved, some of which were also divided into three separate realms.[4] This appears to be a road map to the otherworlds, one to be read by the dead shaman who lay in the grave. Perhaps people thought that the shaman might need a reminder of where to go, or perhaps it was a list of tasks they wanted their shaman to complete once he or she got to the otherworlds. It should not surprise you to find that the grave was also constructed on the shoreline, where the portal between the worlds is close.

The division of the otherworld into three is common to most shamanic societies, although some also further divide the upperworld and lowerworld into many more realms. Even the Christian tradition recognises heaven, earth, and hell; although, in this case, the lowerworld is considered a negative place and not somewhere you would willingly go. As with a lot of Christian imagery, this is a distortion of earlier traditions; the lowerworld is no more connected with hell than the antlered Master of the Animals is connected with the devil. Unfortunately, the easiest way to subjugate existing beliefs is to tell people that what they honour is a devil and where they go is hell. These distortions should not trouble us when we make contact with these ancient and powerful archetypes. Another early tradition surrounding the otherworlds is that they are a mirror image of this world so that everything in this reality is reversed in the other. Some Native American shamans, for example, carry out their most important journeys at night, during the winter, so that, in the otherworlds, it will be daytime, during the summer.[5] Similarly, items that are broken in this world become whole in the otherworlds, and things that are turned upside down in this world appear the right way up in the otherworlds. Some of the shoreline rock engravings at Alta, especially boats, were carved upside down, and it is likely that these images represent a successful crossing to the otherworlds and a continuation of the shaman's journey.

## Getting to the Otherworlds

We have seen before how the lowerworld is often associated with water, from the hunter-gatherer lakeside cemeteries, through the engravings positioned at the edge of the sea, to the graves shaped liked boats. In every case, however, the journey is down, *into* the water. This is also true of your journeys to the lowerworld, when you have always gone *down* through a hole and into the earth. Our Ice Age ancestors used caves as suitable entrances to the lowerworld, but there were also many other ways of getting down into the earth. In Iron Age Scotland, for example, several houses were deliberately positioned over the top of earlier burial tombs.[6] The builders of these houses dug into the tomb and constructed a route from the house to the tomb. Leaving the bones and other funerary remains where they lay, the people living in the house would then have their own private route down into the earth. Imagine them, candle in hand, tentatively descending the steps that led down into the tomb. Aware of the bones that covered the floor, this would indeed have felt like a place of the spirits. Elsewhere in Scotland, but also in Cornwall and Brittany, people dug special underground chambers next to houses, and, with no obvious use, perhaps these were also used as portals to reach the lowerworld.[7] In the Stone Age, people moved around the land, digging pits and filling them with debris from their feasts and also with special pottery. The pottery was special because it carried designs similar to the phosphenes mentioned in chapter 1 (a sure indication of otherworldly association).[8] Perhaps people used the pottery to hold the food and drink of their feasts, taking what remained at the end and burying it in the earth; returning to the lowerworld what belonged in that realm.

The upperworld is more clearly associated with the sky, and you have seen how the shamans whose images were engraved on the Norwegian rocks left their bodies behind and flew up, into the sky. There was another means of getting to the upperworld, however, and this is most visibly demonstrated at a place called Navan, in Ireland.[9] Here, the Iron Age people constructed an enormous labyrinth, fashioned out of tree trunks and set in a concentric circle.[10] Walking through labyrinths has long been known to induce the trance that is vital for any journey to the otherworlds. (They even appear in Christian cathedrals, where intense communion with God was the aim, rather than a journey to the otherworlds.) At the centre of the labyrinth at Navan was a particularly enormous tree trunk, reaching high into the sky. It is likely that, after walking the labyrinth (and feeling the effects of trance), this was the route people used to enter the realm of the upperworld: ascending the tree and flying high into the sky.

Ascending a tree to the upperworld might also remind us of the Master of the Animals, who always seemed to be depicted at the base of a tree. Perhaps he was a gatekeeper for those who wanted to climb the tree and ascend to the sky. Seahenge, found, appropriately, on the shorefront in Norfolk, was another huge tree that our ancestors had turned upside down and driven into the earth; around it was a plank-built fence with a small entrance to squeeze through.[11] Knowing that things in the otherworlds are often represented as upside down in this world, Seahenge was probably another portal to the otherworlds. Perhaps people sat on the bole of the tree, among its roots, and let themselves be carried into the sky or deep into the earth. Interestingly, the shamanic people of Siberia also had their own versions of Seahenge: trees set into the earth and surrounded by plank fencing; they also used them as conduits to the otherworlds.[12] The Sámi of Lapland did similar.[13] It seems that this is a tradition that had very widespread adherence. Even today, Laura, who often journeys to the upperworld, found that her journeys are more intense when she sits in her favourite tree: "I often go to my tree to journey or simply to visit her. At first, I expected it would somehow feel strange to journey there but, actually, it felt rather cosy and familiar. I can feel her presence even when I am in the otherworlds and she is always a source of great strength."

## Journeying to the Upperworld

For your first visit to the upperworld, you will also climb a tree, pushing off from its uppermost braches and flying up, into the sky.

---

### Exercise: Journeying to the Upperworld

*Begin as you would for a journey to the lowerworld, except this time, state your intention as: I am journeying to the upperworld to connect and to look around. Then, imagine a tall tree before you. Begin to climb it (and, do not forget, you are not limited by your physical body, so you can easily climb even the smoothest trunk). When you reach the very top of the tree, jump into the air and you will find yourself flying upwards into the sky. Keep going up until the tree is far beneath you. You might pass through clouds or even reach the edge of space, but keep going up; you have not yet reached your destination. Keep going until you pass through a membrane (rather like coming up for air when you have been swimming underwater) and emerge into another realm: this is the upperworld. Walk around a little and*

*explore this new land. How does it differ from the lowerworld with*
*which you are familiar? When you hear the call-back drumming, pass*
*back through the membrane and fly down, towards the earth. When*
*you see your tree, land upon it and climb back down. Then, return to*
*your physical body as usual and write about your experiences in your*
*journal.*

---

Like the lowerworld, the upperworld also contains allies that can
help and empower you. But whereas lowerworld allies are usually in
animal form, upperworld allies are usually in human form. If you did
not meet anyone on your first journey to the upperworld, journey
again, this time setting your intention as: *I am journeying to the upper-*
*world to find my teacher and guide.* When you get there, look around in
the same way you did when you went in search of your power animal.
Again, trust that whomever you meet will be exactly right for you.

Hannah, for example, went in search of her upperworld guide and
found that Rhiannon, of the Welsh Mabinogion myths, came to her:
"I started climbing a tree near where I live. The tree seemed to grow
higher and higher, up through the clouds. After I had been climbing
for some time, I jumped off the tree and flew through the air, feeling free and weightless. I continued moving upwards until I passed
through a layer and emerged on a hill surrounded by mist. Coming
around the hill was Rhiannon on her white horse. I asked if she was
my teacher and she smiled and held her hand out to me. I took her
hand and sat behind her on the horse. We then raced faster and faster.
When the call-back came, I thanked Rhiannon and she took me back
to the hill so that I could fly back down to the tree."

Kate, who was born in America but now lives in Europe, found
that her upperworld guide was an old Native American chief from a
tribe near her hometown. He teaches her many things about the land
of her birth and the native traditions of its people. John, by contrast,
found that his upperworld guide was a beautiful woman; she turned

out to be his grown-up sister who had died when she was only a small child. "It was her smile that welcomed me to the upperworld," John told me, "her hands that reached out in greeting. I was overcome with the love that I felt inside."

Whereas your power animal grounds you and brings you physical empowerment through shapeshifting and dance, your upperworld guide often brings more cerebral qualities to bear on the issues on which you ask them to help. Of course, these are just generalisations, and you will develop your experience as to whom you should journey to depending on the help that you need at the time. However, if you really do not know where to go, then journey with the intention of going to the *otherworld*, rather than specifying a particular realm. Then, just before setting off, pay attention to your body and notice where you feel "pulled." If there is a tug downwards, go to the lowerworld; but if there is a tug upwards, go to the upperworld. By doing this, you are listening to and trusting your intuition. Try journeying to both your power animal and your upperworld guide with the same question or issue and then compare the answers or help given. Over time, you will develop a feel as to whether you should journey up or down, and you will instinctively know in which realm you will find the best help.

## Journeying to the Middleworld

Think back to the engraved rocks on the Norwegian shoreline; there is one place to which you have not yet journeyed: the middleworld. This realm is very different from the upperworld and lowerworld, as it is not a separate realm but a different way of looking at this world. Whereas in your journeys so far, you have gone somewhere else, this time you will stay right where you are. By listening to the beat of the drum and entering into trance, however, you will be able to see the world in a very different way. In fact, the world will be so different that it is called the middleworld, to differentiate it from the normal, every-day place you are used to.

---

### Exercise: Journeying to the Middleworld

*Begin as you would for any other journey, but this time, state your intention as: I am journeying to the middleworld to connect and to look around. As the drumming starts, just be in your body; feel the heaviness of your body and the space around you. Then, let this feeling of heaviness fall away until you are able to step out of your physical body and leave it behind. This is the middleworld: the world you are familiar with but can now see in a completely different way. Move around; you will find that you can run, fly, and swim just as easily here as you can in the upperworld and lowerworld. Now, look around you. What do you see? Wisps of light? A light mist? These are patterns of energy, now perceptible in your trance state. You might also see other beings as you move around: animals, humans, and possibly shapes that you cannot put a name to. Just let them be. Do not interact with anything at this stage and remember, if you need assistance or feel uneasy, call upon your power animal or upperworld guide and they will come to help you. When you hear the call-back drumming, come back to your starting place and see your body before you. Step back into it. This is much easier than it might sound and you will very quickly be back in your physical body again.*

---

There are no allies to find in the middleworld and this is why, at this stage, it is best not to interact with anything whilst you are there. The middleworld is the realm of many different spirits, however, and you might have seen some on your travels. If not, look out for them on your subsequent journeys. You may have noticed that the quality of objects in the middleworld is different and things that are solid in this world are more opaque when viewed in the middleworld. This is because you are seeing the spiritual essence of the objects: their energy patterns. By observing the way these patterns change, you can discern how energy flows throughout your world. Discerning these energy flows will become especially important later when you discover how to clear negative energy from the places you inhabit.

When in the middleworld, you can move anywhere in space and time. Time travel is not difficult and there are several ways you can begin: you might pass through a mist to reach the time you desire; you might fly up into the clouds, knowing that when you come back to the earth the time will have altered; or you might spin around the world, Superman style, perhaps going clockwise for forwards in time and anticlockwise for backwards. Ask your power animal or upperworld guide for other methods and then practice visiting different times in the past and future. Moving through space is just as easy and, as you have found in the upperworld and lowerworld, you can move far quicker without your physical body to consider.

Since the middleworld is just the real world seen through different eyes, it becomes possible to move to another place and observe what is happening there at the same time you are journeying. Several people have claimed that the CIA has taught them such remote viewing (as the practice is called). I tried it myself once with a partner, Rob. Whilst I journeyed to the middleworld, Rob left the building we were in and walked around. At an agreed signal, I was to observe where he was and what he was looking at. In my middleworld journey, I saw Rob in front of a brick-built house with a blue car outside. I then returned to this world and took Rob back to the place in which I had seen him standing, right in front of the brick-built house. Rob confirmed that this was indeed the place but, unfortunately, there was no blue car. Just as I was beginning to doubt if our exercise had worked, a blue car drove up and a woman got out. Rob and I both laughed: I got the right place, but the wrong time.

## What Actually Journeys to the Otherworlds?

Now that you have explored all three realms of the otherworld, consider what part of you leaves your body and journeys, whilst your physical body is in trance. Most shamanic societies believe that our soul, or at least a part of it, departs (the rest remains with our body and will do so until death, when it all leaves). The word *soul*, however, has many religious connotations and some people prefer to call it our *spirit* or even our *essence*. For the scientists who study the brain, the soul is a nebulous concept because it cannot be identified; for them, the shamanic journey to the otherworld is merely a series of hallucinations experienced solely in the mind.[14] These same scientists, however, still speak of *going into* trance, as if it is actually a real journey. For the shaman, the shamanic journey is a journey to a real place that exists outside of the mind. No scientist can *prove* that the otherworlds do not exist, and for those of us who have actually been there, even the very notion of trying to do so seems absurd.

You know that to put your body into the state in which it is able to journey to the otherworld, you need to enter trance. You have achieved this through listening to repetitive drumming, and you know that this was also a common method in the past. You have seen how the Sámi shamans, who sailed their boats in the Norwegian fjords and engraved images of themselves onto the rocks, also played drums to set their spirits free to journey to the upperworld. These drums were made from reindeer hide stretched taut over a circular wooden frame or pulled tight across a shallow wooden bowl. I own one of the latter drums and the journeys it has given me have been worthy of such a beautiful object. During the Stone Age, when people were making wide-brimmed pots to use around the house, the skin forming the surface of the drum was stretched across the neck of such a pot with the deep ceramic body magnifying the sound accordingly.[15] In fact, the volume and depth of the sound seemed particularly important to people at this time and several of the huge burial chambers, where dead bodies were buried all together, were designed so that someone drumming just outside the entrance would fill the air with a loud and deep noise, rather akin to blowing across the top of a bottle.[16] If people gathered here to journey to the otherworlds, and a burial site was probably considered a very suitable portal between the worlds, then filling the air with the sound of the beating drum would have been particularly significant.

Gathering together to journey to the otherworlds also took place in a different place in the later Bronze Age period. You are probably familiar with the Native American sweat lodge ceremonies, where a tent-like structure contains the heat and steam produced by pouring water over very hot rocks. The almost overbearing heat and humidity within the confines of the lodge can evoke trance states, allowing people to connect with the world of the spirits and, if they desire, journey to the otherworlds. But sweat lodges are not just a Native American tradition; they also were common in our European past.[17] Piles of burnt stones have been found in many places where there was a good supply of water. The occurrence of small troughs, presumably used to hold the water, suggests that the hot stones were added to the water to produce steam rather than the other way round. Intriguingly, the Nenet people of western Siberia still use similar sweat lodges for their journeys to the otherworlds, and it is likely that this is the end of a very ancient Eurasian tradition.[18]

## Entheogenic Plants in Ancient Europe

Our prehistoric ancestors carved images of boats not only onto rocks but also onto small bronze razors that people used for shaving their hair.[19] Rather than carry people, however, these boats carry something else altogether: mushrooms and, in particular, the fly agaric mushroom.[20] Known for its beautiful red and white spotted cap, this mushroom is still used in parts of Siberia to induce trance and, if the razors are any indication, our European ancestors also commonly used it. One of the symptoms of taking this mushroom is excessive movement and muscle spasms and this may explain why the people in the boats in the rock engravings were dancing: they had ingested the mushroom and were feeling the effects.

Chapter 2 mentioned henbane, which is another potent trance plant that may have given the people of Lepenski Vir the impression they were turning into fish. The seeds of henbane, the most intoxicating part of the plant, also have been found on sites dating to the Iron Age, where the seeds had been burned, perhaps to allow people to inhale the toxic smoke.[21] The famous oracle at Delphi also may have burnt henbane seeds to induce the trance necessary to contact the Greek Gods and receive the prophecies that she was renowned for.[22]

During the Stone Age, opium seemed to have been used abundantly, and distinctive pottery was designed to facilitate taking the drug.[23] Some of the small incense burners were shaped like the poppy head. Cannabis was another drug burned in a brazier and Herodotus, the great Greek historian, notes that the Scythian people of the European Steppe burnt cannabis at funerals.[24] Perhaps the shamans of the tribe used it to ensure that the dead had safely passed across the veils to the otherworlds: a last service to their departed kin.

Like fly agaric, ergot is also a fungus that induces trance. It grows on infected heads of rye, a plant whose use expanded greatly during the Bronze and Iron Ages. In one of the famous bog bodies, a man found perfectly preserved in a marsh in Denmark, analysis of the stomach contents showed that the man had eaten ergot shortly before he died.[25] There is even a suggestion that the famous Eleusinian harvest mysteries of the ancient Greek world used an ergot-spiked drink made from contaminated grain as the centre of their rituals, allowing them to communicate directly with the Gods.[26]

The attitude of people to these amazing plants can perhaps best be summarised by what they are called. Enforcement agencies call them *narcotics*, things to be banned; scientists call them *hallucinogens*, things that cause hallucinations; thrill-seekers call them *psychedelics*, things to get inside your head; but shamans generally call them *entheogens*, things that help us communicate with the sacred. The key aspect in all of these descriptive names is that they induce trance. They do this by flooding the brain with the same chemicals that are naturally released however someone enters trance. You have achieved the same results by listening to repetitive drumming. Taking entheogens merely replicates what can be achieved in other, far more controlled, ways. Moreover, if entheogens are abused or taken through mere curiosity, the resulting effects are often unpleasant and dangerous. At best, taking entheogens in this manner can provide a momentary experience of being a shaman, but they can never provide the life to go with it.

Traditional people in many parts of the world take entheogens, and they are a very important part of the spiritual and shamanic culture. Peyote, the small Mexican cactus, is taken as part of Native American Church ceremonies; ganja or marijuana is an important part of Rastafarianism; teonanacatl (now recognised as a psilocybin mushroom) is part of Mazatec shamanic culture; and many South American Indians take a brew containing ayahuasca.[27] In every case, however, the entheogen is contained within the culture, the appropriate dose is known and controlled, and an experienced shaman oversees the ceremonies. The same is not true for ancient European entheogens. So, for the time being at least, they will have to remain interesting curiosities of how our ancient ancestors journeyed to the otherworlds.

In this chapter, you have achieved a full complement of otherworld allies: your power animal and now your upperworld teacher. These spirits of the otherworlds are there for your benefit, to empower your everyday life and make you all that you have the potential to be. Journey to them as often as you can and make use of these powerful sources of strength and wisdom. Your allies are not the only spirits of the otherworlds, however. You may have already seen other beings on your journeys: animals that pass you by, people who carry on with their tasks as if you were not really there, and perhaps other wisps and shadows that might indicate a fleeting presence. In the next chapter, you will meet some of these spirits and find out how incredibly crowded the otherworlds can be.

# 4
# Calling the Spirits:
## Gathering and Using Your Power

You watch as a woman strokes a small model of a deer. She cradles it as if it were truly alive rather than a crudely fashioned piece of river clay. Almost reluctantly, she walks towards a small lean-to structure that roughly covers a shallow pit in the ground. A man stands at the entrance and takes the model deer from the woman. He enters the shelter and sweeps aside the bones that litter the floor. You can just make out a small rounded mound of earth with a hole low in its side; this is a kiln and inside are many other animal models, just like the deer you saw the woman hand to the man. This last little statue is then added to the pile and the hole into the oven is closed. The man then kindles a fire to surround the kiln and you sit to wait for its effect. A small group gathers as the fire reaches its greatest intensity and you have to fight a little to keep your place at the front. Just as the crowd settles, you hear the first explosion from inside the kiln. It is the animal models shattering in the heat but, rather than being upset, the people around you exclaim loudly and turn to each other with smiles on their faces. Another explosion is followed by yet more and you realise that there will be nothing left of the clay animals by the time the fire has burnt down. The explosions come to an end but nobody seems anxious to leave, so you spend some time sitting, watching the flames *fade until, finally, there is only the red glow of the charcoal to remind you that they were there at all. The man who first lit the fire opens the door to the kiln once more and begins to rake out its contents. As you predicted, the models are totally smashed, some beyond all recognition. As they cool, people come forward to take a small piece from the remains before walking silently away. Eventually, you are left all alone, wondering exactly what it was you have just witnessed.*

## Offerings to the Spirits

Dolní Věstonice is a small village in the Czech Republic that was occupied almost 30,000 years ago.[1] This was long before people started making pottery bowls and cups, although, as you witnessed yourself, the inhabitants of Dolní Věstonice certainly had the technology to do so. The problem was that their lifestyle was nomadic; they moved from place to place depending upon the season and crockery was just too heavy and fragile to carry. They did make small models of animals out of clay, however, and they fired these in small earthen kilns. Rather than fire the figurines properly, so that they came out hard and useable, people fired them at such a high temperature that it caused them to explode.[2] This was not a mistake but a deliberate and technically difficult act; whatever made them do it must have been very important indeed.

Hunting societies—and the people of Dolní Věstonice were certainly hunters—often have a close and intimate relationship with their prey. As well as treating the bodies of the slain animals with respect, the people believed that the animals killed in the hunt have to be replaced if there is to be enough game for future needs. For every animal that is killed, the Master of the Animals sends another to replace it.[3] What the inhabitants of Dolní Věstonice appear to have been doing was giving him something in return. The exploding animals were offered as a gift to the Master of the Animals to send more game in return. By being broken in this world, they were passed to the other-worlds, where they became whole once again. This is why the people were so pleased that their animal figures exploded in the fire: it meant more prey for them to hunt.

Making offering to the spirits of the otherworlds is a good practice to adopt. Before doing so, however, you need to be sure what a spirit is. To shamanic people, everything is alive.[4] This is not just a figure of speech but a real belief: everything on the planet is alive. Although we accept that animals are alive, and even that trees and plants have life, it is harder to accept that the hills, streams, and earth are also alive. It is even harder to accept that our cars, computers, and telephones are also living, but to a shaman, this is precisely what they are. Perhaps the books for children with talking trains, or the way we moan at our cars when they begin to play up on an icy morning remind us that it was not too long ago that we all thought the same. It follows, however, that if something is alive, it also has a soul or a spirit and this spirit can be approached in the otherworlds and spoken to, just as you speak with your power animal and upperworld guide.

The spirit of things can be approached in any of the three otherworlds but, in general, I have found that the spirits of groups of things, such as the spirit of Stone (representing *all* stones), or the spirit of Tree (representing *all* trees), or even the spirit of Computer (representing *all* computers), are best approached in the lowerworld or upperworld. The spirits of individual things, such as the spirit of *a* stone, *a* tree, or *a* computer, are best approached in the middleworld. Chapter 5 explains how to approach the spirits of individual things; this chapter concentrates on the spirits of groups of things.

An enormous variety of spirits exists, and they inhabit all sorts of places. This was brought home to me when I visited Siberia and the husband of a modern-day shaman drove me around. Every so often, he would wind down his window and throw out a handful of coins, cigarettes, rice, or whatever else came to hand. Occasionally, when we passed the abode of a particularly powerful spirit, we would stop and

pour vodka on the ground and tie a prayer-flag onto an already fes-
tooned tree. These were all offerings to the spirits of the places we
passed along the road and, by making them, we ensured that we had
the spirits' protection for our journey. Like the people of Dolní Věstonice, we were giving something to the spirits in the hope of getting
something back in return. In your shamanic practice, you should always offer first and ask second; this way, you always keep gratitude at
the forefront of your heart.

## Showing Your Gratitude

Gratitude is sometimes lacking in the modern world. We have come
to expect so much, and we talk of our *rights* as if we owe nothing in
return for them. Most religions attempt to counter this by teaching
their followers prayers: words of thanks spoken out loud to divinity.
These prayers are usually someone else's words, however, and, to be
really effective, a prayer has to come from the heart. When it does, it
becomes a worthy gift to offer to the spirits. If you have not prayed for
a while, it is easy to get out of practice, but there really is nothing to
it. Find somewhere quiet where you get a sense of the spirit you want
to address (and, in my experience, spirits can often tell when they are
about to be addressed and often move a little closer as a result), and
then speak whatever is in your heart. If you speak as if you are address-
ing something real (which, of course, you are) and just say what you
feel, before you know it, you will be praying. There are no formulas,
no special words, nothing that need inhibit you from saying what you
want to say.

Another way of using your voice to make an offering to the spirits
is to sing. This might sound even more off-putting than trying to pray,
but you do not need a good voice to sing to the spirits. Whatever you
sing is a song of the heart and, as such, is always beautiful. In fact, you
do not even need to use words. The Sámi people have a special song
called a *joik*, which is more a series of joined-up sounds than a usual

song. I learnt how to joik many years ago and find that, when I offer my voice to the spirits, it immediately draws them close. Rather than speak words, I express myself in sounds.

Poems are another way of using your voice to make a gift to the spirits, especially if you have written the words yourself. Mandy, who writes wonderful poetry, reads her creations to the spirits and then buries the paper containing the poem deep into the earth. It is a wonderful way of offering something of herself and showing her gratitude for all that the spirits give her. Again, however, the act of giving is important and not how well you can write. A poem could be three words that express how you feel; if they come from your heart, such a poem would indeed be a fine gift to offer to the spirits.

To offer something more tangible to the spirits, bear in mind that one person's gift is another person's litter. In my own practice, I only offer things that are natural or fully (and quickly) biodegradable. If you are out in the country, look out for a piece of quartz or an interesting stone, and use that as an offering to the spirits. Find a beautiful feather and offer that, or give a handful of birdseed, which will also help feed our precious wildlife. The same principle applies as with prayers, poems, and songs: what is in your heart when you make the offering is important, not what you actually give. One of my teacher spirits, for example, lies buried high on a mountain peak in Wales. When she was buried during the Bronze Age, people placed bunches of meadowsweet around her grave. Meadowsweet grows wild near my home and, every year, just as it comes into flower, I pick a few stems and carry them up the mountain to lay near the woman's grave. My offering is not big or impressive, but it comes from the heart; I make the walk up the hill a form of pilgrimage, where I reflect on all the help I have received from her spirit during the year.

If you are inside, lighting a candle can be a good offering to the spirits, especially if you light and extinguish it with a short, spoken dedication. I like to say something like: "I light this candle for the spirits and for my ancestors; may its light be their light," and, when extinguishing it: "As I extinguish this candle, may the light of the spirits and of my ancestors remain within me."

Chapter 3 described how the Scythian people of the European Steppes burned herbs or incense over hot charcoal held in a brazier. The scented smoke was thought to be pleasing to the spirits and, once again, is a tradition we can also follow. Many manufactured incense mixtures and sticks that can be lit with a match are for sale, but for a really worthy gift, collect and mix your own. Many tree barks are scented when burnt, or try dried flower heads (I find that lavender gives a delicious perfume) or even berries, such as those from the juniper bush. Similarly, you can gather and burn the resin that oozes from pine trees, providing a wonderfully thick and beautifully scented smoke. During prehistory, people used pine resin for many things, particularly when something sticky was needed to hold items in place, but I am sure they would have also burnt it and savoured the scent just as much as we do today. Experiment and make your own incense mixture to offer to the spirits.

## Journeying to the Elements

When you make your offerings to the spirits, you make a sacrifice: you give with no intention of retrieving what you gave. The Romans, who invaded much of Europe at the end of the Iron Age, were particularly keen on sacrifice, and they would often strike a bargain with the sprits whereby they offered a certain item but only in exchange for something specific in return.[5] In a way, the sacrifice was a form of legal contract, and perhaps this is not surprising from a people who formed the earliest European laws. The Roman focus on sacrifice, however, may have distorted the way they saw the Iron Age people they conquered. In one particularly infamous passage, Lucan, a Roman poet, commented that the Gods of the Iron Age Celts required human sacrifice in a number of different ways: some wanted their sacrificial victims to be burnt; some wanted them to be hanged; whilst others wanted them to be drowned.[6] If we couple this with the evidence we have for people being buried in deep pits, a pattern begins to emerge.[7] Each method of death corresponds with one of the elements: burning to fire, hanging to air, drowning to water, and burying to earth. Perhaps the Roman poet misunderstood what his Celtic sources told him: instead of actual sacrifices, these were ways of interacting with the spirits of the elements. Shamanic journeys the world over are often compared to a form of death and rebirth. Since our soul or spirit leaves the body for a while (whilst it journeys to the otherworld), it is easy to see where this imagery comes from. Perhaps this is what the Celtic people tried to explain to the Roman but, lost in his own world of sacrifice and law, what he recorded for posterity was something very different.

Just as during the Iron Age, journeying to the spirit of an element is a perfect way of beginning your work with the spirits. Unlike your power animal or upperworld guide, however, the spirit of an element has no predetermined form. The spirit may take the image of a person or an animal, an object, or be something made from the element itself; in every case, you must trust that what you see is exactly what you *need* to see at that particular time. As with any journey to the otherworld, the first thing you should do is to call your power animal or upperworld guide so that you have an ally and a protector by your side. For your first journey, meet the spirit of whichever element you choose. On subsequent journeys you can then ask for help with a particular issue, request the power of the element to help you cope with something you have to do, or obtain whatever advice and guidance you need at this time.

---

## Exercise: Journeying to the Elements

*Decide which element you want to journey to and then set your intention as: I am journeying to the upper/lowerworld to meet the spirit of air/water/fire/earth. When you arrive in either the lowerworld or upperworld (it does not matter which, and why not try both?), call*

*in your power animal or upperworld guide and ask them to introduce*
*you to whatever element you want to meet. You might be taken on a*
*magical journey to the very heart of the element; you might be shown*
*a representation of the element that is for you and you alone; or you*
*might be set some tasks to fulfill to ensure that you are fully prepared*
*for your encounter. Like all journeys, always listen to your helper*
*spirits and do as they advise. Shamanism is about empowerment and*
*finding your own destiny and not always following instructions from*
*a book, even this one, so you must be prepared to listen to what your*
*power animal or upperworld guide tells you. After you hear the call-*
*back and return to this world, is there anything you could add to your*
*neck pouch to remember your encounter with the element? That way,*
*the next time you are stuck in a train tunnel, you can touch the pouch*
*and call upon the spirit of earth to protect you, or, if your car catches*
*fire, you can ask the spirit of fire to take back the flames and keep*
*them for another time.*

---

Marek had a particularly moving encounter with the spirit of earth when he used his knowledge of shapeshifting to become the element and learn something of its mysteries: "I merged with the spirit of earth until I became a standing stone. The age of the stone staggered me. A human life is a mere fraction of time compared to the stone. It was winter and my base was embedded in the frozen soil but I did not feel the cold. I then became a cave, sheltering those who may need my dry interior. I became the sea cliffs, shaped by the sea that pounded its surf against me. I became the exposed rocks of a mountain and felt the wind buffeting my being. And, last of all, I was the ore of a metal. The fire was before me, melting my form until the secrets ran from me. And then, I was the standing stone again. I realised that no one element stands alone but is shaped by the other three. It made me realise just how much all things are connected."

The spirit of an element can also teach you about who you are and the qualities that you hold. In general, water corresponds to your emotional life, air to your intellectual life, earth to your physical life, and fire to your energetic life. Journey to each element and ask what qualities of the element you hold and those that you need to cultivate. Jenny, for example, found that by becoming more aware of her air qualities, she could compensate for her otherwise dominant water personality: "I feel that air qualities are within me: a logical mind, a lightness of being, and clear-headedness; but they are not as naturally strong as my emotional water qualities. Detachment from other people's problems and less over-sensitivity would come from a better balance of air qualities." From then on, Jenny journeyed a lot to the spirit of air and, over time, achieved far more balance in her life.

In addition to the elements, you also can journey to the spirits of the four kingdoms of our planet. These kingdoms were represented in the shaman's pouch described in chapter 2: the snake, weasel, and falcon bones corresponding to the animal kingdom; the conifer cube, the roots, and bark corresponding to the plant kingdom; the amber, chalk, and shell corresponding to the mineral kingdom; and the shaman himself corresponding to the human kingdom. You have read about the head of the animal kingdom before—the Master of the Animals—but this is now a chance to journey to meet him. There are also Masters and Mistresses of the other kingdoms; the ancient Greeks, for example, called the Mistress of the Animals *Potnia Theron*. Your power animal or upperworld guide can take you to meet them all. As you did with the spirits of the elements, meet them in an initial journey and then seek their advice and wisdom to bring the power that they hold into your life.

## The Spirit of Work

Our ancestors sought spirits not only in the natural world, but also in their cultural world and, in particular, in the work they undertook. For the Iron Age people, every task was a sacred duty in itself and had spirits and, later, Gods, associated with it. The Romans recorded some of the names of these spirits so that we know that the spirit of blacksmithing (an incredibly important trade for people who took their name from the metal) was called Govannon; the spirit of healing was called Noden; and, just to show that even more lowly trades had spirits, the spirit of pig-rearing was called Moccus (the Welsh word for pigs is *moch*, after this spirit).[8] Even today, each profession, trade, or task has an associated spirit and since, for most of us, work of some sort takes up a large part of our lives, journeying to meet and befriend this spirit can be very beneficial.

## Exercise: The Spirit of Work

*Begin as you would for any journey but, this time, sense whether you should go to the upperworld or lowerworld in order to meet the spirit of your work. Then, set your intention as: I am journeying to [wherever you are going] to meet the spirit of my work [or, if you prefer, name whatever it is that you do]. When you reach your destination, call in your power animal or upperworld guide and ask for their help in meeting the spirit of your work. Then, follow their lead and see where your journey takes you. You might want to ask the spirit for its help to improve your proficiency at what you do, or you might want to ask for its guidance in how best to advance your career. Whatever it is you ask for, do not forget that you can discuss the reply that you are given with your power animal or upperworld guide before you return.*

When you have met the spirit of your work, journey again to meet the spirit of your company or firm. Journey in the same way you did to meet the spirit of your work but, this time, change your intention to reflect the new spirit you want to meet. However, whilst some people may be very proud of where they work, and this exercise will be straightforward, others may have a neutral or negative relationship with their place of work. If so, then journeying to its spirit may be a means of resolving any difficulties that you have at work or, at least, letting your feelings be voiced. Speaking out in this manner can be hugely empowering, especially with your power animal or upperworld guide by your side.

Jane, for example, was extremely unhappy at the place in which she worked. She felt that the company had little scruples and was having a hugely negative impact upon her well-being. So she journeyed to her power animal to ask what to do: "He took me to a bat, which I took to be the spirit of [my company]. Bat told me that he didn't like what was happening either, but he needed help to stop it. He told me to imagine everything that I didn't like about [my company] and bring them to him. I imagined all the things that were wrong and gave them to Bat. They were like little round globes all across his wings. Bat then carried the globes up to the sun where they shattered into tiny crystals. He then told me to imagine a bright light flooding my office and driving out all the lies and negativity." Jane's journey helped her cope with the next few months of working there but, after that, she left and moved to a much nicer place.

It was quite revealing that Jane saw the spirit of her company as a bat. Many companies have animal spirits and, sometimes, these have become well known, even to those without shamanic knowledge. A tiger represents a fuel company, for example, a black horse represents a bank, and a (famous) grouse represents whisky. Coincidence? Maybe not.

The biggest difference between the work you do today and the work our ancestors undertook is that work today can be very removed from the rest of your life. In the past, people grew or farmed what they ate and, as a result, work was very connected to every other part of their lives. The other big difference was that money had not been invented, so that everything was either produced at home or, occasionally, bartered from elsewhere. To try to bring something of the attitude of the past into your life, work out what you earn against what you spend.

Then, convert these into units of time. So, for example, if you earn £500 per week and spend £200 on rent, £100 on food, £100 on entertainment, and £100 on savings, then you can calculate that on Monday and Tuesday you work to put a roof over your head, Wednesday you work to eat, Thursday you work for all the fun in your life, and Friday is a day of thrift, a day for the future. You are no longer a wage slave but are actively working for the things in your life that you really want. You still have to work to pay the bills too, but looking at work in this manner allows you to connect the different parts of your life and realise the interdependency of everything.

## Animal Spirits

You have been working with your power animal for some time now and drawing on the strength and wisdom it offers. Occasionally, however, you might want to draw on the powers held by another animal, particularly if you are about to undertake some activity or event to which it is especially suited. For example, if you are about to fly, call upon the power of Eagle to calm your nerves or, if you are learning to swim, call upon the power of Seal to help keep you afloat.

Calling upon animal powers was extremely common in the past. The Scythian people, for example, decorated their very finest possessions with images of deer, lions, and even griffins.[9] The latter animal suggests that these were not ordinary animals but animal spirits, and the way that they were depicted, with hooves kicked up as if they were flying through the air, adds to their otherworldly appearance. Moreover, none of the animals came from the grassland territory of the Scythians, but from beyond the edge of their world in the forested uplands.[10]

To journey to obtain the power of an animal spirit, either state which animal you want to meet or ask your power animal to help find an animal that is exactly right for you at this time. Since you are seeking an animal, journey to the lowerworld.

Calling the Spirits   71

## Exercise: Animal Spirits

*Start as you would normally, stating your intention as: I am journey-
ing to the lowerworld to meet an animal spirit that can help me at this
time. If you have any specific issues you need help with, state them as
part of your intention. Next, journey to your power animal and ask
to be introduced to an animal spirit that might be able to help you.
As always, be guided by your power animal and trust that whatever
animal you meet is exactly right. If the animal agrees to help you,
you might find that it gives you a different perspective on a problem, a
bird's-eye view perhaps, or you might shapeshift into an animal such
as a lion if you need strength, or it may be that the exact reason a
certain animal has appeared will only become apparent later. Ask if
there is anything you need to do to keep the spirit of the animal (and
its powers) with you, especially if you need help with a forthcoming
event. Perhaps there is something you could put into your neck pouch,
or a song of power you could learn.*

Yvonne, for example, journeyed to find an animal spirit to help her
give evidence to a tribunal. She was particularly worried about the
questions the tribunal would ask and the grilling she might receive:
"The animal that appeared was Tortoise, which surprised me as I expected a lion or a tiger to give me strength. My power animal assured
me that Tortoise would help so I trusted what had happened. When
I sat in the tribunal, and all my fears were coming to pass, I began to
feel a weight on my back and it slowly closed around me. At first, I
thought I was going mad, but then I remembered Tortoise and realised that she had put her shell around me. It worked! And the grilling I got just bounced off."

Suzy also had a difficult event to attend and, when she journeyed,
it was Horse who appeared to offer her help. She asked if she should
carry something of Horse when she attended the event and was told

that something would be gifted to her in due time. Later, as she was walking past a field near her house, she noticed some clumps of horse hair stuck in the wire fence and knew at once that she had found her gift. She tucked the horse hair into her neck pouch and carried it to her event, which, not surprisingly, went like a dream.

Of course, the hair that Suzy found was a gift from Horse and it represented the power of this tremendous creature. Even the hair itself, however, would have had a spirit that Suzy could have journeyed to and met in the otherworlds. Meeting the spirits of individual items such as this is our task in the next chapter but first, a spirit of a polar bear urgently needs placating.

# 5

# Magical Metal:
## Capturing the
## Essence of Things

You were there when the polar bear was killed. Tracked from the huge soft pugs it trod into the snow and then run down by the speed of the dogs, it was finally cornered and speared by three of the bravest hunters. One blow from the mighty paw of the bear could cleave a human head from its shoulders and you were glad that you were asked to wait by the sled. The bear was immediately skinned, the pelt rolled tightly before being stowed on the sled, and the carcass butchered to provide great slabs of meat. Only the liver was abandoned, buried deep where even the frenzied dogs could not reach it. That was yesterday; today, you watch as a woman treats the skin of the bear, cleaning off the last vestiges of fat before stretching it tightly across a whale-bone frame. Dark stains of grease on the frame show that this is a regular activity and the woman works quickly with a well-practiced skill. When the skin is as taut as it can be, the frame is hung in the strong sunlight. You then watch as the woman hangs some metal objects next to the skin: a pan and what looks like the same beaker and plate that you used at suppertime the day before. The woman utters some words as she arranges the metal items, almost as if she is talking to the spirit of the animal itself. They are soothing words but, from where you stand, you cannot make out what is said. You know *that metal items are rare and precious to this community and are about to ask why these are being left here, when the woman abruptly finishes her work and walks away; you have missed your chance. Not wanting to stay outside by yourself, you return to the lodge, thinking of the warmth of the seal-fat stove and the promised feast of boiled bear meat tonight.*

## The Importance of Metal

To the Inuit peoples of Arctic Greenland, polar bears are dangerous animals. Their size and strength make them ferocious adversaries, and many people have unwittingly met their ends at the paws of a bear. The Inuit believe, however, that polar bears are dangerous not only when they are alive but also when they are dead. Many rituals serve to honour and appease the dead bear, but among the most curious is the tradition of hanging metal implements next to its drying skin.[1] Polar bears are said to like the metal objects so much that, if they are given some, the spirit of the bear will depart in peace and will not stay to cause trouble for the community. The bear does not take the physical object but the spirit of the object; the Inuit, like shamanic people all over the world, believe that all things are alive and have a spirit that abides in the middleworld.

If objects are alive, then they must have an existence of their own separate from any human involvement. In the past, this seems to have been especially true of metal items, and first copper and then bronze acquired an almost mystical significance. One of the first copper items discovered in Europe came from the frozen heights of the Italian Alps and was carried by Ötzi, the Iceman: the Stone Age traveller who was found where he died, frozen into the ice.[2] New research shows an arrow wound to the shoulder killed Ötzi and that a few days before his death, his hand was injured in a fight.[3] Since he was carrying a copper axe-head when he was found, he was almost certainly an important person within his community, perhaps even its chief. Copper items were so rare that only the most important people carried them. Ötzi's murder was perhaps a leadership coup by younger members of the community, keen to take his place at the head of the group. Despite killing him, however, these young upstarts did not take his copper axe. Perhaps the metal item was just too powerful for them to touch.

The first metal items were symbols of prestige and status. Although they might have been made to resemble earlier stone tools, many were for show rather than actual use. Perhaps it was the deep red colour of the copper that first caught people's eyes. In earlier times, dead bodies were sprinkled with red earth, thought to symbolise life because of its resemblance to blood (although *life* in this instance would be in the otherworlds rather than this world).[4] Perhaps the red hue of copper was also thought to symbolise life and reminded people that items made from the metal were very much alive.

## The Birth of Objects

If an item is to live, it follows that it must first gestate and be born. Copper begins its life as an ore and people must mine it in order to obtain it. There are remains of early copper mines in Serbia and, when the ore had been stripped out from the rock, people left pottery vessels filled with food and drink as offerings to the spirits.[5] We have already seen how important it is to give offerings to the spirits for whatever we ask, and clearly the early copper miners thought the same. At flint mines in Norfolk, people also left food and drink, and the pottery vessels they used to hold it were decorated with images similar to phosphenes.[6] The mines probably were seen as places of the otherworld and, therefore, this pottery would have been very much at home there. Intriguingly, some of the earliest metal items also carry the same designs engraved on their surface, an instantly recognisable symbol of their origins in the otherworld.[7]

Once miners had gathered the ore, they smelted it in a furnace to extract its metal. If the time the ore spent deep underground was its gestation, then smelting was its birth. In Africa, traditional societies still decorate their furnaces with breasts and the tattooed designs that a woman wears.[8] Phallic-shaped bellows are inserted into a doorway at the base of the furnace and it is from here that the metal is drawn. The imagery is unmistakable: metal is born, not made. We do not have the remains of any furnaces from prehistory so we cannot tell if they were decorated or not, but the location in which metalworking took place tells its own story. Almost invariably, metal was smelted on boundaries, usually right at the edge of the settled area.[9] Whilst this could have been for reasons of safety, other boundary locations are more figurative. Many metalworking sites are close to water, and in Ireland metal was often smelted on artificial islands called crannogs.[10] Again, having an available water supply was a sensible precaution when smelting metal, but we also know that water was seen as a portal to the otherworlds: exactly where the spirit of the metal would have been thought to originate. Metalworking also took place within cemeteries, places that have no utilitarian advantages but carry symbolic meaning as portals between the worlds. In Denmark, for example, at a place called Sandagegård, a curious walled building contained many cremation burials but also signs of metalworking.[11] At its entrance were slabs decorated with outstretched hands, a warning perhaps that this was a place of the spirits.

In many traditional cultures, metalworking was the preserve of the shaman because of the dangers involved in working in such close proximity to the spirits. Even in our modern society, blacksmiths retain an aura of mystery and superstition.[12] The early metalworkers, however, were probably seen more as midwives than as craft-workers.[13] Following a human birth, midwives in traditional societies often treat the umbilical cords in a particular way. Sometimes, they are dried and sewn into bags that the child can keep with him or her for protection; at other times, the cord is buried as an offering to the spirits as thanks for a safe delivery. The equivalent to an umbilical cord in metalworking is the mould that fashions the item being made. Like umbilical cords, these were not discarded after the metalworking process had concluded but were taken away and buried. In some instances, there even seems to have been a prohibition in using the metal item in a place where its mould lies buried.[14] Occasionally, such exclusion zones can stretch for hundreds of miles where the remains of the moulds bear no resemblance to the metal items used in that area.

In Africa, where the actual process of metal smelting can still be observed, many rituals and ceremonies mark the birth of the metal, just as there are for a human birth. Special words might be spoken, herbs applied to make the process run smoothly, and even songs and dances are performed around the furnace.[15] Although it is impossible to know if similar ceremonies were carried out in the past, it is almost certain that they were; the birth of an object was an incredibly important occasion. When you made your neck pouch in chapter 2, you performed your own ceremony before starting work. This was to mark the birth of your pouch and the crossing of its spirit from the otherworlds. When you think of other objects you own, however, it is most unlikely that you were there when they were born, let alone performed a ceremony to celebrate the birth. Nevertheless, using your knowledge of journeying in the middleworld, you can journey back in time and observe what happened in the past. If you do this for the objects you own, then you *can* be there at the time they were born and befriend the spirit of the item and make it your ally.

---

## Exercise: The Birth of Objects

*Think of a significant object that you own. Perhaps it is something you use in your journeys to the otherworlds, like a drum, or something from your neck pouch, like a stone. Now, holding the item or having it by your side, journey to the middleworld, stating your intention as: I am journeying to the middleworld to witness the birth of my [whatever object you have chosen]. Call your power animal or upperworld guide if you are unsure. See the object as it is now and then ask if you can witness its birth. If the object is agreeable, journey back in time in whatever way suits you best and observe the moment in which the object was born. This might have occurred during a manufacturing process, when a seed germinated, at the time when an animal left its mother's womb, or when a rock cooled from a volcano. Try to see the point that the object's spirit (which you can now see, since you are in the middleworld) enters into its physical form. Speak to the spirit of the object, asking what lessons it has for you, or how it might like to be treated in the future. In many cultures, sacred objects like to be fed every so often and you can ask if this is something the spirit of your object desires. When you return, spend some time with the item in this world and see how your perceptions of it have changed. Does it feel more real, more alive? Will you treat it any differently as a result? Now, repeat the journey with something entirely utilitarian, a fork, or a lawnmower perhaps, something that is entirely functional to you and see what happens. From now on, when that item goes wrong, or you need it to perform better, you will know its spirit and be able to call upon it for help.*

---

Jill journeyed to witness the birth of her blanket, a fine Native American textile, which she wraps herself in when she journeys: "My power animal took me to the edge of a great plain. Cotton Bush identified itself as the origin for the cotton in my blanket and Sheep came forward to say that she gave the wool. I watched as each was gathered by hand and worked into a yarn. I saw the yarn spun and then stretched on a loom. As the blanket was nearing completion, Cotton Bush and Sheep seemed to merge and enter the blanket and I knew that its spirit had been born. I spoke to the spirit of Blanket and asked her to keep me safe as I journeyed, and I promised I would always honour her with care."

Marcus had been given a drum with a plastic membrane instead of a skin, but that did not stop him journeying to witness its birth: "I went back and back in time until I had the most amazing journey in a prehistoric swamp, which later became the oil field from which my plastic drum was made. Awesome!" For Marcus, just because the drum was made from plastic did not stop it being alive and it became a powerful ally and companion through many years of shamanic journeying.

## The Life of Objects

If an object is born, then it follows that it also lives out its life and has an individual biography in the same way that you do. In fact, some objects become so bound up in what has happened to them over their lives that those events completely overshadow their otherwise quite ordinary status. You probably have souvenirs from your holidays, for instance. Why do you keep them? Often, the item is not particularly beautiful or especially useful, but it represents somewhere exotic and holds the thoughts and memories you have of that place. People in prehistory kept items for similar reasons. During the Ice Age, shells were particularly valued in those places farthest from the sea.[16] People pierced the shells and made them into necklaces; you can imagine the stories people told about them and about the huge expanse of water from where they came. It must have sounded very exotic.

Other items people keep are antique heirlooms, retained because of their age and their association with a family's history. Again, prehistoric people kept similar items, and archeologists have found older-style items in among hoards of far more recent pieces.[17] Perhaps these were the antiques of the day and were kept because of the memories they held. Other items are treasured today because of who once owned them: think of the value of John Lennon's guitar, or the scramble to catch the headbands tennis players throw into the crowd at tournaments. These items are special because their lives intertwined with someone famous. The first people to use metal in Britain thought in a similar way, and we know that they chipped pieces off the bluestones of Stonehenge and carried them with them.[18] Not only was the stone itself special, but also its association with Stonehenge and all the people who had attended ceremonies there across the years.

Think about items you own and the reasons why you keep them, especially those items that are neither functional nor decorative. Often their biography gives them value: the story of their lives. To examine those lives in more detail, journey to the past except, this time, follow the life story of an object from its birth up to the present day.

---

### Exercise: The Life of Objects

*Think of a significant object you own (perhaps the same object you observed being born) and journey to the middleworld, stating your intention as: I am journeying to the middleworld to witness the life of my [whatever object you have chosen]. Again, call your power animal or upperworld guide if you are unsure. Start at the birth of the object and follow it forward through its life. Notice how its spirit responds to the things that have happened to it, how this has changed the energy of the object. Observe what happened when you first came across the object and the effect this had, both on the object and also upon you. Speak directly to the spirit of the object and ask it to explain aspects of its life so that you may strengthen the bond that now exists between you.*

---

Kevin journeyed to observe the life story of a turtle-shell rattle he had been given as a gift: "I started on the bank of the Amazon River. I saw a child playing with a washed-up turtle shell before taking it home. After a while, a man took the shell and made it into a rattle. He did not keep it, but traded it to another who used it at the ceremonies in his village. One day, some white people came and they traded the rattle for some machetes. They brought it back to the States and sold it to the shop where my wife bought it. I watched as she wrapped it and, finally, gave it to me."

With some items, when you watch the story of their lives, you may witness occasions when the item was mistreated or harmed. Like people, objects bear the scars of the past, both as scuffs and scrapes on their surfaces, but also at a deeper level in their souls. When you come across an item that has had a traumatic past, ask your power animal if there is anything you can do to restore its equilibrium. In the journeys I have undertaken to restore the energy of a mistreated object, I have been told to wash items in spring water, leave several in bright sunlight, bury some in the earth, blow scented smoke over a few, and lay others on my drum whilst I gently beat its surface. Treating the objects you own with care and respect empowers them and strengthens the relationship you have with them. Rather than merely using an item, work in harmony with it, the object lending its power to the tasks you undertake.

## The Death of Objects

What lives must eventually die, its spirit leaving this world and returning to the otherworlds, and this is as true for objects as it is for us. In the Bronze Age, of all the metal objects that existed at the time, weapons and especially swords were the most prestigious items. When a sword reached the end of its life, it was usually broken and placed into water.[19] Again, what is broken in this world becomes whole in the otherworlds and water is an ideal portal to the otherworlds. In a shamanic context, the way in which Bronze Age people treated their swords is exactly the behaviour we might have expected. However, it seems that they went further still and even performed the equivalent of a burial ceremony for their swords. At a place called Flag Fen in eastern England, a wooden platform was built that extended far across the water of the fens.[20] This platform was then divided into small compartments or rooms and it seems that each family in the area had its own private space where it could lay its swords and, occasionally, other metal items to rest. Lying in the silt below each room are many swords, their close proximity to the platform showing that they were gently lowered rather than thrown into the water. However, before being placed in the water, the swords were broken and marks on the blades show that this happened in a dramatic frenzy of violence with the sword smashed repeatedly against the ground to effect the break.[21] Perhaps this was a deliberate performance, a eulogy acting out the biography of the sword one last time.

In the Iron Age, people took these ceremonies a stage further. Not only did people place their broken swords into water, such as the River Thames in Britain or the River Meuse in the Netherlands, they often placed the severed head of a human to lie next to them.[22] We are used to objects accompanying people in human graves, but what seems to have happened here is that humans were accompanying objects as they made their own transition back to the otherworlds. It must have been a valued piece indeed that warranted such an incredible send-off.

When you consider the items you own, and especially those that are coming to the end of their lives, the traditions of our ancestors would suggest that you need to consider carefully the manner in which you dispose of them. Perhaps the easiest way of doing this is to journey to the spirit of the object itself and ask for its help.

---

### Exercise: The Death of Objects

*Think of an object you own that is nearing the end of its life. Journey to the middleworld, stating your intention as: I am journeying to the middleworld to witness the death of my [whatever object you have chosen]. As always, call your power animal or upperworld guide if you need any help. When you meet the spirit of the object you have chosen, ask if you might witness its death. If the object agrees, travel forward in time until you reach the point that its spirit returns to the otherworld. Try to observe what happens to the object left behind. Whilst this is one possible scenario you are witnessing, ask the spirit of the object if it is happy with its fate or whether it would prefer a different end. Agree how you might mark the passing of the object and what you should do with the remains it leaves behind.*

---

Janice, for example, was clearing out her house after her divorce and came across a brass ornament she and her husband had bought on their honeymoon. It was a lovely piece, but had too many painful memories associated with it. Before throwing it out, Janice journeyed to witness the death of the object: "I followed [the ornament] from my bin to the landfill site. It was buried beneath piles of rubbish and was finally compacted to nothing. I spoke to the spirit of [the ornament] and he told me that he didn't want to die like this. He then told me to find a new owner for the piece. I asked if there was anything I should do to mark our parting and he replied that I should give him a polish." Janice took the ornament to her next shamanic journey group where someone else fell in love with it and gave it a new home.

As Janice found, it is very likely that when you follow this journey, your object will ask you to reuse, recycle, or pass the item on to someone else. This might seem to reflect our modern concerns with the environment and reducing waste, but our ancestors also keenly followed recycling. In the past, however, the objects themselves, rather than their human companions, *always* determined what happened to them.

## The Recycling of Objects

The metal tools and weapons of the Bronze Age were relatively easy to melt down and remake into a new form, and people gathered many hoards of broken items to be reworked.[23] Strict rules on such recycling depended entirely on the status and the life story of the metal items themselves. Swords, the most prestigious items, could only be made from bronze that was exotic.[24] In northern Europe, this meant bronze from southern Germany.[25] Moreover, the swords made from this metal also copied the exotic styles of southern Germany. Tools, on the other hand, were made with whatever metal was available and in a style that was local to the area in which they were made. Some tools were always recycled into other tools; the cargoes of shipwrecks in the English Channel, for example, contain items that have never been found anywhere else and therefore must have been melted down and recycled.[26] Our ancestors accepted that the spirit of the item survived recycling and therefore the spirit of a tool could never become the spirit of a sword, no matter how well it was made. Concern for the spirit of an object when it is recycled is as important today as it was for our ancestors, but is usually something we completely overlook. You can help to redress the balance by journeying to your own objects and listening to what they have to tell you.

## Exercise: The Recycling of Objects

*Think of an item you own that has been recycled and journey to witness its life, using the same technique and intention as your earlier journey. This time, however, when you follow the life history of the object, see what happened to the spirit of the object when it was recycled. Did the spirit pass into the new object and, if it did, what does this add to your attitude and relationship to the item? Do a similar journey to the spirit of an object you want to dispose of and ask if there is anything into which the spirit would like to be recycled.*

## The Essence of Objects

To us, bronze and iron are similar: they are both metals and can be made into similar objects; if anything, iron is superior to bronze since it is harder and keeps a sharp edge better. To our ancient ancestors, however, who considered the spirit of things and not just their physical properties, bronze and iron were entirely different. People during the Bronze Age knew about iron and what it could do, they just ignored it.[27] The reason was that, unlike bronze, iron was not exotic; it was abundant, widespread, and could be collected from the fields that people ploughed to grow their crops. It was everything that people did not want reflected in the items they used. This remained the case until the time when owning land became more important than wearing an exotic sword; we call this time the Iron Age. People now started to get protective about the land they farmed: hillforts were built, villages were enclosed by fences and ditches, and houses got much bigger; people wanted to keep what they had.[28] It was also at this time that people turned to iron, a metal that reflected this new focus on land and locality. The spirit of bronze was exotic and spoke of places faraway; the spirit of iron was local and spoke of the land a person owned. Wearing an iron sword was almost like wearing your field. Iron was invested with the essence of what people now held important; it carried the essence of land.

In the same way that the essence of land was incorporated into items of iron, you can also use objects to capture the essence of something. Many people, for example, believe it is possible to capture the essence of luck, and numerous charms are available that purport to be lucky. If you journey to the spirit of what you want to capture and ask for its help, however, you can obtain many other things in addition to luck.

---

### Exercise: The Essence of Objects

*Take an object such as a stone or perhaps a piece of metal and see if you can capture the essence of something within it. Set your intention and journey to whatever it is you want to capture: perhaps the essence of your family, the essence of health, or the essence of spring. Ask if the spirit of that essence will enter the object and remain with you. You can also capture the essence of strength, of good judgment, or any other quality that you want to bring into your life.*

---

From the time you began your path into shamanism, your world has changed. You are now aware of the existence of alternative realities, you have gained spiritual allies to help you in your travels and, in this chapter, you have seen that even the objects that surround you are alive and filled with spirit. It is now time to meet the last group of spirits that inhabit the otherworlds: the human dead, our ancestors.

# 6
# Dining with the Dead:
## Honouring the Ancestors

**Y**ou have been sitting for hours in the flickering light of a few guttering torches, listening to the repetitive thump, thump, thump of the drums. Ahead of you lies the opening of a tomb, a cavernous yawn into blackness faced on either side by an enormous lump of rock. Around you sit others, some drumming and some, like you, carried along on its insistent, pulsating rhythm. It seems an age since the shaman disappeared into the tomb; dressed only in rags, he cut a dishevelled but dramatic figure as he called upon the spirits to let him pass beyond the gateway and enter into the place of the dead. Eventually, he returns. You notice that he walks as if weighed down with a load and it soon becomes apparent that he has dragged the half-rotten carcass of a woman out behind him. The flesh is so putrid that much of it has already fallen away from the bones, leaving only the barest suggestion that the corpse was once a human being, just like you. Rather than repulsion, the people around you greet the body as if it were an honoured guest among them. Some of the older women coo softly, caught up in their own memories of the past. Others call out, asking to be remembered to their own ancestors who also lie within the tomb. After everyone has had their say, the shaman takes hold of the body and begins to snap each bone free of its neighbours. He forms a small *pile next to him, sorting each bone so that it lies next to its partner from the other side of the body. Eventually, his grisly task complete, he bundles up the bones and returns again into the confines of the tomb. You know that he is now adding the remains of the woman to the ancient piles of bones that lie at the far end of the tomb; she is now no longer an individual, but has taken her place among the ranks of the ancestral dead. This is the most dangerous part of the shaman's task and the drums renew their intensity to help him complete it successfully. It might be dawn before he returns to the world of the living and you pull your woollen cape tighter around your shoulders as you prepare to wait out the night.*

## Two Stages of Death

During the Stone Age, people were not buried individually but were placed in large communal tombs with an entrance and passageway large enough for someone to walk comfortably along.[1] This passageway led to a central chamber and sometimes to subsidiary chambers on either side. Moreover, since these tombs were designed to hold many people, they were not sealed, but were left open so that new bodies could be added when necessary. Newly dead corpses were initially left in the passageway whilst they rotted enough for the bones to be separated and divided into constituent groups. They were then added to the piles of bones that already lay in the chamber itself. The move from flesh to bones was of great significance, being a progression from the individual identity that the person would have held in life to them joining and becoming one of the ancestral dead. In a way, death was divided into two stages: first, leaving the world of the living, and second, joining the world of the dead.[2]

The ancestors, however, were not forgotten in the past and, as you saw at the beginning of this chapter, people often went to burial sites to communicate with the deceased and obtain their help with the issues of everyday life. When I stayed in a modern shamanic community in Siberia, I attended a ceremony where a shaman called down and embodied an ancestral spirit for a local family. The family immediately knew who it was that had returned to them and they talked to the spirit as if she were still alive. Of course, to the family, she was, but just in a different way from that which we are used to. In prehistoric times, people also interacted with the dead in a similar way and there are caves in Croatia where the people of the Bronze Age regularly dined with the two hundred or so bodies buried there.[3] In some cases, people lit small fires and cooked food right next to the remains of a body, as if they were seeking out their own direct relatives and enjoying their company. In Bulgaria, there is even a burial chamber with a sliding stone door and, from the wear on the runners, it is clear that it was often pushed aside for people to enter the tomb and communicate with the dead inside.[4]

## Meeting Your Ancestors

Meeting your ancestors is still a valuable practice today. Many people visit the burial sites of their departed loved ones and even talk to the lingering presence they feel might be there. With your shamanic knowledge, however, you can go further and hear what the dead have to say in return. To do this, journey to the upperworld, not because you are travelling to heaven but because our society thinks of people going *up* to the afterlife when they die. If you go back to your very earliest ancestors, you might find that the beliefs were different, and people went *down* to the lowerworld.

---

### Exercise: Meeting Your Ancestors

*Decide whom you wish to meet and state your intention accordingly: I am journeying to the upperworld to meet [state the person's name or your relationship to them]. (Alternatively, if you do not want to meet anyone specific, just say "one of my ancestors" in place of a name.) When you arrive in the upperworld, call your power animal and upperworld guide to help you. Ask if they will find the spirit of whomever you want to meet and bring him or her to you. (You are not going to the land of the dead—the afterlife—in this journey; you are waiting for your ancestor to come to you.) When your ancestor arrives, greet them and ask if they would like to spend some time with you. As always with journeys, do what comes naturally and, if you are in any doubt, ask your power animal or upperworld guide for help. When you hear the call-back, thank your ancestor and, if you want to, ask if you can visit them again; then return to this world in the usual way.*

---

Journeying to meet your ancestors can be a good way of obtaining help and guidance for the issues you face on a daily basis (after all, these are your ancestors, your direct lineage, and they will have as much interest in you as you have in them). This journey also can be a way of healing past wounds. Grace, for example, had trouble relating to her father and, over the years, their relationship declined to the point that they rarely saw each other. After learning about shamanism, Grace journeyed to her deceased grandfather, her father's father, and asked for his help in coping with her father. Her grandfather tried to help but, sadly, her father remained unresponsive and Grace never attained the relationship with him that she had wanted. In getting advice from her grandfather, however, Grace understood that she had done all she could and that she needed to respect her father's desire for isolation. Although the rift between them never healed, and her father eventually died himself, Grace never carried any guilt that the situation was her fault. In time, she hopes to journey to meet her father in the upperworld and see if a new relationship might be forged now that he has left this world behind. From a shamanic standpoint, death need not be final.

## Shapeshifting Your Ancestors

Shapeshifting into one of your ancestors is another way of making peace with the dead or just embodying the strengths that they hold. You, quite literally, walk a little way in their shoes.

---

### Exercise: Shapeshifting Your Ancestors

*Journey in exactly the same way as you did to shapeshift into your power animal except, this time, set your intention to shapeshift into a named ancestor. As you do not want just anybody inhabiting your body, shapeshift only into those you know and trust. Always ask your ancestor's permission first, and get your power animal to join you as you shapeshift. Shamanic work can be dangerous, but, with the right precautions, you can minimise that risk significantly. As you begin to feel your ancestor within you, move around a little and try to get a feel for how they were. Assume the posture that they took and see what this tells you. What attitudes did the person hold? What were their fears? Their desires? What were their strengths, and are they willing to share them with you now? When you want to return, turn back into your form as you did when you shapeshifted into your power animal and your ancestor will return to their realm.*

---

Alison, who had never known her birth mother in life (she had given Alison up as a baby and had then died without ever meeting her), got to know her in the otherworlds and, after many meetings, decided to shapeshift into her form. In particular, she doubted her mother's sincerity and wanted to feel for herself whether what she said was true: "My first impression of my mother was arrogance but this was tempered by uncertainty. I realised I was experiencing her younger self but that her ambition was limited. It seems that she relished the opportunities that she had but did not know where to direct her energy. As I went to leave my mother, I felt a small spark of life within her womb—myself. I felt my mother's love for the child. It was overwhelming. I could also feel the knowledge that she must give me up. Why? I felt now I could talk about these things with her: she was sincere in her love for me; I had felt it for myself."

## Cutting the Ties

Although journeying to your dead ancestors can be a way of healing past wounds, some ties with the past you may feel incapable of severing, however much they harm you. If this is the case, embody physically whatever it is you wish to leave behind and cut the ties that bind you to it.

---

### Exercise: Cutting the Ties

*Find a symbol of what you wish to let go of, such as a piece of wood, a stone, or something that is appropriate to the issue you want to resolve. Write upon its surface what it is you wish to sever the ties to or, if you cannot write directly onto the object, put your words onto paper and attach them to the item. Take a length of string and attach the item to your waist, so that it drags behind you as you walk (this might take a little ingenuity but it is important that you physically feel the weight of whatever it is you want to let go of). Drag the item around for as long as you want but, when you feel ready, make a conscious decision to let it go and cut the string that ties you to it. Say in a firm voice what you are doing and then feel the lightness and freedom you have achieved. You might want to burn the object, or put it into a fast-flowing river, or perhaps even bury it in the earth. Whatever you do, return whatever you have now left behind back into nature and ask that its energy be dissipated and turned into good.*

---

I once followed a similar exercise with a large group, where we selected our symbols and, after carrying them with us all day, we released them that night into a large bonfire. Everyone drummed or chanted to support the person releasing their ties to the past, and it was an incredible experience to witness so much determination and bravery. When it came to my turn, I released my ties with the past into the fire and felt liberated and reborn. I felt the people around me but I also felt my ancestors, supporting me and carrying me through.

## Trapped Spirits

When you think of mummies, you probably think of Egypt, where ancient Egyptians routinely preserved bodies before burying them in their tomb. Mummies also existed in Europe, and at a Bronze Age village South Uist, in Scotland, prehistoric people preserved several bodies and then kept them through several generations.[5] Imagine the scene: People retrieve the mummies from wherever they were kept and bring them into the light of the fire. They share food and drink with the bodies before whispering their problems and hoping for some help in return. Eventually, during the Iron Age, the mummies were buried, still under the floor of the house, but their spirits were finally allowed peace and could move on to the afterlife. Earlier, you read how death was divided into two stages: leaving the living and then joining the dead. The mummies of South Uist had done the former but it was a long time before they achieved the latter. In the meantime, they were trapped, condemned to an existence between the worlds. Since their spirits could not move on, they remained in this world: in the middleworld, effectively trapped by their living descendents.

Today, dead spirits still can be trapped in the middleworld, unable to move on to the afterlife, although it is very unlikely that this will be because of any deliberate ploy by the living. It is far more likely that when spirits become trapped, it is because of the manner in which they died. Sometimes, a very sudden death, or a death that was particularly traumatic, can so disorientate and confuse a spirit that it does not know where it should be going. It therefore becomes trapped and, occasionally, may even be unaware that it has died at all. A friend of mine, Alicia, lives near a large hospital and she spends a lot of her shamanic life helping those spirits that have become trapped as a result of their untimely deaths. She keeps her work necessarily secret but provides a very real and much needed service to her community. In other cases, the draw to life is so strong that the dead spirit does not want to leave their life behind, a situation that is sometimes exacerbated by the living unable to say goodbye. Losing a loved one is hard, terribly, terribly hard, but we must always let them go. Venus, who also works with the dead, says that not letting go of the dead is really not letting go of our own suffering; we must always let the deceased go, however much it hurts.

When dead spirits are trapped in the middleworld, they wander aimlessly and, unsurprisingly, they often are attracted to the living and those whom they used to know. Over time, when everyone they knew in life has passed on themselves, the trapped spirits often remain at locations that were once familiar to them, seeking out the world they used to know. We call these spirits ghosts and, although they are completely harmless, they often inspire fear and attempts to exorcise their presence. What these spirits need, however, is not exorcism but help, and we are ideally placed to provide it.

## Exercise: Trapped Spirits

*Think of a place in this world where you believe there might be a trapped spirit. Journey to the middleworld and go to this place. When you get there, call your power animal and upperworld guide. Calling your power animal and upperworld guide is very important; they will know how to help the trapped spirit and how to keep you safe. Then start looking for the trapped spirit. If you find it, think of a way of moving the person to the afterlife (their departure is usually*

*marked by their spirit rising upward towards the upperworld). You*
*may just need to point out the way, but if a spirit seems reluctant*
*to go, ask your power animal for help. There are many methods for*
*coaxing a spirit to move on, so listen to your power animal for advice.*
*Being trapped in the middleworld is a miserable existence and do not*
*think you are helping the dead if you leave them there to suffer; mov-*
*ing spirits to the upperworld is natural and right. When you see the*
*spirit ascend and disappear, your work is done, but, before returning,*
*ask your power animal to check that no lingering essence has attached*
*to you. If you are working with a partner, ask them to undertake a*
*brief journey to the middleworld and make sure you are completely*
*and spiritually clean.*

---

Moving spirits on to the afterlife is called *psychopomping*, an ancient word formed from the Greek *psyche*, meaning "soul" and *pomp*, meaning "to guide." One of my most moving experiences of psychopomping came when I stayed in a tiny fisherman's cottage with my wife, Vanessa, on an island off the coast of Northumberland. The first night we had similar dreams: a man had entered our room and was standing over Vanessa. The following afternoon, when I was preparing to undertake a shamanic healing journey, I could feel the man's spirit again, very interested in what I was about to do. Abandoning the healing, I journeyed instead to meet the spirit of the man and see if I could help him pass over to the afterlife. When I caught up with him, my power animal by my side, it turned out he had been a fisherman who had lost his life at sea. The cottage was where his betrothed had lived and, every time a new woman stayed in the cottage, he would peer over her to see if she was his beloved. His name was Joseph, hers was Mary; it was a match made in heaven. Joseph had no idea that he was dead and only seemed interested in finding Mary. Not knowing what to do next, I asked my power animal for help. He immediately disappeared and came back with a young woman. From Joseph's reaction,

I knew that it was Mary returned to him; she had died herself many years past. Joseph followed her to the afterlife without hesitation. The joy on his face is what makes shamanic work so rewarding: I still had tears in my eyes as I returned.

Very occasionally, a dead spirit, desperate to cling to life, can attach itself to a living person and even try to share that person's body. This is called possession and, unlike shapeshifting, is uninvited and unpleasant. I once spoke to Terry, who had been possessed for a time by a spirit he had tried to help: "I developed a drinking habit and a craving for cigarettes. These weren't my desires but belonged to the spirit. I became uncouth and aggressive and people started avoiding me. I would say to anyone attempting psychopomp work to be careful."

By calling in your power animal and your upperworld guide before you meet a trapped spirit, you can make sure that nothing untoward will happen to you. Moreover, if you ask your otherworld allies or your working partner to check you out afterwards, you can sort out any problems before they have a chance to develop. Chapter 8 explains more about possession and how you can help someone who is suffering from it.

Working with a partner when you undertake psychopomp work is good practice, and in some occasions such assistance can be extremely important. Where there are likely to be a considerable number of trapped souls, for example, as a result of an accident or perhaps at a hospital, a single individual trying to help is likely to become rapidly overwhelmed. In these instances, a group of people can journey together, all with the same intention, and all touching the people on either side. Physical contact among the group makes sure that people stay together when they journey and everyone has the support of the others as they go about their work. These group psychopomp journeys can be incredibly powerful and I have had the privilege of being involved in several. Every time, I have felt almost crushed by the size of the task, but I have looked around and seen my companions, diligently working away at this tremendously important and sacred task, and it has given me the strength to continue.

## Caring for the Dead

If you are concerned that a newly departed spirit might be trapped, journey to your power animal and ask them to check if the person has passed over or not. In almost all cases, the answer will be yes; but if not, you now know what to do.

Unlike humans, animals are far more likely to pass over to the afterlife unhindered and unimpeded. In the case of our pets, however, it is often nice to know that they have made the journey successfully and have not become trapped in the middleworld.

My own experience was with Chester, my beloved cat. He had a personality so big that it had touched many lives during his seventeen years and yet, when he finally succumbed to the tumour growing in his stomach, I knew that it was time to say goodbye. A fighter by nature, one day Chester did not want to leave the comfort of his bed. The day before, he had been living normally, but this day was different. I journeyed late in the afternoon and met the Master of the Animals. I asked if Chester was going to die and I was told that he was. I asked the Master of the Animals for his help: I asked that Chester be taken quickly and with no pain. The Master of the Animals told me that he would come for him that night. The following morning, Chester was dead; the Master of the Animals had been true to his word. I carefully wrapped the body and journeyed. The Master of the Animals was there and, at his feet, was Chester. He did not notice me as he walked away, perfectly content to leave this life and follow the Master of the Animals to the next. I still grieve the loss of my beloved cat but I know he is safe and that gives me great comfort.

## Preparing for Your Death

Your passage to the afterlife will be easier if you prepare now, whilst you are still alive. Of those who have undergone near-death experiences, many describe that, at the moment of death, their entire life plays out before them (many also speak of a tunnel leading to another world, something you are now very familiar with).[6] This point-of-death review can be painful, especially if you have never come to terms with things in your past or if you still have unhealthy attachments. At worst, the pain can even distract you from a smooth passage to the afterlife and you may become trapped in the middleworld yourself.

To make this point-of-death review easier, you can start reviewing your life now. That way, you can face any difficulties that arise in your own time, using your power animal and upperworld guide to help. When I took time to review my own life (and it took a few months of regular journeys to achieve), I first went to my power animal and he took me to a cave. At the centre of the cave was a pool of water and, looking at its surface, I began to see my life played out before me. On each subsequent journey, I watched either a whole year or a period of time that was distinct and significant to me, working backwards until I had reviewed my entire life. At the end of every journey, my power animal would gather up all my memories into a huge book, which I eventually left behind in the cave. I found it helpful not to judge anyone or anything that I saw during my review (and especially not myself) but to remember any instance that needed my attention and to go back to it during another journey. This way, at the end of the review, I knew that I had come to terms and dealt with many of the demons that had once lurked in my past. Of course, some demons undoubtedly may emerge in the future, but by conducting such a review you are better prepared, both for dying and, perhaps more pertinently, for living.

## Past Lives

I finished the review of my life when I reached the point of my earliest memory: a zoo trip with my granddad when I was not yet three years old. There is no reason, however, why you cannot continue your explorations and move back into the previous lives you may have lived. If you journey back to past lives however, keep in mind that life in the past was often short and hard, and death was often sudden and traumatic. If you truly want to know about your past lives, be prepared for what you might find, in all of its unsavoury detail.

Rather than reviewing your past lives in their entirety, it is better to start by journeying to a point where you were happy and successful and see if there is anything arising from that time that you could apply to your life today. Later, if you feel able, journey to times that were not as happy and see what lessons you can learn from those.

---

### Exercise: Past Lives

*Journey to the middleworld and state your intention as: I am journeying to the middleworld to experience a past life where I was happy and successful. When you get to the middleworld, call your power animal and travel back in time in whatever way suits you best. When you arrive in the past, watch yourself going about your previous life, or even talk to yourself and ask questions. Whether you reveal who you are is up to you, but be prepared for some disbelief! As always, when you hear the call-back, thank your old self for the help you have been given and retrace your steps back to this world.*

---

After you have looked at your past lives, you may begin to wonder about your future lives and who or what you might be in your next incarnation. Our Iron Age ancestors, the ancient Celts, certainly believed in reincarnation and the Roman historians who studied them recorded their beliefs.[7] Unlike the philosophers who followed Pythagoras (and whose views are often mistaken for those of the Celts), our Iron Age ancestors believed that humans always reincarnate as other humans and never change into an animal form. This echoes their approach to metal recycling, where a tool could return as a tool but never as a sword, and a sword could never return as anything else. Again, it is the spirit that determines how it is reborn and not necessarily the form it takes through life.

When journeying to a future life, seek the time when you have fulfilled your highest potential and become all that you are capable of becoming. Journey with this as your intention, using the previous exercise as a guide. Having seen yourself reach your full potential, reflect on how this makes you feel now. You have this potential with you in this life: it was *your* future you saw. That knowledge should fill you with a renewed sense of confidence to know that you can achieve so much.

Looking at your future lives can reveal much about your untapped potential for this life. To learn what the more immediate future holds, however, you need to look for appropriate signs and omens that might portend events yet to unfold. You need to look around you and know how to read the signs that you find.

# 7
## Flying Birds and Running Hares:
## Dreams and Portents

*Y*ou stand in battle formation, one of thousands of warriors waiting for your queen to speak. Around you, men and women have arrayed themselves in brightly coloured tunics and breeches, with swords strapped to their waists and shields attached to their forearms. Some have released their swords and are beating steadily on the rim of their shields, quieting the crowd and drawing attention to the magnificent woman standing at the very front of the line. Queen Boudica, for it is she who leads this war band, turns away from her horde and surveys the ground before her. The grass stretches endlessly from where she stands; only a few dark copses break the monotony. The sky leans hard upon the earth and storm clouds gather at the juncture. Boudica takes a step forward and drops to her knees. Screaming toward the heavens, she unclasps the hem of her skirt and a shape darts out from beneath it. It is a hare and it zigzags wildly over the short grass. The horde is silent now as all eyes watch the hare. It veers left and there is a gasp but then it turns again and runs towards the right. There is acclaim; Andraste, the Goddess of Victory, has spoken through the hare: triumph will follow. Boudica rises from her knees, her red hair catching the early morning breeze, and she turns to face the horde again. Her eyes still fixed on the heavens, she utters a terrible shriek;

*then, in a voice all hear clearly, intones, "I thank you, Andraste, and address you as kinswoman. As queen, I pray to you for victory and liberty from the Roman foe." Her arms raised, she seeks out the eyes of each of her warriors. As she meets yours, you feel the strength of this woman and you know you will follow her through anything.*

## Finding Your Portent

Queen Boudica is one of the most famous individuals to step out of the Iron Age past.[1] Left destitute when the invading Romans took her lands, she raised an army that sacked the Roman towns of Colchester and London, before marching against the might of the imperial army itself. Before committing herself to the task, however, she first divined the outcome by releasing a hare and observing the direction in which it ran. The Romans, against whom she later took up arms, recorded the events and some of her speech afterwards. Whatever happened after the hare was released was considered auspicious, and Boudica believed that Andraste, the Goddess of Victory, was with her.[2] In the end, her army was defeated, and Boudica took her own life; but, for a while, the prophecy held true and she met with success after success.

Running hares were not the only way that the Iron Age people obtained portents of the future. The task of divining fell to the Ovates, a group of seers who came just below the Druids in the priestly hierarchy.[3] Their methods were legion and virtually every occurrence had some bearing on future events.[4] The flight of birds across a winter sky may portend a great event to follow, or the white of an egg cracked on the earth may show if a person would heal from a wound. The most infamous method of divination was the killing and disembowelling of a sacrificial victim in the belief that the future may be read from the entrails.[5] The convulsions of the limbs and the pouring of blood were also thought to be particularly important.

# A Walk of Divination

Fortunately, in following the path of your ancestors and predicting the future, you do not have to resort to sacrificial killing or, indeed, to violence of any sort. All you need to do is go for a walk and, like the Iron Age Ovates, take notice of your surroundings.

---

### Exercise: A Walk of Divination

*Think of something in the future upon which you want guidance. Do not make the event too specific but set an intention such as: What path will bring me the most contentment? Then, holding this as your intention, go for a walk. Where and how far is entirely up to you, but make this a walk of purpose, a walk of divination rather than just a leisurely ramble. Repeat your intention over and over, like a mantra to focus your mind. Take notice of everything about your surroundings and look for three things that really catch your eye, things that make you stop and take notice. These are your portents. Finish your walk and interpret them. Meanings might come easily to you or you may want to journey to your power animal or upperworld guide for help.*

---

David, for example, wanted to know whether he should look for another job. He decided to walk out in the countryside in order to look for his three portents. His first was a sheep that had escaped from its field. Next, he saw his first primrose of the year, and, lastly, he saw a crow flying far overhead. He interpreted the sheep as showing him that he should leave his field too: his current job. The primrose he took as a sign of good things ahead: a new flowering. However, the crow he took to be a warning that he should get a good overview of the situation, a bird's-eye view, before proceeding. He did this, decided to move, and his new job is going well. Sally, in contrast, wanted to know if she should go out with a man who had repeatedly asked her but whom she had kept turning down. She walked through the town where she worked during her lunch hour. Her first portent was a DVD display featuring the film *Single White Female*. Next, she saw a bunch of dumped flowers, and finally two cats fighting. Needless to say, she left the man well alone!

## Scrying the Future

The most wealthy women of the Iron Age, women like Queen Boudica, were often buried with mirrors in their grave.[6] Before you get any notions about the vanity of Iron Age women, know that these mirrors were polished sheets of bronze, enough for a vague reflection but little more. Moreover, on the back of the mirrors were finely engraved patterns, very similar to phosphenes.[7] Generally, such imagery was associated with items of the otherworlds and it appears the mirrors were no different: these were divining tools and, just like a modern crystal ball, staring at their surface could induce images of the future. This is called *scrying*, from the Latin word meaning "to reveal," and you can easily follow this practice yourself.

Obtain either a flat piece of brass or copper to replicate a mirror, or, alternatively, find an object made from one of these metals with a large enough surface area for you to work with (junk shops are full of items that will be suitable). Polish it so you can see vague shapes reflected in the metal but not so much that these become readily identifiable. Now, you are ready to scry.

---

*Exercise: Scrying the Future*

*Think of an issue around the future that you want help with but, again, do not make the event too specific. Holding the "mirror" or other object before you, have some drumming playing in the background or ask a companion to drum gently for you (this is not so that you journey to the otherworlds but is to shift your mind slightly into a more responsive state). Keeping your intention at the forefront of your mind, look into the metal and see what appears. Do not try to analyse what you are seeing, just let it flow before you and, when you feel you have an answer to your query, stop the drumming and let your mind return to its normal state. Think about what you have seen and try to discern its meaning in the same way you did with the portents after your walk of divination.*

---

Another means of scrying is to use a bowl of water or, if you are outside, a still pool of water. You are familiar with the idea of water being a portal to the otherworlds and you have seen how people in the Bronze and Iron Ages placed swords and other items into the water as a way of passing their spirits to the afterlife. What you are trying to do now is draw something across from the otherworlds: an image or brief glimpse of something that might augur what the future has in store. Chapter 1 described how Ice Age people did something similar inside their sacred caves, when they scraped at the surface of the walls, attempting to penetrate the membrane through which the spirits of the otherworld appeared. They also put their hands flat against the wall and blew paint around and over their skin, so that their hand disappeared and seemed to merge with the wall.[8] Perhaps this was a way for people to reach out to what lay beyond, a means of seeking knowledge about their lives and about what the future might hold for them.

As well as gazing at the surface of water, observe the clouds as they flit across a summer sky and see what shapes and images they hold that might shed light on the future. There can be few better excuses for lying on your back in a warm spot and observing what is happening above you. Alternatively, on a winter's evening, watch the flames of a fire as they dance and entwine in a myriad of shapes and forms. I spend many evenings looking at the dance of the flames and it is always deeply revealing; there is much wisdom to be found in a fire.

The aim, in every case, is to obtain a clue, a fleeting indication of what the future might hold. Like the ink blot tests of psychiatrists that are designed to unlock the deepest desires of the mind, however, you might think that with any portent of the future, all you are finding out is what *you want* the future to hold. There is nothing wrong with this. Sally, for example, never wanted to go out with the man who kept asking her; her walk of divination made her resolve stronger. In fact, when someone comes to me with an issue with two possible paths and they do not know which one to take, I often tell them to flip a coin. Despite their dubious looks, just before they throw the coin I ask them: What do you want it to be, heads or tails? On most occasions, people admit to secretly wanting either heads or tails, and, with that, they have their answer.

## Determining Your Destiny

The future is not fixed for any of us; if it was, then what would be the point of doing anything? You might as well just sit back and let it happen. That is not to say you do not have a role or a destiny to fulfill in your life and finding out what this is can be a challenge in itself. What you attempt to discover when you scry into the future is one possible version of that future. Often, this is the version you want to see happen, although sometimes it might be the opposite. What you must do with either version is to discern the path that will lead you to it and then decide whether you want to walk down it or not. At some level, you will walk down all possible paths to all possible futures, and the recent discoveries of multiple dimensions and multiple realities suggests how this is possible; what you must decide is which of those futures you will manifest in this world and in this reality. Life might be determined; how you live it is not.

Occasionally, an omen is just so strong that you cannot ignore it. That happened to me a number of years ago when Vanessa and I were undecided about where we should live. Our dream was to buy a remote farmhouse in the Welsh hills, but was it right to do so at that stage of our lives? We agonised over the decision. One week, I spent time with a shamanic colleague on her smallholding. We discussed the possibility of my moving to Wales and I decided to work shamanically with the issue whilst I was there. A new animal power also arrived to help me: Buzzard. I spoke to Buzzard in the lowerworld one afternoon, as I sat in a yurt my friend had erected. Buzzard was keen on my move but I resisted: What about the practicalities? Was it really the best thing to do at that particular time? I was beginning to doubt what Buzzard was saying. Rather abruptly, he told me to leave the yurt, walk around to the back, and I would find something there that would be meaningful to me. I did as he said, but found nothing other than a small feather; what did that mean? I returned to Buzzard and, rather half-heartedly, thanked him for the feather. "No, no," he said, "that's not it. Go back and look again." I did so, and, this time, found the remains of a buzzard egg, newly hatched; *that* meant something to me. I was finally resolved: I would move to Wales. I then pushed my luck and asked Buzzard to help me choose the house I should buy. "I'll tell you when you get there," was his response. Several months later, Vanessa and I drove to a remote farmhouse deep in the folds of a mountain valley. As we left our car, a buzzard started calling above us. It did not stop. We spent more than an hour at the house and the buzzard did not pause. The owner even apologised for all the commotion. We bought the house that same day. Buzzard had been true to his word.

Buzzard pulled me into a future that I wanted but, if I am honest, was too frightened to pursue on my own. In another reality, perhaps I did not move, and I am still at my old house, wondering what I should do. The omen Buzzard gave me, the hatched egg, I took to represent a new life for me in Wales, a hatching of my hopes and dreams. I trusted what I had been shown, even if Buzzard had left me in no doubt at the end.

A more direct way of determining your inner desires for the future is to stand up and talk about your life. The same colleague I stayed with when Buzzard came to me suggested that I do this when thinking about my move. She asked me to speak about my life where I was living at the time, and then how I saw my life would change if I moved to Wales. She just sat and observed. Afterwards, she told me that, when I had discussed my existing situation, my shoulders were slumped and I had crossed my arms. I had not noticed this. When I spoke about the possibility of moving, however, I became more animated and moved my arms, as if I was drawing the future towards me. I was unaware of what I was doing, but it was clear what my body language had revealed about my innermost desires. I needed the confidence to follow my dream, and it was Buzzard who gave me that. If we want something to come true hard enough, then maybe it will.

Like spinning a coin, however, sometimes it is good if the predictions for your future are more random and have less personal input from you. Perhaps you do not mind what the future holds; you just want a clue as to what might be around the corner. You have already seen that Sámi of Lapland used to paint their drums with images. They used alder sap mixed with saliva to give the images a deep red colour that stood out sharply against the white reindeer hide of the drum. Taking three or four small interlocked hoops of brass and iron (called a frog for reasons that will become apparent), they placed the metal on the flat skin of the drum and then began to beat its surface. How the frog jumped across the skin, and the images it touched when it landed, determined what the future had in store. I have often used my own Sámi drum in this way, watching how the frog dances across its surface and wondering what secrets it might reveal to me.

# When Things Go Wrong

Although the future is not necessarily fixed and you can, to an extent, determine your own destiny, what happens if you have a bad omen and cannot see anyway to avoid it? In one of my first jobs, the secretary who had been allocated to me, Moyra, had been told by a fortune-teller that someone she worked for, driving a red car, would have a serious accident on a local stretch of road. With every new person she worked for, Moyra would ask them if they had a red car. She was horrified to learn that I did and that I regularly drove the stretch of road in question. Since I could not avoid the road any more than I could change my car, we needed a different solution.

The best way of dealing with this type of warning is to make it come true: live out the bad thing that you have been forewarned about and make it happen. However, you do this in a manner over which you have complete control. In effect, you *act* it out. For the car accident, I arranged some chairs into the shape of a car and pretended to drive the road in question. Another person drove their "car" into me and I mimed being hurt. An "ambulance" arrived and I was rushed to "hospital." Fortunately, after some emergency "surgery" (and a very real cup of tea), I was fine. The prophesy had come true; it had happened, and that was the last Moyra worried about it. If you ever have a premonition that something bad will happen, act it out in a similar manner and make it come true. Such make-believe makes belief.

Omens that fail to come true may also trouble us. In prehistoric times, people were far more cavalier in their treatment of the spirits, and if they felt they had been let down, then they took their revenge accordingly. In the Netherlands, at a place called Bargeroosterveld, the people of the Bronze Age made a shrine to the spirits.[9] They fashioned a ring of stones with a wooden framed entrance and decorated the structure with a horned roof. This place of the spirits was built on the edge of a peat bog, at the juncture where the water met the land. Although the shrine stood for many years, it was eventually torn down and deliberately and quite utterly destroyed. Whatever had happened, someone was very upset with the spirits who lived there. Today, we can take a more philosophical view and realise that our interpretation of the omen was wrong, or the event we foresaw has not yet come to pass. This once occurred to me. I met someone, years ago, whom my power animal told me would be very important to my future career. As it turned out, she was not, and, since I felt that she had wasted a lot of my time, we parted company. I was a little cross with my power animal and I told him so; he just smiled. Years later, and quite out of the blue, the same person sent me a brief note giving me the details of someone else who *did* advance my career significantly. My power animal had been right all along; I just needed more patience.

Generally, if you feel a portent is important, it probably is; you just need to understand it, or perhaps, as in my case, have the patience and trust to see it through. I often do the same thing if I make an error; I stop and think: am I being told something? Often, it is just that I should slow down but, occasionally, I notice something important that I would have otherwise overlooked. The key is to remain open to the possibility that the spirits are trying to tell you something; and then to trust whatever it is that you are told. If you think it is important, trust that it is; if you think that it is nothing, let it go.

## Dreaming Your Future

One of the oldest and most widespread methods of foretelling the future was to sleep and observe what dreams might reveal. In fact, we still tell someone with a problem to *sleep on it* and see what turns up.

In prehistoric times, dreams were tremendously important and reached their highest development with the Greek healing temples or *asklepieia*, sacred to the healing God, Asklepius.[10] People came to the asklepieia when they needed healing; they spent the night at the temple and recorded their dreams. By analysing the dreams, the priests divined a cure for whatever illness the person was suffering from. Asklepius himself is often depicted holding a staff with a snake entwined around it and this is still used by the World Health Organisation as its logo. In the ancient temples, snakes were often kept loose in the dormitories in the belief that they would aid the healing process.

Although it is much older than the asklepieia, when I visited the Hypogeum on Malta, a vast, underground sanctuary, I wondered if it could be a very early form of dream temple.[11] The myriad underground chambers that make up the Hypogeum seem womblike in their form and almost invite you to enter into them and sleep. One of the chambers (tellingly called the Oracle Room by its excavators) has patterns drawn on the roof that seem similar to phosphenes, a sure sign of otherworldly connections. Finally, one of the items found within the Hypogeum was a clay model of a woman lying, fast asleep, on a couch. Could this be the final confirmation that this most enigmatic of places was once a dream temple?

Whatever else it was, the Hypogeum was also used as a burial site and many human remains were buried under its floors. These bodies might have been deliberately placed there in order to facilitate dreaming. The Iron Age Celts, for example, slept on the grave of their ancestors in the hope that the deceased spirits would impart some of their wisdom through dreams.[12] You have journeyed to your ancestors to ask for their assistance in your life; Iron Age people, and perhaps the ancient people of Malta, were doing the same through their dreams.

Clearly, the intention in every case was to have dreams that were meaningful and useful. People were not seeking just any dreams, but prophetic dreams that would benefit them. You can probably recall at least some of your dreams and, for the most part, they are probably quite ordinary. In particular, you may dream about the previous day (a useful thing in itself given what we know about the importance of reviewing our lives upon death), run through what you have to do the following day, or stress about the problems that afflict all of us now and again. These are not usually prophetic dreams. What you look for in a prophetic dream is something different; you want the sort of dream that you wake up from and have the sense it was significant. Trust your intuition and take notice. For some, these types of dreams are frequent and commonplace; for others, they may happen rarely. If you are to use your dreams actively as a means of obtaining information, however, you need to cultivate your prophetic dreams, and you can do this through dream incubation; exactly what people were doing at the asklepieia so many years ago.

---

### Exercise: Dreaming Your Future

*Before you incubate your dreams, you first need to remember them. Have a pen and paper by your bedside and, immediately upon waking, write down all that you remember. Some people suggest recording your dreams if you wake in the middle of the night. I have never managed to be quite that disciplined, but, if you are, then an alternative to writing is a portable voice recorder; this has the advantage of not requiring a light to be switched on (a sure way of clearing your mind of anything). After a week or so of this practice, you should find that you recall your dreams far more easily. It is almost as if the mind, aware that there is now a point to remembering, suddenly decides to do so. At this stage, you are ready to start dream incubation. Before going to sleep, hold an intention in the same way that you do before you journey to the otherworlds, something along the lines of: I am incubating a dream to help me with [state the subject]. Then, go to sleep! Do not expect instant results—dream incubation takes practice—but note down anything you consider relevant and look for a pattern emerging.*

---

Occasionally, a dream can be so precise and accurate that you are left in no doubt whatsoever as to its value. This happened to me when my dog, a great big deerhound called Mabon, suddenly developed a huge swelling on the side of his face. Rushing him to the vet, I feared that all sorts of things might be wrong but, despite a good deal of attention, the vet could not find what the problem was (except for the obvious swelling). That night, I decided to incubate a dream to find out what was wrong with Mabon. I dreamt very vividly that a snake reared up and bit me on the hand; not only that, but it would not let go, however much I tried to shake it off. The next day, in some desperation, I took Mabon back to his breeder to see what she thought of the swelling. She took one look at him and said: "Snakebite!" My dream had been correct and, to my relief, the swelling went down a few weeks later.

To help incubate dreams successfully, craft a dreaming bundle, rather like the neck pouch you made in chapter 2. For this pouch, however, everything you gather should have a connection with sleep and dreaming. Place all the items into a small piece of cloth, bring the ends together, and tie them securely. Keep the bundle by your bedside. I keep an owl feather in my bundle; the bird's connection with night and also with wisdom makes it an especially suitable item. Vanessa keeps a piece of ancient pottery in hers that she collected from a rubbish dump just outside an asklepeion we visited on the southern shore of Crete. Nancy, another shamanic dreamer, keeps a piece of black jasper in her bundle, a stone that is said to generate prophetic dreams. Whatever you choose, make sure that the items have some meaning for you and are in some way associated with night and with dreams.

When you work with dreams, you may experience bad dreams, or even nightmares. To avoid them, Native Americans put a dream catcher above their beds: an intricately netted hoop that allows the good dreams through and traps the bad ones in the net. Whilst some bad dreams can be extremely disturbing, be careful that, in avoiding them, you are not losing useful information. Use your discernment and decide for yourself if the dream has any merit, or whether you should hang a dream catcher and avoid repeating it. Where a nightmare is particularly troubling, a good way of diminishing its power is to journey the next day with the intention of re-entering the dream and finding out more about it. Call your power animal or upperworld guide if you want help to alleviate your fears. Most often, however, nightmares rapidly lose their terror when you face them during the day.

Through journeying, re-enter any dream when you think there might be more information to obtain or when you did not get to the end of an important sequence. How often are you awoken from a dream just when it starts to get particularly interesting? Through journeying, you can go back and finish the dream. Re-entering your dreams through journeying is not quite the same as lucid dreaming, which is becoming aware that you are dreaming whilst you are still asleep. Lucid dreaming allows a degree of control over the dream and enables you to ask questions about the dreams as they arise. Although this can be very useful, I actually prefer letting the dream happen in whatever way it is meant to happen and then going back to it in a separate journey the following day.

When I was trying to decide what to call the next chapter of this book, a friend of mine, Val, recounted her dream of the night before. "I found a snake in my bed," Val told me in a rather excited email. Knowing about the healing power of snakes, what to others might have been a nightmare, to Val, was wonderful. However, for me, it gave me exactly the heading I wanted for the next chapter: *Finding a Snake in Your Bed*. But do not fear, because, like Val, you also will find the experience rather wonderful.

# 8

# Finding a Snake in Your Bed:
## Spirit Intrusions and Extraction

You hear the commotion long before you see its source. Three large men half-drag, half-carry another into a small lean-to hut. The man they lead is unwell and you follow them as they pass through the doorway. Inside, a fire smoulders and a woman sits on its far side. You look around, and from the myriad bones, herbs, and animal parts that are scattered at the edges of the floor, you know the woman is a shaman. The sick man now lies by the fire and the shaman moves quickly towards him, squatting low by his head. Catching sight of the woman, the prone man begins to have a fit and the others have to hold him firmly. The shaman reaches for a small flint knife and, in a single movement, scalps the man in a broad arc over his left ear. His fit intensifies and the others struggle to hold the man still. You move closer and, taking hold of his shoulders, add your own strength to the task. The shaman cuts deeply into the flesh of the skull, peeling back the skin to reveal the bone underneath. She then scrapes slowly at the bone. The man is still and his breathing is shallow. Surely, the shaman is killing him. You watch as the shaman works at the bone, sawing continuously until she has completely cut through. She continues the procedure again and again until she has formed a crude circle. She prises the circle of bone upwards until, with an audible snap, it *breaks free; there is now nothing between you and the man's spongy grey brain. You notice that the circle of bone is retrieved and wiped clean of the gore that covers it. The wound is then covered and the man is left to sleep out his ordeal. Some months later, when you next visit the village, you notice the man in the fields, tending the cattle. He not only seems unaffected by his ordeal but actually looks healthier than when you saw him last. As you pass close by you notice that he wears something around his neck: small, round . . . it is the piece of skull that the shaman had removed from his head. You nod a brief greeting to the man and inwardly wish him well; the healing from the shaman has obviously done its work.*

## "Bad" Spirits

Cutting into the skull and removing a piece of bone is called *trepanation*, from the Greek word meaning "to bore."[1] Many ancient societies, including that of our Stone Age ancestors, practiced this procedure. At a burial site in France, for example, of the 120 bodies discovered, 40 had been trepanned. Whilst it seems incredible that a people with no surgical tools, anaesthetic, or medical facilities would contemplate such a radical surgery, the most amazing thing is that some people survived the procedure and went on to live perfectly normal lives. We know this because, on many remains, the cut bone shows signs of healing, which could only have happened over a long period of time. Our ancestors probably practised trepanation for a number of symptoms (including bouts of epilepsy such as those suffered by the man in the hut), but the belief behind the procedure was that bad spirits had invaded the patient and a hole needed to be cut through the skull to let them out. They treated the cause not the symptoms of the illness. Modern science has radically altered the definition and understanding of illness by focussing almost exclusively on the symptoms of disease rather than its underlying cause: the *dis-ease* of the individual. Our ancient ancestors remind us that, for every symptom, there is a cause and we neglect this at our peril.

From a shamanic perspective, you know that everything is alive and has a spirit in the middleworld, and the same is true of illnesses. When you get ill, modern medicine focuses on the symptoms, whereas a shaman would focus on its cause: the intrusion by the spirit of the illness into your body. Moreover, to a shaman, physical and emotional illnesses are no different; both stem from an intrusion by a spirit. These spirits are not bad or evil, however; they are merely bundles of energy in the wrong place. It is like finding a snake in your bed. The snake is only bad because it is in the bed; put it outside where it belongs, and it is no longer bad. You adopted a similar approach when you helped trapped spirits cross over to the afterlife. Trapped in the middleworld, these spirits could haunt places and be considered bad, even evil, yet they were just lost, confused spirits, and, with a bit of compassion, they moved on to their rightful place. Keep the same principle in mind when you confront the spirits that cause illness. Our ancient ancestors realised the reality of spirit intrusions and sought to rid them from the body through trepanation; you will use less intrusive but just as effective methods when you do the same.

## Spirit Intrusion

First, however, consider how the intruding spirit enters the body in the first place: how illness is spread. Illness enters when negative energy attaches itself to a person. Generally, this energy is formless and pure although, as you will read later, it often takes a more recognisable form when you begin to work with it. Such negative energy generally enters the body when someone is tired or low, either mentally or physically. If that person feels power-full, there is little space left for negative energy to enter; if that person feels power-less, negative energy can fill the void. Nature, as we know, abhors a vacuum. Negative energy can enter when something bad happens and a person absorbs the negativity surrounding the situation instead of letting it go. Cruel words also can enter the body as a spirit intrusion, the negative energy contained in the words finding a way past its defences and lodging themselves firmly within. A person can help the intruding spirit unwittingly by endlessly replaying the unpleasant scene over and over, hearing again the words said. Words, to a shaman, are things and should always be used with care. Even negative thoughts can cause spirit intrusions, and this is the origin of the curses prevalent in many modern shamanic communities. Like words, thoughts are also things, so be careful when you think negatively about another. When these spirit intrusions, the manifestation of negative energy, enter a body they weaken it and, over time, various symptoms become evident. This is when people usually consider themselves ill. For a shaman, however, this is just the culmination of something that may have happened a long time ago and can only fully be cured by extracting the intrusion and dissipating the negative energy attached to it. In a perfect world, where every individual is filled with power, negative energy would never attach to anyone and would dissipate naturally; spirit intrusions and their associated illnesses just would not happen.

Some illnesses are contagious and we can readily catch them from others. Most of us suffer from colds and flu sometime during the year, and we accept that these are passed on through viral infections. In a shamanic sense, however, people will only catch the virus if its associated spirit can gain entry to the body; if they are sufficiently power-full, they will not catch it. Conversely, if they are run-down and generally power-less, they may find that they catch everything and spend a considerable time laid low with one illness after another. When you work with spirit intrusions and draw them out of your patients' bodies, there is a risk, therefore, that the spirit may travel from your patient's body into your own. Before starting any healing work, it is important to make yourself as power-full as possible, so no space exists into which the spirit of the illness can enter.

Think of all the experiences you have had since you began your shamanic path; perhaps the most powerful (and the experience leaving you most power-full) was when you shapeshifted into your power animal. You were filled with an energy and vitality that was so strong it felt unlimited. That is exactly how you need to feel when you attempt spirit extractions; shapeshifting into your power animal once again is how you will achieve that feeling. I once had a salutary lesson of what can happen when I overlooked this tremendously important step. A friend, Liz, called me to say she was suffering from sinusitis and had just come back from the doctor who prescribed antibiotics. I said I would journey to see if I could help. I met up with my power animal and we gathered healing energy and took it to Liz in the middleworld. As I saw my friend and spread the healing energy about her, I noticed a black form in her head, just above her eyebrows. Without thinking, I reached into her head, gathered up the dark energy, and drew it out. I returned from the middleworld and thought no more about it. The next day I awoke with an awful headache and a terribly blocked-up nose. After a few hours, I realised what had happened. In drawing out the bad energy from Liz, I had left myself unprotected and it had immediately moved into me. The fact that I was not physically next to Liz was irrelevant; spirits inhabit the middleworld and I was in the middleworld, next to Liz, when it entered me. I had two very painful weeks to rue my impetuosity. Preparation is essential to successful spirit extractions; if you go ill yourself, you are of no use to anyone.

## Spirit Extraction

When a patient comes to you looking for healing, make an initial journey to your power animal or upperworld guide to ask what help you should offer and which technique you should use. You can then plan your work accordingly. In rare instances, you may be advised to do nothing at all. Some people who come to you may not be ready to be cured, or they may need to effect some life changes before a cure will work. Always listen to your power animal and follow their advice.

## Exercise: Spirit Extraction

*Make your patient comfortable; unlike you, they can sleep if they want; it will not make any difference to the healing. Ideally, have someone drum for you, perhaps a friend or relative of your patient or, failing that, use your drumming recording but make sure it is set to repeat to give you a continuous, unbroken beat with no call-back. Then, call your power animal and fill yourself completely with power. This is extremely important. If you are not full of power, you might leave a gap where the bad spirit you extract from your patient can move straight into you. Remember how you shapeshifted into your power animal earlier and do the same now; you can drum, make noises, sing, even dance around the room; do whatever it is that puts you into the state where you know that you are brim-full of power. Now enter the middleworld. Look over your patient and examine the person closely. Since you are in the middleworld, you can now see the patterns of energy both around and within your patient. Does anything look out of place? Generally, negative energy, the spirit intrusion you are seeking to extract, will stand out and assume a form that is immediately recognisable as an alien object. I have found bricks, ants, a rat, thick black tar, and shards of metal, along with a myriad of other foreign objects within patients' bodies. When you come across anything similar, you have found the spirit intrusion.*

*Crouch over your patient and open your eyes and take a closer look at where you think the intrusion might be, or feel the energy emanating from that place; smell or even listen to the spot; do anything that helps to determine exactly what you need to extract. If you are in any doubt, ask your power animal for help. When you are sure you have located the intrusion, make absolutely certain that you are completely full of power, and pull it out. Some people suck it out; some people gather it in their hands; my power animal generally plunges into the patient's body and thrashes it out. However you extract the intrusion, make sure everything is extracted and gather it all together in your hands. Next return the intrusion back to where it belongs. Since you will not necessarily know where this is, the best thing to do is to put it in the earth, into water, onto a fire, or throw it to the winds; as you probably recognise, these are all portals to the otherworlds and the spirit can find its own way home. Remember, nothing is bad, it is just in the wrong place; all you are doing is giving it a little help to go on its way.*

*At this stage, your task may be complete or you may need to re-move other intrusions. Check with your power animal whether you should go back and look for more now or whether your patient needs another healing at a later date. When everything is finished, return from the middleworld back into your physical body. Then help your patient to rise. Some people like to talk about what has just happened to them, whilst others just want a bit of space. Whatever else you do, however, do not tell the person what you found. The form the spirit took was for you and you alone: who wants to be told that they were carrying a rat, or worse, inside their bodies?*

---

When I carried out an extraction for Giles, he did not tell me be-forehand what was wrong with him; he just asked for a healing. I jour-neyed to my power animal and he confirmed that Giles needed an extraction. When I looked at Giles's body, whilst I was in the middle-world, I saw thousands of black ants running over his shoulder. With the help of my power animal, I gathered them all up, pulled them out, and threw them towards the nearest water source, in this case, a nearby river. When I told Giles afterwards that he had something in his shoulder (without mentioning what it was) he asked me which one. I said the left and he nodded. He told me he had recently had an operation on that shoulder but that it was being slow to heal; that was why he had come to me in the first place. With another patient, Rosie, after I had journeyed to the middleworld, I saw that her head above her right eye was covered in thick, gloopy tar; it took quite a while to get it all out. Afterwards, Rosie told me about her migraines, with the pain always gathering above the right eye. The extraction did not end the migraines completely, but Rosie reported a marked improvement in the severity of her symptoms.

With Giles, I threw the spirit I had just extracted towards the nearest river; with Rosie, I threw it towards the sea, since this was the nearest water to where I was working. During the Iron Age, people also threw spirit intrusions into water but they went a stage further. In southern France, at the source of the Seine at Dijon, was a Celtic healing sanctuary, and people used to make small models of various body parts and throw them into the water.[2] Some threw in model arms and legs, others threw in models of eyes, ears, and internal organs. Perhaps the shaman, having extracted an illness from a patient, made a small model of the part of the body affected and moved the spirit into this before depositing it into the water. Over time, people got to know the spirit of the river into which they were depositing the model body parts and called her Sequana, later to become Seine, which is still the name of the river today.

The Sámi taught me a similar healing technique that mirrors what the ancient Celts were doing in France. Instead of pulling out the spirit intrusion, they rub a speckled stone over the affected part of the body and the spirit moves from the body into the stone. They drop the stone into a stream or river and the negative energy is naturally dissipated.

Once you have extracted an illness from a patient, make sure the space that the illness occupied is not left empty for another spirit to invade; you need to make your patient power-full. The easiest and best way of achieving this is to teach your patients how to journey for themselves and let them find their own power animal. Next to the healing itself, this is the greatest gift you can give to anyone who comes to you for help. Take them through the initial chapters of this book and, if they want to explore further, let them work through the rest on their own. If a patient likes the thought of having a power animal but does not want to journey for themselves, get a power animal for them (chapter 9 explains this technique). If someone resists the idea of a power animal altogether, do not force one upon them or surreptitiously find them one without them knowing. Aside from the invasion of personal and spiritual space, if a person does not want to engage with a power animal, then he or she is unlikely to gain much by having one anyway. Some people need the space to make their own choices and find their own path and, even if you disagree with their decision, you must respect it nonetheless.

## Possession

Generally, when you undertake a spirit extraction, you find pure energy, which, although naturally formless, usually appears to be something mildly unpleasant and certainly inappropriate to be in a human body. This is how you know you should extract it. Occasionally, the energy you find may take on a human form, as if another individual squats in the body of your patient. This is called possession, and is something you must be prepared for.

Chapter 6 described how some dead spirits do not move on to the afterlife after death, but become trapped in this world. These spirits are deeply attracted to the living and may even haunt the places with which they were once familiar. Occasionally, this attraction can go too far and the dead spirit can actually invade a living body and take up residence there. This is what happened to Terry; the dead spirit battled with Terry for the use (and abuse) of his body.

Healing possession is not difficult but you must always remember that, when you treat it, you have two patients: the person who came for the healing *and* the spirit of the dead person inside that person. Disregard anything you have seen or read about exorcism as this is not the technique you shall use; all you will do is persuade the dead spirit that it is in the wrong place and convince it to move on to the afterlife. In effect, this is just another form of psychopomping, except that the dead spirit is inside a person rather than wandering about in the middleworld. Sometimes, the dead spirit will not want to give up its new home and this is quite understandable; none of us would want to be evicted from where we live. Our task, however, is to persuade, cajole, or, if things become desperate and our power animal agrees, even trick the dead spirit to leave. Remember, though, that wherever you find suffering, you must be prepared to help and this includes offering your support and healing to the dead spirit. Sometimes, for instance, offering to find a power animal for the dead spirit will be sufficient inducement for it to leave the body it inhabits. With a power animal beside them, moving the spirit on to the afterlife should be that much easier.

When you have persuaded the dead spirit to move on, you do not need to extract it; just let it leave of its own accord. Moreover, once a dead spirit has passed over into the afterlife, it cannot come back and so there is no danger of it returning to your patient in the future (providing it did actually go in the first place; get your power animal to check if you are in any doubt). Like any extraction, do not unwittingly become the new host to the dead spirit; keep up your defences and maintain your power-full state when you are healing someone of possession.

## Self-Healing

Although you have learnt the technique of spirit extractions and can help people who come for healing, it is not always so easy helping ourselves. In traditional shamanic communities, healing was obtained from another and even the shaman would go to another shaman if anything was wrong. In our society, people are encouraged to cope on their own and so-called *self-help* books typify this attitude. Unfortunately, many shamanic techniques rely on a supportive community and ready access to a healer that is not always possible in our modern world. Whilst your power animal and upperworld guide will always help you when you are ill (and it is always beneficial to journey to them if you need healing), you cannot extract an illness from yourself. You can, however, do many other things to help maintain your health and, of course, the health of others.

Chapter 5 described Ötzi the Iceman and his marvellous copper axe. Ötzi also carried a knapsack that contained several pieces of birch fungus, an inedible but incredibly useful plant.[3] Ötzi suffered from intestinal worms (very common during this period) and they probably caused him considerable discomfort. Whilst Ötzi might have gone to a shaman for a spirit extraction, the birch fungus would have also helped his healing. Being a gentle laxative, the fungus, if taken at the correct dosage, would have purged Ötzi of his worms and helped him to recover. The extraction would have dealt with the underlying cause of what was making Ötzi ill, whilst the medicinal fungus would have helped treat the symptoms.

The modern world has many drugs and medicines available to treat the symptoms of a huge range of illnesses. Just because you know that healing the spiritual side of the illness is of equal importance does not mean that you should reject what modern medicine has to offer. Rosie, for example, despite coming to me for an extraction, still takes painkillers when she gets a migraine, and I would certainly encourage her to do so. If you truly want to help your patients, make use of every tool available, and this includes modern medicine.

## The Pharmacy of the Hedgerow

Before modern science synthesised and produced the range of medicines used today, people looked towards the pharmacy of the hedgerow to provide the remedy they required. Whilst even herbal medicine is big business today, some simple remedies are easy to make and use.

Among my favourites are herbal teas; these are simple to prepare and very gentle to ingest. Feverfew and camomile make a very soothing tea for headaches and migraine, and Rosie found that it helped to lessen her pain. Mint tea is wonderful for stomach problems as well as a whole range of other ailments. I keep several varieties growing just outside my kitchen door and drink almost nothing else in the summer; moreover, mint is such a hardy plant it will grow almost anywhere, even in a shady window-box. For colds and flu, the old favourite of squeezed lemon, chopped ginger root, and a good dollop of honey is hard to beat, and it almost makes it worth getting ill to have some. Aside from teas, most people know to rub nettle stings with a dock leaf. To make it really effective, rub the dock leaf between your hands first and extract some of the juice before you apply it to the sting; the juice really seems to help. A useful remedy when you are out picking blackberries in the autumn and snag your hands on the thorns is to wrap the wound in a bruised blackberry leaf. This not only stops the bleeding but also helps close the wound, an example of nature providing the cure right next to the problem.

Whilst picking and using herbs is a good practice, use your knowledge of shamanism to go a little further. Once, I was picking gorse flowers with a friend, Lucy, to make into tea. I was picking away quite happily, managing to avoid the sharp spines of the bush, whereas Lucy was wincing and yelping so much that she eventually announced that collecting gorse flowers was far too dangerous. I asked her whether she had sought the permission of the bush before she started picking the flowers. She replied that she had not but would do so now. That was the end of her difficulties and she was not troubled by the spines again. Your shamanic practice tells you that everything is alive and has a spirit and, in this instance, Lucy had communicated with the spirit of the gorse bush and gained its permission to pick the flowers. If you journey to the spirit of the plant whose leaves or flowers you want to pick and ask permission first, not only will the process be easier, as Lucy found, but you will also gain an ally for your later healing.

## Exercise: The Pharmacy of the Hedgerow

*Choose a plant you wish to use for healing and sit with it a while. Explain why you are there and what it is you want from the plant, whether it is some leaves or flowers, or even a length of branch. You might find that you want to journey to the spirit of the plant in the usual way, or you might find that you can maintain a "conversation" whilst you remain in this world; just do whatever works best for you but make sure that you also listen for a response. If the plant agrees to your request, take what you need. You might also want to give something in return, such as a handful of birdseed, a tidy of the foliage, or a song. Take your cuttings home and journey again to the spirit of the plant (this is also appropriate if you have bought some herbal medicine from a shop or received some from an herbal practitioner). Ask if the spirit of the plant will work with you in your healing, listen to any advice it might offer, and thank it again for its help.*

Herbs need not necessarily just treat physical ailments. The gorse flower tea Lucy and I prepared is said to be good for restoring hope and is also used in the Bach Flower Remedy range to counter despair. In prehistoric times, herbs and trees were used in similar ways. For example, an Iron Age house in the wetlands of the Netherlands had an animal byre that was made from woven willow withies.[4] This would not appear unusual but for the fact that willow is poisonous to livestock and would seem to be unsuitable wood for the byre. Willow has other properties, however, and an extract from its bark provides an effective painkiller (and has now been synthesised to give us aspirin). Perhaps the people making the byre thought that the willow would be beneficial to the livestock, even healing their ailments, in the same way that the bark helped the human inhabitants of the dwelling.

Mistletoe was a sacred plant to the Iron Age Druids and is mentioned by the Roman historians as having the ability to cure all illness; I carry some in my neck pouch.[5] Other trees, such as hawthorn, were cultivated for their protective qualities, perhaps because they make good barriers against intruders. At the start of my driveway is a hawthorn tree and it is both a sentinel and a guardian watching over the approach to the house. Finding out the hidden properties of herbs and trees can be rewarding and is easy to achieve by journeying to the spirit of each. Lesley, for example, owned a house with an enormous pear tree that dominated her garden. Journeying to the spirit of the tree, she encountered a woman dressed in flowing green and white robes who became both a teacher to Lesley and a guardian for her house.

A more traditional house guardian for many of us is a dog. In prehistoric times, however, people also saw dogs as healers. At an Iron Age healing sanctuary at Lydney in Gloucestershire, deerhounds were kept to help heal the sick.[6] The dogs would be encouraged to lick open wounds and the antibacterial properties of their saliva would prevent infection and help healing. Even now, we put our fingers in our mouths when we cut them, echoing this very ancient healing technique.

This chapter has been all about extracting spiritual intrusions from the body: the cause of the illnesses we suffer. Spirits entering our body are not the only thing that can make us ill, however; we can become ill when a part of us leaves. This is called soul loss and learning how to treat it is the next step on your shamanic path.

# 9

# Bringing the Soul Back Home:
## Healing the Traumas of Life

The battle has raged all day and you have returned to the king's hall for some rest and, if there is any available, some food. As you pass through the huge wooden doors, you are struck again at the immensity of the hall; it is truly fit for a king and you walk purposely towards the massive oak trunk that stands at its centre. To one side of the trunk lie those who have been wounded during battle; some look so close to death that you wonder why they have been brought here at all. At the rear of the hall waits the shaman; his healing powers will be sorely needed this day and you can tell at a glance that he is already deep in trance, calling in the spirits that will aid his task. Suddenly, the shaman beckons the first of the wounded and a man is lifted and carried to him. Before the shaman is a bronze cauldron, filled to its brim with water. The shaman indicates that the wounded man should be cast into the cauldron, head first, and, after a little manoeuvring by those who carry the patient, this is done. The shaman lifts his hands and, whispering an entreaty to the spirits, seems to draw something from the air, which he gathers and thrusts towards the cauldron. Almost at once, the patient revives and you can hear him splutter in the water. His legs thrash wildly and it is not without difficulty that he is extracted from the cauldron and set on his feet.

*Almost miraculously, he seems quite unscathed and, whilst a moment ago it seemed certain that he would die, he is now strapping on fresh armour and calling for his horse. You watch as he strides through the doors of the hall and casually accepts his mount. Inside the hall, the next of the wounded, a woman this time, whose head lolls as if her spirit has already passed on, is carried towards the shaman. Again, she is thrust into the cauldron, and again, the shaman revives a person who was surely dead.*

## Back from the Dead

Chapter 2 described the Gundestrup Cauldron, which had the Master of the Animals engraved upon its side. A similar tableau was engraved on another section of the bowl, this time showing a horizontal tree with warriors walking beneath it.[1] Their focus is a huge figure who lifts each warrior in turn and thrusts him, head first, into a cauldron. Once they are removed, the warriors, now on horseback and above the tree, ride off in the opposite direction. A tree can act as a portal between the worlds and you ascend such a tree when you journey to the upperworld. The same seems to be the case for the cauldron: the warriors beneath the tree are in the otherworld and are, in fact, dead. By moving towards the shaman, however, they are thrust into the cauldron and reborn; their souls are reunited with their bodies. The warriors can then mount their horses and ride away, this time on the other side of the tree: in this world.

Dramatic confirmation of this interpretation comes from an ancient Welsh story that tells of a war between the Iron Age tribes of Wales and Ireland.[2] The Welsh were struggling badly, whereas the Irish warriors seemed almost without number. The reason was because the Irish had a cauldron of rebirth, whereby any of their dead thrust into its waters would be brought back to life. This seems to be precisely what is depicted on the side of the Gundestrup Cauldron, a rare case where a later myth accords with an object recovered from the ground.

Whilst the scene on the Gundestrup Cauldron and the Welsh story both point towards the revival of the dead, we must be wary of accepting things on face value. The Iron Age Celts were well known for their love of boasting, and the world that they lived in was far more metaphorical than ours. Rather than actually bringing the dead back to life, the cauldron (and the story) probably depict a form of healing where the patient's soul, or at least part of it, was restored to him or her following the rigours and trauma of war.

## Soul Loss

Chapter 3 explains how, when you drum and enter trance, part of you leaves your physical body and journeys to the otherworlds. We refer to the part that journeys as our soul, spirit, or essence, depending upon our preference. (Although the word *soul* carries a lot of modern connotations, in the case of soul loss and retrieval, it is still the most commonly used term.)

Accordingly, when you journey, part of your soul travels to the otherworlds; when you end your journey, it returns. If your soul part did not return from the otherworlds, you would probably feel quite ill. Part of you would be missing and your energy would plummet alarmingly. You would feel listless and empty and might, if asked to describe your condition, say that you felt half-dead. This would be more accurate than it might seem, since, on death, all of your soul departs, so if a part of your soul is missing then you are, in a way, partly dead.

Perhaps the warriors engraved on the side of the Gundestrup Cauldron were not actually dead but, rather, had lost part of their souls through the trauma of battle. The shaman, through his or her healing, was bringing the soul parts back. It is the ancient healing technique of soul retrieval that is depicted on the side of the cauldron: restoring the soul to those who have lost it.

*Losing the Soul*

When you are threatened, your survival instinct tells you to run away; out of *flight* or *fight*, most of us would, quite sensibly, choose the former. Our soul is no different. When something happens that is completely overwhelming and potentially damaging, part of our soul can break away and flee. This is particularly the case if you are physically unable to get away from whatever threatens us. Situations that lead to such a response can be physical, such as an accident, assault, rape, or abuse, or can be emotional, such as the grief of death, pain of divorce, or feelings of worthlessness. All these situations sap energy and leave people so power-less in the face of external circumstances that part of their soul escapes and retreats to the otherworlds. This is not a weakness or flaw in their personalities but a survival mechanism that helps them cope with whatever is assailing them. Having part of the soul escape is a way of shutting down, of putting a part of themselves in a safe place, and then finding the forbearance and will to survive the terrible experience in which they find themselves. Soul loss is a noble response, not a sign of frailty.

Soul parts hide in the otherworlds since this is the only place the soul knows to journey to. Even if a person does not practice shamanism, they still dream at night, so their soul part will have no difficulty finding the way. Often, the soul part will return on its own once the ordeal is over; this is perfectly natural and demonstrates the value of the body's survival mechanism. Sometimes, however, the soul part will not return and the person remains listless and ill, their energy depleted and their vitality gone. Soul loss that outlasts the initial period of trauma that caused it becomes a problem that needs intervention to heal.

Although soul loss is often involuntary, occasionally, a person can willingly give part of their soul away, not realising the damage this will cause them. The love for a child, for example, can induce a parent to give up part of their soul to their offspring, especially if the child is gravely ill or in serious trouble. Unfortunately, the parent's soul part has no effect; only our own souls sustain us, and the parent will have left themselves depleted for no reason. Never think that giving away a part of your soul is ever in anyone's interest.

Soul theft is sometimes spoken about in traditional shamanic communities but it is unlikely that you will come across it in your practice. Each society has its own way of explaining things and if a community is steeped in sorcery and magic, then the explanation for soul loss is more likely to be linked to malignant forces and theft. This book explains shamanic traditions in another way and, when you begin to use the technique on your patients, you will need to find an appropriate way of explaining what you do that will satisfy *them*.

### Symptoms of Soul Loss

The main symptoms of soul loss are a chronic loss of energy and a general feeling of malaise. Emotionally, enthusiasm for life diminishes and depression forms. In some cases, the personality changes so that the person becomes a mere shadow of their former self. Phrases such as: "I'm not all here"; "Part of me just seems to be missing"; and "I've not been the same since . . ." are strong indicators of soul loss. Often, people with soul loss remain stuck in the past, unable to move on from the experience that caused their soul to depart. Unfortunately, the departing soul part does not take the pain and trauma of the event with it. People quickly become trapped in a downward spiral from which, without a soul retrieval, there is no way out.

Since the pain of the trauma does not depart with the soul part but stays with the body (where it may or may not come to an end), in retrieving a soul part we are not retrieving the pain associated with its loss. This is important: what we bring back to our patients is the soul part as it existed *prior* to the trauma that made it depart. We do not retrieve the trauma itself or the pain and suffering associated with it. By returning the soul part to our patient, we also return all the gifts and strengths that the soul part holds; we make our patient whole again.

*Tracking the Soul*

Since soul parts always depart to the otherworlds, you will find them there. Given that the otherworlds are vast, however, you first need to hone your skills as a tracker.

---

## Exercise: Tracking the Soul

*Work with a partner and, whilst you drum, your partner should journey to either the upperworld or lowerworld and hide something distinctive that you have both agreed upon beforehand. Tell your partner not to hide it too thoroughly but to leave it somewhere where you are likely to come across it. Then, your partner should return from the journey and drum for you. State your intention as you do at the start of every journey but wait for a little tug that tells you to go up to the upperworld or down to the lowerworld. Call your power animal and ask it to help you find whatever it is you are looking for. Trust that it is the expert and follow wherever it leads. After a while, you will probably find the object and return to your partner and describe where it was. Although your description may not match theirs exactly, there will probably be enough common points to convince you that you were in the right place and managed (with the help of your power animal) to track something in the otherworlds successfully. If not, try again.*

---

The first time I tried this exercise, I was convinced that I stood no chance of finding the object that my partner, Sue, had hidden. I journeyed to the lowerworld and, following my power animal, I eventually found the object on the side of a pool formed by an enormous waterfall. I returned and described the location to Sue. She nodded enthusiastically: that was exactly where she had left it. Tracking is easy if you leave the work to your power animal and follow behind in their wake.

# Bringing the Soul Home

After you have successfully tracked and found the soul part of your patient, you need to catch it and bring it back. To do so, you need a container to hold the soul part, whilst you negotiate the path back into this world.

The Native Americans of the Pacific north-west coast use small hollowed-out pieces of wood or bone as soul catchers.[3] These are often carved or painted to depict the power animals that help the shamans to track the lost soul parts. In the European past, if anyone used wooden soul catchers, then the evidence will have long since rotted away. During the Stone and Bronze Ages, however, some people were buried with hollow bones and it is possible that these served the same purpose (they are often described as rudimentary flutes by excavators and there is no reason why they could not have been both).[4] Objects placed in the grave of their owners were considered extremely important and likely served an equally important service, such as holding a person's soul part whilst it was being retrieved by a shaman.

For your soul catcher, try also finding a hollow bone. You can find them in the countryside, especially in wilder places where scavengers break up fallen carcasses. If a bone is not completely clean when you find it, place it near an ant nest. Once the ants have spent a few days removing anything remotely edible, you will find that your bone is a lot cleaner as a result. Leave the bone out in the sun for a few days to bleach it and then give it a quick scrub. Before you use the bone in your shamanic work, journey back to the animal it came from and ask if it will let you use the bone in your healing and, if so, whether they will also help you in the task. Do not be concerned with what type of animal the bone came from but trust that whatever it is, it is exactly right for you (our ancestors often used sheep bones although some used swan and even bear bones).

If you are unable to find a hollow bone, use a stone as your soul catcher, rather like the Sámi use a speckled stone when they extract spirit intrusions from their patients. The principle is the same: the spirit or, in our case, the soul part, enters the stone and allows the shaman to carry it between the worlds. In the past, stones containing quartz crystals were especially treasured and these can serve as very effective soul catchers.

Whatever tools you use to catch the soul parts, be careful that you do not come to depend on them so heavily that you are unable to work without them. Although I have caught soul parts in quartz crystals, hollow bones, and speckled stones, my power animal has also taught me to catch the soul part in a song and hold it there until I am ready to restore it to my patient. As a song is something you will never be without, such a technique allows you to work and heal anywhere without being overly dependent upon tools.

## Soul Retrieval

Chapter 8 explained that, before you offer any form of healing to a patient, you should first journey to your power animal or upperworld guide and ask exactly what is required. Sometimes, you will be told to do a spirit extraction, on another occasion, you will be told to do a soul retrieval, whilst other times you will be told to do both. Generally, do the extraction first and the soul retrieval next, so that the soul part you find is restored to someone free from any negative energy. Similarly, if you find evidence for possession, deal with that before you attempt soul retrieval. Occasionally, you might be told that soul retrieval is not appropriate, even though your patient is clearly suffering from the loss of part of their soul. Conditions must be right to bring back a person's soul part successfully, and for it to remain there permanently. For example, if soul loss occurred due to abuse, and that abuse is ongoing, any soul part returned to the person probably will leave again soon afterwards. In this instance, help your patient in other ways, perhaps by teaching them to journey and find a power animal that can help them cope and, hopefully, stop the situation. This approach, however, would not apply to a person with problems that largely originate in the past, such as a person unable to come to terms with the death of a loved one, or someone who has suffered but has now recovered from physical trauma. Although the suffering is ongoing, the situation that caused it is not and, with the restoration of their lost soul part, such people will find coping that much easier.

In every case, always listen and follow what your power animal or upperworld guide tells you. Whatever healing they suggest, follow what you are told. Whilst the following exercise shows how a typical soul retrieval is achieved, if your spirit allies tell you to change any aspect or to do something differently, listen and follow what they advise. Shamanism is all about our personal relationship with our spirit guides and not our ability to follow instructions from a book.

## Exercise: Soul Retrieval

*Make your patient as comfortable as possible, either by lying them down or reclining them in a chair. Lie or sit next to them if they are comfortable with you doing so and touch them at some point as a focus for the bond between you. Although you should set an intention for the journey, do not state your destination but allow yourself to be gently tugged to wherever you need to go. Ask a partner to drum for you or use your drumming recording (set to repeat to give you the same continuous drumming beat you used when looking for spirit intrusions) and then call your power animal. Tell them what you are doing and ask for their help in tracking the soul part. They may take you to either the upperworld or lowerworld, even moving between each, or they may go to places you have never been before; just stay with them and keep looking out for the soul part of your patient. Like spirit intrusions, soul parts do not have any particular form but are essences of pure energy. To make our task easier, however, soul parts usually, although not always, appear in the form of the person at the age they were when the soul part left. So, for example, if you see your patient as a three-year-old child, you know that you have found the soul part that left them when they were this age. Talk to the soul part and tell it who you are and why you have come. Explain that the soul part is missed, reassure it that whatever caused it to go has now passed (assuming that it has) and emphasise that your patient wants it to return. Sometimes, a soul part will tell you why it originally left and be anxious to know that the situation has now changed. Give every reassurance you can. You may also want to ask the soul part if they are bringing with them any particular gifts or strengths that might help your patient. If so, remember what these are, and be sure to tell your patient after you return. After the soul part has agreed to return, gather it up and place it in your soul catcher. Ask your power animal if there are any more soul parts you should retrieve and, if so, go through the process again.*

*When you have gathered all the soul parts your power animal tells you to collect, return to this world and crouch over your patient. Place your soul catcher over their heart and blow in the soul part or parts you have brought back (either all together or, if you prefer, one by one). At this stage, Sandra Ingerman, one of the most experienced soul healers in the modern world, likes to look into her patient's eyes and say: "Welcome home."[5]*

---

On some occasions, the soul part you are tracking will not appear in human form. Whilst this can make it more difficult to recognise, often you will just get a feeling that you have found what you are seeking. Julie, for example, was only seventeen when she got married. It was not exactly what she wanted, and it was not exactly to the man she wanted but, for a variety of reasons, she went ahead. Unable to cope, her health suffered and she became more and more lethargic; she describes it: "As if part of me had exploded and gone to the stars." Years later, I met Julie and, without hearing her story, I gave her a soul retrieval. I eventually found her lost soul part in the upperworld, among the stars. It took the form of a seventeen-year-old girl but had divided into so many pieces that I had to spend a long time sweeping them all up. It was like collecting star dust. When I told Julie what I had found, she shared her story with me, confirming all that I had discovered.

Veronica's soul part appeared to me as a seven-year-old girl, sitting by a swimming pool and looking lost and abandoned. When I returned and told her this, it meant nothing to her and yet, slowly, the memories of a holiday in France returned: "I was staying with other children but, one afternoon, they had left me all alone. I remember sitting by the pool and feeling devastated." Such a small incident in childhood resulted in Veronica losing part of her soul. Although, as an adult, Veronica realises that the incident was trivial (the other children soon returned), the damage had already been done and it took many decades before the problem was put right. Following her soul retrieval, Veronica says her confidence has blossomed.

## Holding the Souls of Another

Occasionally, you may find that the missing soul part is held by another person; this is common when your patient has given away a part of their soul. Hugh for example, had given a part of his soul to his dog, Charlie, when Charlie was fighting for his life following an accident. When I asked Charlie to give the soul part back (it appeared to me as a ball of light), he did so without question and I was able to restore it to Hugh. Sometimes, however, the person (or animal) who holds the soul part will not give it up so readily.

When you meet such resistance, remember that the person only wants to keep the soul part because they think that it is doing them some good. Explain that it cannot help them and that the person who it really belongs to desperately needs it back. Offer to find them a power animal, on the condition that they give up the soul part. Occasionally, you may find that the person holding the soul part is a dead spirit, trapped in the middleworld because they still hold a living soul part. Again, explain the situation and offer to find a power animal for them. Then, psychopomp them to the afterlife. Remember that these people are not thieves but that they have something which is incredibly precious to them, and you are asking them to give it up. Never just take the soul part or use force of any kind, but negotiate and persuade, using the many gifts you have at your disposal to offer them something in return.

You may have inadvertently taken other people's soul parts yourself (or those of your animals or even the places where you have been). If this is the case, it is important to give them back as the real owners will be missing them. Journey to your power animal and ask for their help in gathering up the various soul parts of others that you hold and ask for a ritual to hand them back. The ritual need not be complicated but must be deliberate and meaningful. When Vanessa was working on giving back the soul parts that she held, we were staying on the west coast of Scotland. Her power animal told her to put the soul parts that she needed to return into a stone and throw it into the sea. She was told that a seal would be there to collect the stone and would then return the soul parts to their rightful owners. She did this and, just as she threw the stone into the sea, a seal momentarily appeared on the surface of the water. It watched the stone fall and then dived under the swell. It was an incredibly moving confirmation of the power behind shamanic work.

## Healing After Soul Retrieval: Finding a Power Animal for Someone Else

If soul retrieval is the cure, then you must also give your patients the power to heal and recover afterwards. The easiest and most effective way of doing this is to teach them to journey for themselves and to find a power animal of their own. However, if a patient is unwilling to journey but likes the thought of having a power animal, you can find one for them.

---

## Exercise: Finding a Power Animal for Someone Else

*Journey as you did for the soul retrieval except, this time, your intention is to find your patient a power animal. Think back to when you first found your power animal; you may have seen it several times or had a strong feeling of connection. Do exactly the same this time, except call your power animal to help you. When you have found your patient's power animal, put it into your hollow bone, return to this world, and blow the power animal into your patient as you did with their soul part.*

---

After I had retrieved Melanie's soul parts, she asked if I would find her a power animal. Tiger appeared, and I brought him back and blew him into Melanie's heart. She was delighted: "I always thought my power animal was a cat; but a tiger: wow!"

In addition to power animals, you also can find other spirit powers for people. Whilst these can certainly help your patients to heal, they can also be a wonderful gift for anyone at any time, the shamanic equivalent of a present. The technique is just the same for finding a soul part or power animal except that, this time, the spirit power you find can, quite literally, be anything. For example, I have given people the power of hope, of bat, of molten iron, and of rain, among many others. Journey with the intention of finding a spirit power that is exactly right for the person you are journeying for and then just trust whatever turns up. Once, when I was journeying for Roger, I got absolutely nothing; it was just black all around me. I tried to move but there was nothing else there. I did think about coming back and trying again but then it dawned on me: the first spirit power was the power of *dark.* I gathered up some of its essence and, almost immediately,

I found myself in a frozen landscape. The next spirit power was *ice*. When I had given them to Roger, he immediately saw their relevance: he was going to the Arctic the following week, just before Christmas, when it would be dark and covered in ice. I had known nothing about his travel plans but had been right to trust whatever turned up when I journeyed.

## Animal Healing

Many people wonder: if humans have power animals, do animals have power humans? In fact, animals have power animals, just as we do, and, like us, they also respond well to spirit extraction and soul retrieval. This was revealed to me when I healed my own dog, Mabon, at a time when he was getting so dependent upon me it was becoming a problem when I was not there.

After an initial journey to find out what healing I should do, I was told I should do an extraction, a soul retrieval, and find him a power animal. I lay Mabon down and went over him whilst in trance, feeling for anything that should not be there. In Mabon's stomach area, I came across some black pitch and my power animal freed it up by entering Mabon's body and thrashing around. Mabon started licking at his stomach furiously as this happened. I gathered up the gloop and threw it towards the nearest river. I could detect nothing else and Mabon settled again. I then journeyed to track Mabon's lost soul part, but rather than going to the upperworld or lowerworld I was pulled to the middleworld, outside by the gate to my house where Mabon, when he first came to me, had stood in bewilderment. I remembered him being completely distressed and unwilling to come into the house; I could do nothing to comfort him. Part of his soul had obviously remained at the gate. I gathered up the soul part (which appeared to me as a puppy), first in song and then in my arms, and brought it back to Mabon. As I blew the soul part into him, he squirmed and then became extremely animated. I thought I might have to stop working as he got so excited but, eventually, the storm blew itself out and he settled. I then journeyed to find a power animal to help him integrate the soul part that had returned. I found Goose and carried her back for Mabon. As I blew her into his heart, he became animated again but, this time, he settled down quickly.

Following his healing, Mabon has never again had any difficulty being on his own and, although he is still devoted to me (as I am to him), it is no longer a problem when I am not there. In some respects, since dogs are far more in tune with the natural and spiritual worlds, they make ideal patients for shamanic healing. The same is also true for other animals and also for plants and trees.

When part of the forest at the rear of my house was recently cut for timber, it left huge swaths of cleared ground as well as the incidental damage caused by the heavy machinery. I was concerned for the souls of the trees, sliced down suddenly and with enormous violence, and so I began to do soul retrievals for the forest. Although I was concerned at the size of the task, the work was straightforward and much appreciated by the trees that I helped. I walk through the remaining forest almost every day and, since completing the healing, I now feel as if I am surrounded by friends.

You can also heal entities such as businesses and organisations, many of which are sorely in need of soul retrieval work (see chapter 13). You can also heal buildings such as your home. You will probably carry out most of your shamanic work around your home; where you live should become both a sanctuary to hold the power that you raise and also a place worthy of the spirits that you call upon to help you in your tasks. This is easy to achieve and, as ever, our ancestors will show you how to begin.

# 10

# Beating the Bounds:
## Making Your Home
### a Sanctuary

The rising sun on your back feels warm after a night spent out in the open. You are in the far north and, despite the signs of spring all around you, it is still extremely cold. To your left, just across the sandy dunes, lies the broad sweep of the sea, and its gentle caress of the shore is incessant and intoxicating. You walk along the shoreline towards a large tower you can just see in the distance. As it gets closer, you notice an open doorway; its inhabitants must have left to work their nearby fields. You stand in the doorway and, because the sun is still on your back, your shadow enters the interior before you. The walls to the tower are wide and faced with sturdy blocks of stone and, as you pass through the door, you have to squeeze into a narrow passageway. At its end is a stone wall, causing you to turn left in order to enter a dimly lit chamber. A fire smoulders and, as you suspected, the place is abandoned. A water trough pushes you to the outside of the room and you walk to the left of the central hearth. Another doorway leads to a farther chamber with a much smaller hearth but, again, the configuration of the room forces you towards the outside, passing the central fire pit on its left. Eventually, you have walked through every chamber, the configuration of the house and the positioning of its hearths, water troughs, and various cupboards always forcing you *to walk in a certain direction. As you reach the entrance passageway, again you realise that you have walked around the entire house in a sunwise direction. As you turn to leave, the sun blinds you momentarily as it is now shining straight down the entrance passageway and illuminating the chamber beyond. Since it is springtime, the direction you face must be east. It seems that whoever built this house had very definite ideas as to how people should enter and move around within it, and all of these focused on the sun. For now, though, you are just enjoying the warmth of the morning, seeping into your bones.*

## Facing the Sunrise

Tower houses, or brochs as they are known, were commonly built during the Iron Age on the coastline of the Scottish Islands.[1] You may recognise the significance of the shoreline as a place betwixt and between, where the veil to the otherworlds is thin. Moreover, the people who built the brochs not only built their houses high, into the sky, but also excavated chambers beneath them that went down, into the earth; the brochs seem designed to mirror the three worlds of the shamanic universe. The Iron Age designers, however, went further still. The doorways to the brochs faced east, towards the rising sun, and their internal arrangement forced people to walk sunwise around the house: the direction the sun takes across the sky and what we now refer to as clockwise.[2] Old Gaelic (Scots and Irish) refers to the sunwise direction as *deosil* (pronounced *djee-zhul*), which is opposed to *widdershins* (a Saxon word adopted into Gaelic), or anticlockwise. There is a strong feeling that *deosil* is the correct and proper way to proceed and the same seems true of the Iron Age brochs. Intriguingly, the Inuit peoples of Greenland, when they made igloos, always spiralled the ice blocks they used to make the dwelling in a deosil direction.[3] This tradition was clearly very important in the European past and people from widely differing times and places followed it.

In prehistoric times, the east-facing entrance was also an important tradition, and most of the roundhouses built during the Bronze and Iron Ages in Britain had doorways orientated to this direction.[4] Continental houses were rectangular rather than round but were still built so that the end housing the livestock faced east. This alignment was so important for people that even the long mounds that covered burials pointed towards the east, as if the dead were also arranged according to the sun. Even the fields, where people planted their crops, were orientated towards the rising sun.[5] The walls demarcating each individual field were arranged in a grid with the east-west walls given priority.[6] Even in steep river valleys, the alignment was unwavering, despite making ploughing the field very impractical; facing the rising sun was clearly so important to people that it overrode all other concerns. Something of this is reflected in modern Welsh, where the word for the right-hand direction is *de*, which is also the word for "the south." If you stand with your right hand towards the south, you are facing east and the rising sun. Even in language, there seems to be a right way for us to orientate ourselves in the world.

## Ancient Feng Shui

This overriding concern with orientation began with the first European villages in Stone Age Bulgaria.[7] Surrounding their houses, people built enclosures, which, when viewed from above, made almost exact squares. Furthermore, each side of the square was orientated towards one of the cardinal directions: north, south, east, or west. Since the people at the time had no compass or other means of orientation, these walls had to be aligned according to the pattern of the rising and setting sun. These villages are one of the earliest examples of humans arranging the space that they inhabit according to the movement of the sun. People probably thought of this arrangement as the correct and natural order of the world: if the sun rose in a certain direction and moved across the sky in a certain way, then this is how people thought they should also behave. People were aligning themselves and the places they inhabited with the natural order and movement of the sun.

The ancient Chinese held similar views and, over time, this developed into a complete system of arranging and organising anything that people constructed. *Feng shui* is the correct alignment of things to maximise the flow of *qi* (pronounced *chee*), the energy of the natural world. Although ancient Europeans did not formulate their ideas to quite this level, they also tried to preserve the flow of *qi* through their villages and houses except that, to them, the energy they sought to maximise originated from the sun. By bringing the sun into their houses (both by aligning the doorways with its rising in the east and arranging the interiors so that people had to walk *deosil* around them), people made sure that the energy flowed correctly and their homes stayed positive and healthy. Effectively, this was ancient European feng shui.

Consider your home; your front door probably does not face the rising sun and  the layout of your rooms probably does not force you to walk *deosil* around them—these traditions have been long forgotten. Looking at the flow of energy around your home, however, can still be beneficial. You can notice where there might be blockages, causing the energy to stagnate and become oppressive. Whilst a feng shui practitioner might consult books and charts, you know an easier way. Journey to the middleworld and walk around your home; you will see the energy for yourself and observe how well it flows.

---

## Exercise: Ancient Feng Shui

*Journey to the middleworld stating your intention as: I am journeying to the middleworld to observe the flow of energy around my home. Then, leaving your physical body, walk around your home from room to room as you would normally do; go through your routines of getting up, leaving the house, and returning home, all the things you would generally do in a day. As you are doing this, see the energy flowing around you; observe a pattern for how that energy moves as you pass. Notice whether the energy stagnates in any corners, and whether it seems to drag you back or spur you on as you pass. Then, return to this world and, making a simple plan of all the rooms in your home, plot the energy flow as you saw it. You now have a sketch of your home showing the way that the energy flows around it. What does it tell you? What areas need attention?*

Energy that does not flow smoothly around your home quickly stagnates and loses vitality. House builders always have a show suite to lure potential buyers to their development, rather than let people walk through an actual house; empty houses are full of stagnant energy, which is very off-putting.

There are many ways of breaking up stagnant energy and getting the *qi* to flow. You have seen how Iron Age people, for example, walked through their entire house in a *deosil* direction to stimulate the energy in their wake. To achieve something similar, do not ignore parts of your home but deliberately keep the energy flowing through your daily activities; an unused spare room, for example, can quickly feel musty as the energy stagnates. Similarly, a sick-room can rapidly deteriorate into an unhealthy space; counter this by flinging open the windows and letting sunlight fill the room. This is just what ancient Iron Age people were doing when they built their houses with the doorway facing east. Feng shui manuals suggest that wind chimes are a good way of breaking up stale *qi*, and I like to place mine near a window so that they catch the breeze and fill the room with their sound. In fact, any form of sound or movement works well to break up stagnant energy; singing whilst you vacuum, for example, can be very effective. Similarly, introduce plants or pets into stagnant areas to bring back the vitality and get the *qi* flowing again.

## Removing Negative Energy

When you viewed the inside of your house in the middleworld, in addition to stagnant energy, you may have also noticed areas where the energy seemed negative and even slightly threatening. Just as spirit intrusions can enter your body, negative energy can enter your home and, once there, has much the same effect. Building specialists call this sick building syndrome, and whilst they recognise the symptoms, the ignore the cause. Like spirit intrusions, negative energy can enter your home in much the same way. Arguments, for example, give off their own energy which can accumulate in your home (especially in those areas where the energy does not flow well to start off with). Similarly, sadness, grief, depression, and a myriad of other human detrimental emotions affect our surroundings and can also accumulate as negative energy in your home. Even trauma to the house itself, such as a leaking roof, can cause negative energy to accumulate. Buildings in need of repair often exude a heavy atmosphere; even a sadness. These are sick buildings indeed.

Homes that accumulate a lot of negative energy begin to feel uncomfortable and may be described as haunted. A friend of mine, Alistair, once described to me his attempt to sleep in an old Victorian hotel that had definitely seen better days: "I just couldn't sleep that night; the room felt heavy with a very dense atmosphere. It could have been my imagination, but it might have been that there really was some presence in the room. I'll never know, but it was really scary." Needless to say, he left the next morning.

Removing negative energy from homes uses very similar techniques to those used to extract spirit intrusions from your patients. First, however, establish that you are actually dealing with negative energy—which needs removing—rather than stagnant energy—which just needs to be dissipated. An initial journey to the middleworld should establish which is required and, of course, you can also consult your power animal or upperworld guide. If you find negative energy, journey again to extract it.

## Exercise: Removing Negative Energy

*Have someone drum for you (and follow you as you move around your house) or put on your drumming recording so that it is loud enough for you to hear it wherever you are. Call your power animal and fill yourself with power as you are now used to doing. Then, lie down and enter the middleworld. Spend time looking over your house and identify the areas of negative energy. As with extracting spirit intrusions from people, the negative energy may take on a definable form. When you know exactly what you are going to clear, stand up and, keeping your consciousness in the middleworld (but opening your physical eyes to enable you to move around), walk to the place you identified. Make sure you are completely filled with power and gather up the negative energy as you did when removing spirit intrusions from your human patients. When you have gathered everything (and you may need to return for more if you cannot carry it all the first time), walk over to a window or doorway and fling it outside. Remember, the energy is not bad or evil; throwing the energy back into nature lets it dissipate naturally. When you have removed all the bad energy from your home (or your power animal indicates that you have done enough for this time), return to where you started and return to your physical body.*

## Healing Your Home

In the same way you offered your human patients healing after a spirit extraction, care for your home in a similar way. Filling your home with scented smoke is a good way to attract positive energy and fill any gaps left by removing the negative energy. Blowing a fine mist of spring water through the air has a similar effect. When I was in Siberia, the shamans used vodka in the same way. Finally, do as ancient people did and fling open the windows and let in the sun.

Sometimes, the negativity you feel in a home can be down to the building itself. When Vanessa and I stayed in a converted barn in Norfolk, the accommodation was wonderful. Every morning, however, I would awake to find Vanessa already up, dressed, and sitting downstairs. She is an habitually early riser so, at first, I thought nothing of it. Several nights later, I was aware of her getting up at midnight and going downstairs. When I asked her why, she said the house was so miserable she could not sleep. I immediately journeyed to the spirit of the house and found that it was, indeed, particularly grumpy and unhappy. When it had calmed down, it told me it was tired of everyone who "lived" there moving out after a week or two: "Why will no one stay with me?" I pointed out that everyone who came to the cottage was on holiday, and the house had a wonderful opportunity to make people happy. This seemed to work. The next night, Vanessa slept without difficulty and the atmosphere about the place was completely different.

## Living Patterns

During the Iron Age in Britain, people divided their roundhouses into two main parts: a sleeping part in the north of the house (right of the door upon entering) and a living part in the south (left of the door upon entering).[8] Whilst this ensured that people always moved *deosil* when entering the house, the arrangement itself also reflected the journey of the sun across the sky. When the sun was in the south, during the day, people were in the southern part of their houses, whereas when the sun was in the north, during the night, people slept in the northern part of their houses. It was another way that people attuned their houses to the patterns of the sun.

The Sámi also divided their tepee-like dwellings, called *kåhte*, in a similar way, so that residents and visitors all had prescribed places to sit on either side of the central fireplace.[9] When I worked with Sámi shamans out in the wilderness of the Arctic, we followed similar rules when we arranged ourselves in the kåhte we used as our living space. Although the central fire pit was replaced with a modern stove, the spot on the far side of the doorway was still reserved for our tools and utensils. To the Steppe nomads, who occupy round frame-built tents (called *yurt* in Turkish or *ger* in Mongolian) the area on the far side of the doorway is considered a sacred place and objects relating to the spirits and photographs of the ancestors are kept there.

You can also make a small part of your home a sacred place where you keep items that relate to your shamanic practice and any other sacred objects. Andy, for example, devoted the top of a cupboard in his living room as a sacred space and keeps images of various Gods and Goddesses there, along with his shamanic tools; he also gathers flowers from the garden to maintain a link with the natural world. When he uses the room for his shamanic journeys, he lights a candle and places it on his altar, so that it can radiate its light whilst he is in the otherworlds.

Although the Steppe nomads brought pictures of their ancestors into their dwellings, our Bronze Age ancestors went one better and brought the bodies inside instead.[10] Whilst corpses can be mummified and kept for generations, more often, bodies, or at least various parts of bodies, were buried beneath floors or under the doorway into the house. Whilst you cannot do this today, you can bring your ancestors into your home through photographs and other reminders. One of my friends, Asia, keeps photographs of her ancestors on the mantelpiece and, every morning, offers them gifts of food and drink, whilst asking for their blessings on her day. It is a wonderful tradition and one that you can adopt yourself.

## Spiritual Boundaries

In ancient times, boundaries were extremely important to people; the earliest European villages had those square enclosures around them that related to the cardinal directions. Although these were physical boundaries, they were also important for their symbolism. In later times, the physical existence of the boundary was ignored altogether and the act of making the boundary was emphasised rather than its continued existence. Bronze Age people, for example, surrounded their houses with ditches that they dug and almost immediately filled in again with earth.[11]

These people were constructing a spiritual boundary rather than a physical boundary. When they backfilled the ditches, they added to the soil various items, including pottery vessels, metal items (which were extremely valuable to a farming family), and various human bones, hinting at an ancestral presence. These probably relate to the rituals carried out when the boundaries were dug and refilled, and with people invoking the spirits and leaving offerings of food, drink, and even metal objects. It is even possible that, after invoking the aid and protection of the spirits, maintaining a physical boundary would have been considered rude and disrespectful and this is why the ditch was filled in again.

Although physical boundaries around your property are a real need today, you can secure your home spiritually, just as your ancestors did. Undertake a middleworld journey to meet your power animal and walk around your home to see what needs to be done. Since you are in the middleworld, walk straight through any walls and, even if you live in a high-rise flat, you will be able to reach all your boundaries. Some people like to surround their homes with light, which acts as a shield for negative energy as well as a protection against intruders. Others plant particular trees or shrubs to protect the entrances to their property, either in the middleworld or in this world, rather like the hawthorn tree that guards the entrance to my house. Occasionally, you may be drawn to build something substantial, like a wall or a gate. Desiree, for example, was having difficulty with her neighbours, who disapproved of her shamanic practice. In a journey, she noticed that these neighbours aimed a lot of negativity her way, and so her power animal told her to hang polished metal around the boundary to her property. These act as mirrors, protecting Desiree's house and repelling any negativity aimed her way.

## Beating the Bounds

Another ancient tradition is *beating the bounds:* ritually reaffirming property boundaries. The practice probably arose in the Steppe area, where deceased kings took one final trip around their realm before burial.[12] This reaffirmed the boundaries of their former kingdom and let the neighbouring tribes know that the king, even in death, would still observe and look after his lands. In more recent times, when parish boundaries were afforded similar prominence, the boundary was struck, over and over, marking its route not just physically but, like boundaries in the Bronze Age, also spiritually. This continuous striking of the boundary provides the name for the practice: beating the bounds. Often, a willow stick was used for this and some of the old folk dances, such as *"Stripping the Willow,"* may be connected to the tradition.

Walking your boundaries (in this world or, if access is difficult, in the middleworld) and ritually affirming their presence connects you with the place you inhabit. In ancient cultures, the ruler and his or her lands were often seen as one, and you should adopt a similar care for and appreciation of your place in the world. When beating the bounds in the past, large trees, milestones, or even springs and wells would have marked the boundaries to a parish and these significant landmarks were often afforded a beating in their own right.

During the Ice Age, people marked and protected the entrance to their sacred caves by placing the skulls of cave bears on prominent rocks and platforms.[13] These not only marked the boundary from profane to sacred space but the skulls probably also represented the spirit of Cave Bear, standing ready to repel any intruder trying to enter the caves. You can put guardians at significant points on your boundaries, either by leaving a symbol of an animal at a significant point, or by journeying to the middleworld and enlisting the help of an animal spirit. Remember, however, you are not looking for a ferocious monster that will terrorise the neighbours and bite the postman, but a sentinel that will keep watch over your property and care for its inhabitants. The guardian of my house, for example, is a fox, who often walks a complete circuit around the building. In his honour, I keep a fox jaw bone hanging in the tree above my shamanic working area and give thanks for his presence whenever I am there.

## Boundaries of Skin

Another far more intimate boundary around us is our skin, which also needs caring for and, occasionally, a little help in repelling the forces of the outside world. When I feel my personal space being invaded, my power animal has taught me a simple technique to keep me from harm. All I do is shrug on an "imaginary" pelt of his skin. I draw it over my shoulders and across my chest, pulling it tight around me. Now, in additional to my own skin, I also wear the skin of my power animal. In a way, it is a form of shapeshifting but is done with the minimum of effort and, more importantly if you are in public, the minimum of attention. Whatever power animal you have, ask if it will allow you to share its skin, scales, feathers, or shell, whenever you feel the need for extra protection.

This chapter focussed on your home, since, for most of us, this is the most important place in our lives. However, you can adapt all the techniques for other environments, such as your car, place of work, or even a train or aeroplane that you inhabit only temporarily. All of these are indoor, artificial places, however, and yet there is another, far greater world beyond their doors. How you should interact and care for this world, the world of nature, forms the next step on your shamanic path.

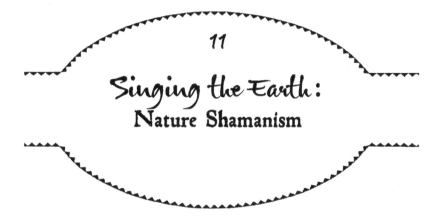

# 11
# Singing the Earth:
## Nature Shamanism

The shaman dips his hands into the water of the cauldron and then thrusts them towards the sky. Howling an incantation to the spirits, he takes more water and douses the rock pillar before him. You stand among the quarry workers who have spent the past week gently and slowly chipping at the rock outcrop until the human-sized pillar that stands before you eventually emerged. The shaman is now calling on the spirits of the land to give up the stone, and you follow his gaze as it rests on each feature of this mountainous place. Before you is the jagged outcrop of rock from where the pillar was hewn; on either side, the moorland stretches until it is swallowed by the sky, and at your back, the land slopes sharply away until it finally falls into the sea. You bring your attention back to the shaman, who is now telling the quarry workers to sever the last hold the pillar has to its mother rock. They do so and the great stone topples forward, only to be caught in the elaborate rope cradle that has been designed to make its passage to the ground as gentle as possible. Before the stone is a wooden sledge that will serve as its home while it is rolled, first down the slope, and then across the shore, to where a boat waits in the surf. From there, it will sail around the coast and across the vast inland channel that slices the land to the east. When it can go no farther on the boat, it *will be transferred to a raft and floated along rivers until it finally reaches its new home. Before the journey begins, however, a crippled boy moves forward, hobbling painfully, and stands before the stone. He touches his legs to its surface and the shaman utters words of heal- ing. Then, more people move forward, some with ailments that are obvious, and some who have inner pains they wish to shed. All touch the stone with reverence. It will be some time before it is ready to leave this place.*

## Healing Stones

The first ring of stones erected at Stonehenge was of bluestone, a slate-blue rock brought from the mountains of Preseli in Wales.[1] Why people brought stone from such a long distance has never been sat- isfactorily answered, although current thought is that the mountains where the stone originated were sacred and recognised as a place of healing.[2] Below the outcrops of rock, which provided the raw material from which the bluestone pillars were hewn, are numerous springs; oral tradition suggests that they have powerful healing properties. This was likely recognised by our ancestors as many of the springs were modified to make access to them easier or to catch the water in an enlarged pool. Perhaps the rock outcrops above the springs were also endowed with healing properties and, by using them to construct Stonehenge, people were building a temple for healing. Certainly, of the numerous bodies that were buried in and around Stonehenge, many were crippled in some way, and it may have been that they were brought to the temple for healing before they eventually succumbed to their ailments and were buried there. Perhaps the way the cairns of Preseli stand like jagged sentinels first gave people the idea of erecting them in a ring and perhaps they even looked at the blue stone with its flecks of white and were reminded of the night sky and the origin of the world.

## Relating to Nature

Our very earliest ancestors, those who lived through the age of ice, or who hunted in the first primeval forests, did not need to get closer to nature, or even really consider their relationship to nature; *they were nature*, part of the natural world. This began to change when humans learnt to farm. No longer were people at the whim of the natural world; now they could start to control it and bend it to their needs.[3] To some, learning to farm was the original fall from Eden; and in the story of Cain and Abel, the farmer murders his brother. At the same time, our ancestors started to construct monuments.[4] As farming tamed and domesticated plants and animals, people also sought to tame and domesticate the landscape and order it according to their demands. They started to build monuments to order the world around them. Often, however, the natural attributes of a place are magnified and concentrated by the building of monuments—as with the bluestones transported to Stonehenge. These were not so much artificial constructions but more of an exaggeration of what could already be found in the natural world.

The first monuments, for example, were round.[5] This shape reflects the shape of the sun (an important ordering principle in slightly later times as described in chapter 10) as well as mirroring the circularity of the horizon when it is viewed from inside the monument itself. Occasionally, prominent landmarks may be reflected in the design of the monument or it may be built so that the sun, moon, or stars are seen to rise in a significant position when they are viewed from inside the structure.[6] The midsummer sunrise at Stonehenge is perhaps the most famous of these but there are many others.

At first, these circular monuments were no more than a bank and ditch, called a *henge*.[7] Unlike bank and ditches built for defence, however, where the ditch is always outside the bank, henges are constructed so the bank is outside the ditch. Perhaps ironically, the most famous henge monument, Stonehenge, is not really a henge at all, since the ditch is outside the bank. The reversal of bank and ditch is puzzling, unless it was designed to keep things in rather than—as is usual with defensive bank and ditches—being designed to keep things out. Since these were undoubtedly special and even sacred places, perhaps the bank and ditch was constructed to hold the power that was raised there and to ensure that its energy was contained.

## Sacred Land

In prehistoric times, humans did not build all the sites they considered sacred.[8] People viewed rivers and bogs as special places, where the portal to the otherworlds was thin, and where any items left in these places could easily make the transition to the afterlife. Similarly, caves were considered sacred during the Ice Age, when some were decorated with images that still fill us with awe today. The trouble is, however, that unless people changed these places in some way, as they did in the caves, or left items there, as they did in rivers and bogs, we cannot tell today if people considered a place significant. The Sámi, for example, hold prominent rocks as sacred, and I have visited a number when I have travelled through Lapland. Whilst they are certainly large and impressive, nothing inherent in the rock itself tells us that it is sacred (at least, no more than any other rock) and so we need to rely on the Sámi shamans and others who still hold to the old traditions to identify them. The same was likely true in the past and much of what our ancient ancestors held to be sacred is now lost to us.

Through your shamanic practice, however, you know everything is alive and filled with spirit and, in a way, this makes everything sacred and worthy of your respect. The Toltec shamans say that nature is the visible face of the spirits and this is certainly how you should approach the natural world. All of nature, from the weeds that grow around unused land in the city centres, to the majestic mountains of the Alps, is sacred and should be held in regard. Like our ancient ancestors, however, you may find some places particularly special and

that they draw you in with their magic. Some may be wild and remote places but others may be close to where you live. Perhaps others
in the past recognised their sacredness and a round ditch and bank or
a circle of standing stones marks its place. Alternatively, the place we
are drawn to may be, so far, unrecognised and uncelebrated. Either
way, find time to visit the place and observe it anew, with the benefit
of your shamanic eyes.

## Exercise: Sacred Land

*As you approach your sacred site, whether it is enclosed by a huge
ditch, ringed by stones, or identified in some other, unseen way, look
at how the place fits into the landscape. Is there an obvious entrance
and, if so, does it face anything special, like a distant hill or the midwinter sunrise? If possible, walk around the site without actually entering it, first deosil and then in the opposite direction, widdershins.
Can you feel the energy flowing. How does it change as you pass? If
there is an entrance to the site, can you feel anything as you pass over
it? (I often experiment with dowsing rods and, if you have a pair,
try dowsing as you walk across the threshold to your site.) Finally,
stand within the sacred space. How do you feel? What impressions do
you get? Next, either where you are or close by if you need to find a
place where you will be undisturbed, journey to the middleworld and
look again at the energy flow around your sacred site. Journey to meet
the spirits of the place and ask if they will show you around. Journey back in time to see how the site was used in the past; if you feel
drawn to the place, others probably felt the same. Finally, ask if there
is anything the spirits of the place might want from you.*

I was once with a shamanic group and we journeyed to find out
more about a place that one of our members felt to be a particularly
sacred location. One evening we walked to the site and, after looking

around and getting a feel for the energy of the place, we all found somewhere we could sit and journey. The stories we brought back with us were many and varied and yet all seemed to relate similar facts about the place. By the time everyone had shared their contributions, we had built up a detailed history of the place, as well as got to know many of its spirit inhabitants. It made for a wonderful summer's evening.

## Hearing the Myths

Although some sacred sites might come with their own history, others can be completely unknown. Journeying to find out about the history and mythology of a place can be rewarding, as my shamanic group found, and, occasionally, can introduce us to spirits and guides that become very significant to your life.

In chapter 4, for example, I related my annual pilgrimage to a remote mountain peak near to where I live, so that I can leave an offering of meadowsweet flowers near the grave of one of my upperworld guides. The grave had been excavated and was found to hold a woman from the Bronze Age, and she was buried with bunches of meadowsweet (hence my offerings today). Below her grave is a lake and there is an old Welsh myth that a woman lives in the lake who has the gift of healing. In my many journeys sitting beside the lake, I have made my own additions to the story and feel that the woman from the grave is the same as the woman who dwells in the water. She has become both a teacher and guide to me and I feel privileged to have had the opportunity to get to know her.

People have always explained their world through stories. In particular, many societies tell myths about their origins and these often speak of a land from where the people first came. In the Stone Age, at the time when the first farmers colonised the primeval forest that covered most of the continent, people built huge rectangular houses of wood and thatch. They aligned these houses in a particular direction so that each faced the place from where the community had originated.[9] By following each settlement back along the line of its orientation, it is possible to follow the spread of farming throughout ancient Europe, right back to its roots in the east. People probably told stories of this mythical homeland and perhaps, over time, it merged with the otherworlds to become a realm beyond the known world. Certainly, when people buried their dead, they made sure their heads faced the direction of this mythical homeland, as if people had to travel east to reach the afterlife.[10] Over time, this myth probably merged with the stories told about the sun so that for generations to come, houses would always be built to face east.

In the Iron Age, the Bards held the myths and traditions relating to the tribe.[11] Without the written word, everything of importance had to be remembered and orally passed down from generation to generation. Public recitations of the history and myths of the tribe probably formed an important part of any gathering; we could perhaps imagine the rapt attention a Bard would command. These gatherings likely took place in forest clearings, called *groves*. Julius Caesar, for example, writes that groves were particularly sacred places, and another Roman historian adds that they seemed to be a world apart from this one: where no worldly animal would knowingly enter, where the ground would shake with power, and where the trees would blaze with a fire that did not burn them.[12] Poetic license aside, these were clearly special places; when the Romans conquered Britain at the end of the Iron Age, they made it their priority to destroy the groves: the seat of spiritual power.

## The Spirits of Place

Since groves were always located within forests, the trees and their spirits became especially important to people. Some Celtic tribes took their names from the trees: the *Lemovices* are the People of the Elm, and the *Eburones* are the People of the Yew. The tree spirits became the *genius loci* or the spirit of the place (from the Latin meaning "local spirit"). Every location has a *genius loci* and, if you have not yet met the one for your sacred place, you can journey to meet it now.

---

## Exercise: The Spirits of Place

*Either at your sacred site or, if you cannot get there easily, at the place you usually journey (travelling the rest of the way in the middleworld), call your power animal and ask to be introduced to the genius locus of the site. Remember that the spirit can take any form: an animal, a tree, or even an indefinable shape that just feels right. Ask it to tell you about the place and see if it adds anything to what you discovered earlier. When you have met the genius locus for your sacred site, meet the one for your home, place of work, or any other destination.*

---

When you have met the *genius locus* of your sacred place, ask what you can do to honour it and keep something of its power with you. You could collect some flowers from the site, or a stone, feather, or leaf, and keep them on your altar so that you have a reminder of your contact with the place and its guardian. You may feel drawn to tidy the area around your site, collecting rubbish and doing any other tasks that may need your attention. When I visit the grave of my upperworld guide, for example, I give it a tidy and take away any litter. If appropriate, plant some trees on the site. Constance, for example, looks after many sacred places around the town where she lives and the Council has given her permission to plant trees on some of them. When planting, she always dedicates one particular tree to the *genius loci* of the site.

In prehistoric times, people also honoured the *genius loci* of a place through trees, although, instead of planting them, they left figures carved from wood.[13] The most common wood they used was oak, perhaps because it represented strength and permanence, but they also used yew, ash, and alder.[14] The figures themselves were roughly human shaped and some had features such as eyes and sexual organs. A Roman historian, however, called them grim, rude, and uncouth, so perhaps their beauty is in the eye of the beholder.[15] Interestingly, some of the figures were deliberately damaged in their left eye and this brings to mind the far later tradition of Odin, the Norse God, giving up an eye to obtain the power of the spirits.[16] Perhaps the figures of our more ancient ancestors hint at the beginnings of this tradition.

Some of the wooden figures from Germany were placed next to tracks, especially where they crossed dangerous areas or where the track had previously collapsed.[17] Perhaps these figures were designed to watch over the tracks and to protect those who were passing along them. It is very similar to my experience in Siberia, which I related in chapter 3, where my driver offered gifts to the spirit of a place (what we now know as a *genius loci*) to allow us safe passage along the road. Many of the wooden figures from the past were also found with pottery and other offerings around them as if people were doing the same.[18]

Making an image of the *genius loci* of your sacred site, and either placing it on the site itself or keeping it on your altar, can be a powerful way of connecting and interacting with the spirit. You do not need any particular carving skills: grim, rude, and uncouth is the look you are aiming for. Clothe your figures or give them some jewellery to wear. A figure from Ireland, made by our Iron Age ancestors, clearly wore something around its neck as the wood has not been weathered there, whereas the rest of the body became battered during the time it was kept displayed in the open.[19]

## Weather Shamanism

Some wooden figures were placed in wet areas, especially in the raised bogs close to villages. Whilst the wet area of the marsh is recognised as being a portal to the otherworld, and therefore an entirely suitable place for a representation of a spirit to reside, there may be another reason as to why the figures were placed here. Climate change is something relevant to us today since the earth is rapidly warming due to the burning of fossil fuels. The climate, however, has always *naturally* warmed and cooled throughout its history and people were clearly aware of that fact. After the melting of the ice sheets following the Ice Age, and bar a few wobbles along the way, the climate gradually warmed throughout the Stone and Bronze Ages until people were able to farm areas of upland that had previously been too cold and wet. From the middle of the Bronze Age, however, and through the Iron Age, the climate got gradually colder and wetter until many of the upland villages had to be abandoned. The raised bogs then expanded, possibly even threatening the villages, and perhaps this is why people placed figures of the *genius loci* at their edge: they were trying to change the weather and prevent the spread of the bog.

Whilst all of us should try to reduce our reliance on fossil fuels and live in a more environmentally aware manner (and this is as much the path of the shaman as anything else written in this book), influencing the weather on a more local scale is also something you can attempt. Although weather systems are vast and, as a consequence, difficult to alter, journeying to the spirit of the weather, be it rain, wind, or snow, can be a powerful way of attuning yourself to the natural world and, just sometimes, the weather may change at your request.

I was once at a large shamanic gathering with my friend, Clive. Since it had rained constantly throughout the day, much of our work was necessarily conducted indoors. That evening, however, we were due to have a ritual outside with a large fire; it did not look promising. Knowing that Clive had a good relationship with the spirits, I asked him, about half an hour before our ritual was due to take place, whether he would journey to the spirit of the rain and ask it to stop the downpour for a few hours. He was doubtful he could do it but agreed to try. Almost immediately, the rain stopped. We were able to light the fire and conduct our ritual until, just as we had finished, it started to pour again. Weather shamanism can work.

Experiencing all forms of weather is another way of attuning yourself with the natural world and also of getting to know the weather spirits better. I often journey outside, and I am used to the rain dripping off the end of my nose as I do so. Unlike the irritation I feel when I am caught in a downpour on my way somewhere, however, when I have actively chosen to be out in the rain (or any other inclement weather) it is strangely liberating and the raindrops begin to caress my body rather than attack it. Shamanism is a path of nature, and you should experience nature in all her moods.

## Moving Through the Land

To our ancient ancestors, nature was not static or something only to be looked at; moving through the land was tremendously important and they marked out the routes that were especially significant. These walkways are called *cursuses* because they reminded the old antiquarians of the Roman cursuses, where they held chariot races.[20] The cursuses our ancestors constructed, however, were not for racing around but for walking along. One, in Dorset, is positioned so that anyone standing within its boundaries on the evening of midwinter will see the sun falling towards and then setting behind a burial mound on the nearby ridge.[21] The sun seems to disappear into the tomb, perhaps to start its journey through the otherworld of night. Clearly, people deliberately positioned the cursus so that they could watch the spectacle after walking along its designated route; it must have been an amazing occasion.

Elsewhere, in Britain, Ireland, and northern France, numerous tall stones were arranged in straight lines, as if they designated routes that people walked during rituals.[22] Even where I live in Wales, there are numerous standing stones and some seem to mark routes through the landscape, often ending at a stone circle or another significant place.

These were not ordinary tracks from village to village but were pilgrimages to be undertaken through a sacred landscape. Chapter 3 described how people in the Stone Age walked the land and had feasts at the end of their journey. They buried the special pottery they used (marked with patterns resembling phosphenes) in specially dug pits along with the remains of the feasts. Their next journey would follow the same route but go a little farther, where they would dig another pit. Eventually numerous pits marked the walk, providing a history of past gatherings and ceremonies. It was a means through which our ancestors first began to inscribe their existence on to the land.

We cannot say what our ancestors did as they walked, but in many shamanic communities today, people sing. The Australian Aborigines believe that the world was sung into being and their land is crisscrossed with song lines, along which people make pilgrimages, walking in the footsteps of their ancestors.[23] Indeed, humans probably learnt to sing, or, at least, to hum, before they could talk.[24] Singing is therefore a powerful way of interacting with nature and bringing its sacredness into the centre of our being.

---

## Exercise: Moving Through the Land

*Devise a walk near to where you live, either through your neighbourhood, a park, or in the countryside. Link places that are meaningful to you and start and end somewhere particularly significant, such as your sacred site. Before you begin the walk, shift your consciousness slightly, as you have done before, so that you can be more receptive to the energy flowing around you. Invite your power animal to join you. Then, as you walk, sing the route. Sing everything that catches your eye and then repeat it until you see something else. For example: "Little bird, little bird, singing so loud, little bird, little bird, large tree, rough bark, rough bark, cloud over sun, cloud over sun." It does not matter what you say or how loud you say it; just sing anything that grabs your attention. You will be amazed at how such a simple practice can totally transform your outlook on the world. When you are half-way around your walk, include yourself into your words, for example: "Little bird, little bird, sing for me, fill me with your song, large tree, be there for me, share with me your strength." You are now calling in power and offering a song in return: a beautiful bargain with nature.*

## A Quest for a Vision

Spending time in nature and getting to know the spirits who live there is common in almost all shamanic traditions. The Plains Native Americans, for example, spend three or four days alone in the natural world, barely moving from one place and going without food or water, in order that a vision might come to them. They call these pilgrimages *vision quests* as a result.[25] Such an undertaking is difficult, potentially dangerous, and relies on the support of considerable backup. Not least, the sponsor of the person on the vision quest, generally a spiritual elder, agrees to pray for them during the entire period they remain in the wilderness. A vision quest, if conducted correctly, is a large commitment and is generally carried out only once or twice in a person's life. In our modern lives, such an enormous undertaking is beyond the reach of many of us (and some Native Americans object to non-natives appropriating their traditions). A day spent walking and singing the land, however, can be a form of vision quest, *a quest for a vision*, that you can achieve almost anywhere. The act of singing itself will be enough to induce the light trance necessary for you to see behind the veil and communicate with the spirits that live there. Even in a crowded city, you can sing the earth: observing, integrating, connecting, and listening to the natural world.

When I worked with the Sámi shamans, they showed me the Sámi way of walking, which is to place each foot upon the earth quite deliberately, heel followed by toe, and to push a little energy into the earth. When you lift your foot, just as deliberately, heel followed by toe, you take a little energy back from the earth. On the days you feel strong and power-full, you give more than you take, but on days you feel empty and in need of help, you take a little more than you give. In this way, you walk in balance with the earth, and the way you walk becomes a metaphor for the way you live: taking what you need and always offering something in return.

The joik, or song, I use in my spiritual practice also originates from the land of the Sámi. A joik is a means, not just of singing about something, but actually bringing it into existence. In a way, creating a joik is a form of shapeshifting where the singer embodies the subject of his or her song. The technique, however, was not taught to me whilst I was in Lapland. Rather, the spirit of Fire gave me my joik. One evening, when I was drumming in front of the flames and offering my thanks for their light and warmth, I was told to open my throat and sing. Out came my joik and I have used it ever since. You should never worry about finding your voice; you just need to ask the spirits to give you what you need and begin. Furthermore, whatever you think about your singing ability, a song, offered in a sacred manner, always sounds beautiful to the spirits.

Playing an instrument is another means to connect with the world around you, especially if you play it in the same way as you sang on your walk: improvised by what you observe in your surroundings. In prehistoric times, people used bullroarers, which are flat pieces of wood swung through the air at high speed that give out a note not unlike a bull roaring.[26] They also used flutes and, of course, drums. Taking your instruments outside and playing whatever rhythm moves you is an ancient way of connecting with nature and bringing the spirits forth. Adding your voice to the sound only enhances the effect.

Walking through nature, either in the countryside or the heart of the city, is a journey through space but also through time. The physical act of travelling takes time but your interaction with the natural world also exists at a level outside normal time. In the modern world, watches and clocks artificially govern time and dissect a moment into milliseconds. Much of life adheres slavishly to a schedule that depends almost entirely on time. You can try to avoid it (and I never wear a watch for anything other than the most pressing engagement, when I have to borrow one) but the passing of time is always there. Our ancient ancestors did not have clocks or watches and their sole means of measuring the passage of time was through observing the movement of the sun, moon, and stars. This was a far more natural way to live and still has much to teach us today.

# 12

# A Year and a Day:
## Celebrating the Seasons

Y ou rise from among the group gathered at the entrance to the tomb. Some are beating a steady rhythm from their hide-covered pottery drums, whilst others chant gently to themselves. It is just before dawn and your breath crystallises in the frozen air of midwinter. Moving forward, you take your place among the four that will enter the confines of the tomb. A shaman calls upon the spirits to protect you as you move into the realm of the dead, and she briefly passes a smoking brand around your body. When the shaman has finished her entreaties, you walk silently into the tomb. The entrance is large and you can walk upright under the huge lintel stone that marks the upper edge of the doorway. Above the lintel is a small rectangular slot that seems to serve no purpose. Inside, the tomb is dark and you are glad to be following another as you grope through the blackness. Under your feet the ground is smooth and polished, although you occasionally knock things aside with your feet. Eventually, you reach the burial chamber itself and are grateful to be able to squat against the far wall. The darkness within the tomb is complete and all you hear is the sound of breathing; nothing else stirs. It is some time before you become aware of a faint glow from the far end of the entrance passageway. It is the first light of dawn and you silently pray that the sun will follow. The *drumming from outside the tomb intensifies and its sound now filters through to you. It throbs around the small chamber and makes you dizzy to hear it. Then, quite suddenly, there is sunlight on the floor of the passageway. It is bright and dazzling and, for a moment, you shield your eyes. Incredibly, the origin of the light is the small rectangular slot that you noticed above the doorway; the sunlight is shining straight through it. Inexorably, the shaft of light moves along the passageway and towards the chamber where you squat against the wall. Your legs begin to hurt but you find yourself unable to take your eyes from the encroaching light. Eventually, it reaches the chamber itself and sunlight floods the floor. To your disquiet, you now see bones and skulls all around you, neatly sorted and piled upon the floor. The sunlight creeps up the walls, momentarily blinding you as it reaches the level of your eyes. And, then, just as quickly as it arrived, it is gone.*

## Watching the Sunrise

At Newgrange in Ireland, a massive burial tomb was constructed during the Stone Age so that its entrance directly aligned with the rising sun at midwinter.[1] Furthermore, the shaft of sunlight enters the tomb through a small slot directly above the doorway; this was a design of incredible complexity and sophistication. Due to the cramped interior, very few people could have witnessed the sun moving along the passageway of the tomb and lighting the central chamber; most people probably remained outside. This was not a ritual for the living, however, but, rather, a ritual for the dead. As the sun was reborn at wintertime, after the longest night of the year, so the occupants of the tomb were reborn for those who witnessed the ceremony, providing a reassuring presence among the uncertainties of daily life. Through their ritual, people celebrated death and rebirth, of the sun, certainly, but also of themselves and their ancestors.

The sun always rose from the same position on midwinter's day because the movement of the earth around the sun is constant, year on year (although today, we add a day every four years to make it fit with our calendar). This means that the earth and the sun will be in the same position every midwinter day and the phenomenon of the sun shining into the tomb at Newgrange will happen every year (including this one).

Aligning monuments to face the rising sun was a complex and time-consuming process and designing the rectangular slot at Newgrange, so that the rays of the rising sun shined straight through it, was an incredible feat. Although other monuments, such as Seahenge in Norfolk[2] and a similar fenced enclosure at Gosek in Germany,[3] have alignments to the rising midwinter sun, the complexity at Newgrange is unequalled. Clearly, celebrating the sunrise following the longest night of the year was incredibly important to these people and a significant event in their year.

The differing length of days and nights throughout the year is well known to us and occurs as a result of the changing positions of the sunrise against the sunset. The closer together these two points are, the shorter the day will be. The extremes of these movements occur at midsummer and midwinter. At midsummer, the sun rises in the north-east and sets in the north-west. Since it has a lot of sky to travel through between rising and setting, this is the longest day of the year. Conversely, at midwinter the sun rises in the south-east and sets in the south-west. Since it has very little sky to travel through between rising and setting, this is the shortest day of the year.

In addition to the rising midwinter sun, some monuments align to the rising midsummer sun, and perhaps the most famous of these is Stonehenge.[4] Here, the sun rises above the heel stone and shines directly into the centre of a horseshoe formed from enormous sarsen trilathons. Those who set out the final form of the monument during the Bronze Age witnessed the rising midsummer sun, and it still thrills those who see it today. Again, this event must have been very significant to prehistoric people and was another means of marking the turning of the year.

The days of midsummer and midwinter, the longest and shortest days of the year, are called *solstices*, from the Latin meaning "to stand still." This is an apt description, for, at this time of year, the position of the rising sun does appear to stand still and remain at a fixed point on the horizon for a number of days. Clearly, even when Latin first originated, watching the sunrise was still considered important.

Between the solstices, the position of the rising sun moves back and forth in a giant arc along the eastern horizon. As the rising sun moves from north-east to south-east and back again, however, it reaches a mid-point that is exactly due east. Furthermore, the sun will rise here once in the spring and once in the autumn, on the equinoxes. *Equinox* is another Latin word meaning "equal night" and these are the times when the day and night are exactly the same length. More-over, since the sun rises exactly due east, it sets exactly due west.

Scholars used to think that prehistoric people ignored the equinoxes; after all, equinoxes are far more fleeting than the solstices and take more effort to calculate. Before people can plot the equinox, they must work out the positions of the sunrise on both solstices and divide this distance accurately on the ground (remember, there was no calendar on which the dates could be looked up). For a long time, scholars considered this beyond the capabilities of our ancestors. A tomb on Jersey in the Channel Islands, however, was excavated recently where the entrance was aligned to the rising sun on the equinoxes;[5] our ancestors were probably more accomplished than people once thought. Moreover, a mass of standing stones at Almendres in Portugal may also be aligned to the equinoxes.[6]

Taken together, the solstices and equinoxes divided the year neatly into four and provided way stations for its turning. Unlike in modern times, however, where days and dates are functional, in prehistoric times, the turning year was measured and observed through the alignment of burial sites and other great monuments. Time had a sacred element for people, which has been largely lost today.[7]

## The Turning Year

Becoming aware of the turning year and the journey of the sunrise along the horizon is a powerful way of attuning yourself to the spirit of the times and the eternal rhythms of the earth. As the sun journeys throughout the year, map your life onto its progress to gain insight and strength from its power.

The spring equinox (March 21) is a time of anticipation and planning, when the longer days have not yet arrived but you become aware of winter losing its grip. This is a period for looking forward to the summer; use this time to identify your hopes and dreams for the year to come. Journey to your power animal and identify your goals and aspirations for the year and also plan how best to achieve them. This time of year is also a good time to follow the divination methods explained in chapter 7 to gain a glimpse of what the future months might have in store for you. Journey to the spirit of Hare, who is at the height of its power at the spring equinox (and may even be seen whilst the grass in the fields remains short). The equinox hare gave rise to the tradition of the Easter bunny and you could incorporate other aspects of this festival into your celebration of the equinox. With nature stirring all around you and the trees and hedgerows coming into leaf, it truly is a time of resurrection.

The summer solstice (June 21) is the midpoint of the year when the sun is at the height of its glory. From this day onwards, however, the sun begins to diminish and so any celebration needs to balance these opposing aspects. Look at your life at this time and check that, in trying to fulfill the aims and dreams you identified at the spring equinox, you still retain your equanimity and balance. Watch the sunrise on midsummer's day and celebrate as the first rays of light touch the earth. This is also a good time to review the past year; stay up through the short night beforehand, looking back at all you have achieved since the spring equinox and assess whether, like the sun, you are achieving your full potential.

The autumn equinox (September 21), like its counterpart in spring, is a time of anticipation but, this time, for the end of summer and the coming of the dark winter days. It is a time of reaping and bringing in the harvest; spend time looking again at your goals for the year, the seeds you sowed back in spring, and determine whether you can now reap the benefits of your efforts.

At the winter solstice (December 21), the sun is at its weakest and the night is at its longest. This is both an ending and a beginning because, from this day forward, the sun gains in strength and the days lengthen until the summer solstice. Watch the sun set on the longest night and review the year, asking the sun to take with it into the darkness everything you wish to shed from the previous twelve months. These may be emotional attachments, bad memories, or the worry and stress that you do not want to carry with you anymore. Pour whatever it is out to the sun and ask that it be taken to the otherworld of night and left there. The following morning, watch the sunrise on the new year and, as the first rays of light reach you, speak of your hopes for the year and ask that they develop in the same way that the sun's power intensifies from this day onwards.

## The Daily Cycle

The sun rises in the east, journeys through the south of the sky—rising high in the summer and keeping low in the winter—and finally sets in the west. The roundhouses of the Iron Age were designed so that their doorways always faced the rising sun. By measuring the progress of the light cast on the far wall of the house, people may have been able to keep track of time throughout the day using their equivalent of a sundial.[8]

Prehistoric people certainly saw the daily journey of the sun as sig-nificant and, at Trundholm in Sweden, they crafted a beautiful model of a horse pulling behind it the enormous disc of the sun.[9] On one side, the disc is golden, and this represents the day; on the other, the disc is dark, and this represents the night. Since the golden side is on the right, the sun-horse is aligned correctly to journey through the sky in a deosil direction. The same horse is also engraved onto contem-porary bronze razors, except that each razor shows a slightly differ-ent scene. By putting all of these scenes together, a pattern emerges where the sun, carried in a boat and pulled by a horse, rises in the morning, journeys through the sky during the day, before setting in the evening and being pulled through the otherworld of night.[10]

Chapter 3 described images of boats on the engraved rocks by the shore in northern Norway, and that chapter also described how the shamans at the time used these boats to carry them to the other-worlds. The same is true for the sun and, at a grave in Sagaholm in Sweden, it also seems true for the dead.[11] Here, slabs of stone, each engraved with scenes of horses and boats, surround the grave. These slabs helped the spirits of the deceased take their final journey to the afterlife, depicting the means that would carry them to the otherworld of death.

## Celtic Fire Festivals

At the end of the Iron Age, people had clearly formulated a more de-tailed way of measuring time and, at Coligny in southern France, they created one of the first calendars in Europe.[12] The calendar marked several significant dates, which some have identified as relating to the ancient Celtic festivals that celebrated the turning of the year.[13]

The four festivals mark and celebrate the events that would have been significant to an early agricultural people. These festivals began with Imbolc, at the beginning of February, when the land was ploughed and the ewes provided their first milk after lambing. Beltane is next, at the beginning of May, when the livestock was moved to its summer pastures. Lughnasadh is in early August and was the time of the first grain harvest. The year then closed with Samhain, at the beginning of November, when the stock was moved to its winter quarters and any surplus was slaughtered and preserved to provide food through the winter. Since each of the festivals falls on dates exactly between those that mark the solstices and equinoxes, these people may have deliberately formulated a system to divide the year into eight equal parts and thereby celebrated its turning every six weeks or so.

Replicating the Celtic festivals is more difficult than following the passage of the sun, since many of us are removed from the agricultural cycle. Moreover, because of new methods and different planting regimes, agriculture in the modern world sometimes bears little resemblance to that practiced by our ancestors. To follow the festivals of the past, therefore, make their timings relevant to your life. For example, I celebrate Imbolc with the first snowdrops, Beltane with the first blossom on my hawthorn trees, Lughnasadh when the grass sets seed, and Samhain at the coming of the first frost. The aim in every case is to attune with the changes that I *observe* in the natural world and let the passing of the seasons be my guide. Depending upon where you live, you may choose different signs to those above, but, whatever signs you choose, *they* should determine when you celebrate the festivals and not an arbitrary date on the calendar (especially since our calendar has significantly changed from that used by our Iron Age ancestors).

To mark each festival, observe what is happening in the natural world and make this the focus of your celebration. In addition, however, several themes have been handed down in folklore and tradition and you can also incorporate them into your festivities. Some may have even originated with the ancient Celts themselves.

At Imbolc, honour Brighid, the feminine aspect of nature, who was a Celtic Goddess and later became a Christian saint. Since she is the patron of poetry and of fire, perhaps the best way of honouring her is to read poems by the light of the flames. For the Celts, Imbolc was also the time of the first ploughing, so "plough" and prepare yourself for the "seeds" you wish to sow at the spring equinox. Journey to Brighid and ask for her help in preparing yourself for the year ahead.

At Beltane, honour the Celtic God, Bel, who was the God of fire. Beacons were lit in his honour and people used to drive their stock between two fires in order to protect and purify them. To replicate this tradition, light two candles and pass between them anything you want Bel to protect. Write down your goals for the year (which you identified at the spring equinox) and pass these between the two flames, asking Bel to help you to achieve your aims. May Day is the modern incarnation of Beltane and, unlike the other festivals, has lost few of its Celtic roots. If you should get to dance around a may pole, then you are most definitely following in the footsteps of your ancestors and honouring their God, Bel.

Lughnasadh is another festival that honours a God: this time, Lugh, the God of light and of the harvest. Prepare a feast to honour Lugh, perhaps bake your own bread and even make your own wine. Lugh is also the patron of horses and many horse fairs are held at this time of year. Journey to the spirit of Horse and ask if it will lend you some of its strength as you seek to harvest the results of your goals for the year.

At Samhain, the Goddess Ceridwen is honoured. She is the Celtic Goddess of the wintertime and, in Welsh mythology, had a cauldron in which she mixed a brew containing all the knowledge of the world. Journey to Ceridwen and ask to taste a drop of the mixture to obtain some insight into what the next year might hold. This is also a time when you should honour your relations who have died and moved on. Using the techniques from chapter 6, journey to meet them and ask if they would like to join you for a short time. It is perhaps revealing that Remembrance Sunday, the day we honour those who have fallen in war, lies close to the ancient festival when the Celts remembered their dead.

At each festival, gather appropriate tokens from the natural world and use them to decorate your altar. You may already do this at Christmas, when you hang up bunches of holly and ivy, but plenty of other plants could liven up your home at other times of the year. I like to keep a vase of flowers on my altar, picked from the land around my house, and manage to do so through all but the most barren months. I do not always have the most colourful display, but the flowers exactly mirror what is happening in nature and keep me attuned to the turning of the year.

Our ancestors probably celebrated each festival with a feast (the Celts in particular seemed to have loved their food) and this is something you can easily replicate. Make your feast as seasonal as possible, however, finding out what is available and limiting your ingredients accordingly. The more locally you can source your food, the better; there is nothing shamanic about air miles.

Even if you are unable to celebrate the festivals, lighting a candle and spending a few moments attuning yourself to the turning of the year can be hugely beneficial. Human beings were once as much a part of nature as any other creature and, whether you acknowledge it or not, you are still driven by the forces of the natural world. You may also feel drawn to journey to your power animal at these times and, if you do, you may find yourself as a guest at an altogether otherworldly celebration.

## Months of the Moon

In addition to highlighting significant dates, the Iron Age calendar from Coligny also divides the year into thirteen months, each determined by the cycle of the moon. The Celts seemed particularly preoccupied with the night, and Julius Caesar notes in his writings that they measured time by the number of nights passed rather than the number of days.[14] We retain a faint echo of this when we speak of two weeks being a fort*night*. Perhaps the night was considered special because of its association with the otherworlds, and this chapter describes a Bronze Age reconstruction of the nightly journey of the sun through these realms.

The moon itself was important to people, and several swords found in Austria, and also fished out of the River Rhone, were marked with the crescent moon.[15] Other markings may show the full moon or, equally, may depict the sun. Iron Age people started their months either at the full moon or at the new moon—Roman historians make different claims. One historian, however, suggests that months actually started at the waxing quarter moon (that is, when the moon has grown to a half circle following the new moon).[16] This makes sense as it divides the month into a bright half, when the moon is half-complete or more (the two weeks either side of a full moon), and a dark half, when the moon is half-disappeared or more (the two weeks either side of a new moon).

Aligning yourself to the cycle of the moon can be a powerful way of connecting with the natural world. I have a shamanic friend, Kristin, for example, who was delighted when her menstrual cycle matched that of the moon: "It makes me feel joined to an ancient power, as if I really am part of nature." Even the oceans of the world move to the energy of the moon and, since humans are made up of so much water, we are similarly affected. Walking in the moonlight is perhaps the best way of aligning yourself with the energy of the moon and, since the moon is so bright, this can be achieved in even the most artificially lit city. You do not always need to see the moon to be able to connect with it, however. Journey to the Moon Goddess herself, or to some of her animal powers such as Hare or Wolf. I like to make an elixir of moonlight every month by leaving a bottle of spring water out in the light of the full moon and asking the Moon Goddess to shine upon it. I drink a little of the water every day for the next month, obtaining the Goddess's blessing and remembering her when her face was full.

## Star Light

The other bodies in the night sky are the stars and planets. It is difficult to say whether our ancestors aligned their monuments to the stars since each star gradually shifts its position over hundreds of years. Unless we know exactly when something was built, and we very rarely do, we cannot say where the stars were at the time. If there is a detailed record of when something was built, however, such as the Great Pyramid in Egypt, star alignments have been recognised,[17] so some of our European monuments probably were similarly arranged. Nevertheless, until the dating of these monuments becomes significantly more accurate, these will have to remain a mystery.

Our ancestors, however, were definitely interested in the stars and had star maps so they could follow their nightly routes across the sky. One such map was made during the Bronze Age at Nebra in Germany, and is a bronze disc with appliquéd representations of the stars, the moon, and perhaps even the Milky Way.[18] Most of the stars are impossible to identify, but a cluster of seven may be a representation of the Pleiades, a constellation that can still be seen in the winter sky today. As with all stars, the Pleiades has shifted its position over the years, but, during the Iron Age, it first rose at Samhain. Since this was a festival associated with remembering the ancestors, the Pleiades developed an association with mourning and with death; this association has persisted into modern times despite the timing of its rising now being much earlier in the year.

Although most of our star constellations are named for classical figures, there are also many Celtic names for the same stars. The Milky Way, for instance, is *Caer Gwydion*, or the Fortress of Gwydion, a shaman from Welsh mythology who pursued the maiden Arianrhod down its silvery route. Arianrhod also has her own constellation, the

Corona Borealis, or, to the Celts, *Caer Arianrhod*. Interestingly, this constellation is a semi-circle of stars, appearing in the summer sky, and the name Arianrhod means "silver wheel." There are many other Celtic star constellations for which we have the names but, sadly, no means of identifying to which stars they refer. Perhaps, sitting out on a summer's night and looking up at the stars above, you could fashion your own names and stories for the patterns and shapes you see there. This is all our ancestors did: they looked at the sky and imagined what lay there. Over time, their stories were remembered and retold from community to community until traditions were established.

Belonging to a community was extremely important to our ancestors. In the beginning, during the age of ice, people's very survival depended on their community, and by the end of the Iron Age, these relationships had developed to provide an identity and sense of belonging. Today, many communities are disjointed or have failed entirely and our world is the poorer for it. Using your shamanic knowlege, you can now care for those with whom you share your life and bring back the spirit of community that was so familiar to your ancestors.

# 13

# Twenty-First Century Tribe: Caring for Your Community

*You were not there when the kill was made but you heard the whoops of delight and quickly hurried over. A deer with enormous antlers lies with a spear through its side and a hunter you recognise as being the best in the group quickly makes an offering to its spirit so that it will pass quickly to the afterlife. After that, the deer is rapidly butchered, its innards discarded, and you begin the long walk back to the camp. You have been adopted into a small group of hunters, four men, six women, and a number of children; each is related to the other although, in some cases, you are not exactly sure how. Each member of this extended family group wears a pierced shell around their neck. It seems to mark them out as belonging to the group and you were pleased when you were offered one to wear yourself. That evening, just as the meat is being prepared for cooking, a shout of alarm comes from the edge of the camp. One of the children hurries over to say that three strangers are approaching. Pausing only to grab a spear, you run to join the others who are moving to intercept the small band of interlopers. By the time you arrive, there is shouting between your group and the other and gestures are made that clearly suggest that they should stay away. You notice that the strangers wear pierced fox teeth around their necks, a symbol you have not seen worn before. Suddenly, one of the strangers lunges forward and it is only by chance that he avoids the answering spear that is jabbed at his chest. The cord around his neck breaks and is quickly retrieved by one of your companions. He looks intently at the items strung on the cord and then exclaims loudly: the man wears a pierced shell; he is not a stranger after all but kin. Questions now fly back and forth, each trying to ascertain the relationship that exists among them. Although it makes no sense to you, a consensus is reached and the small band is invited to stay and eat. Much later, as you tuck into your own slice of venison, you look over to where the group of three are eating. The man who claimed ties of kinship has a huge slab of meat but you notice the other two have only a small piece between them, and most of that is skin. It seems that family counts for a lot in these times.*

## The Tribe of Family

During the Ice Age, when small groups of people struggled to survive in the inhospitable lands of Europe, being part of a group was essential for survival. People just could not live in any other way.[1] In order to mark their membership in the group, often no more than an extended family, people would wear a symbol around their necks. Chapter 2 discussed how these symbols may relate to particular animals, such as a power animal, and chapter 5 explained how they could represent exotic places, such as the sea. In every case, however, they could also denote membership of a group. Since everyone else in the group wore the same symbol, members could tell who belonged and who did not.

People first may have started using symbols to identify themselves when another species of human lived alongside those of our own kind: Neanderthals. Neanderthals were neither brutish nor thugs (in fact, they lived in a very similar way to our species of human), but they could not understand symbolism.[2] Show a Neanderthal a shell and that was all it was: a shell. He or she could not fathom that the shell might stand for something else. Perhaps early people began to use symbols precisely because the Neanderthals did not understand them; a way of poking fun at the neighbours. Over time, the Neanderthals tried to copy what they saw our ancestors doing and started wearing things around their necks too, but they probably did not know what they were doing. Indicating membership of a tribe through wearing a symbol of it was the preserve of our ancestors alone.

In modern times, with family break-ups and a transient society, you may feel like you do not belong to any particular group. Yet, if you think about it, you belong to at least one tribe. Parents, grandparents, and siblings form the first tribe you belonged to: your tribe of family; and, for many, this remains the most important group throughout their lives. To emphasise this closeness, most families share one or possibly two surnames. As you get older, however, your immediate relatives may lose some of their significance and a group of close friends may take over as your tribe of family. You no longer share a name but you may share other similarities and perhaps a symbol demonstrates your solidarity: a joke understood only to members of the group; a special ringtone on your mobile; or even sharing the same intimate memories. At some level, everyone belongs to a tribe of family.

## Caring for Your Tribe

Not all groups will be harmonious all the time and at these occasions pay particular attention to the energy of the group and how it flows among its members, rather like you examined the energy flow around your home.

---

### Exercise: Caring for Your Tribe

*Take some time to think of your own tribe of family, the things you share and the ways you display this to the world. Then, journey to meet your tribe in the middleworld, setting your intention as: I am journeying to meet my tribe of family and observe how the energy flows among us. When you arrive in the middleworld, you may see the members of your tribe in person (although they will not necessarily interact with you) or you may see something else that represents them. When my shamanic friends journey to see me in the otherworlds, for example, they generally get an image of my power animal, which they take to represent me. Try to observe the way the energy flows around the group as a whole and then around each individual member. Are there gaps in the energy and, if so, are these associated with specific individuals? Could they need healing, some help with a problem, or perhaps just someone with whom to talk? Where one member of the tribe suffers, the rest of the tribe will also suffer, so when you find any energy imbalance, see if you can find out what is causing it and then set about repairing it. You are now the spiritual healer for your tribe, its shaman, and it is your task to ensure its well-being.*

---

If one of your group needs help or healing, offer them an extraction or soul retrieval, obtain a power animal for them that will keep them filled with energy, or there may be another way in which you can help that was revealed to you during your journey. Vanessa, for example, once helped me through a very low patch by journeying to my spirit and offering her love. She described it to me later: "I journeyed to a cave where I saw you as your power animal, pacing up and down; you were clearly in distress. I called in my own power animal and asked what I could do. He told me to surround you with love and reassurance and so I pictured a warm glow all around you. Gradually, your pacing stopped and you looked calmer as you were surrounded with love."

If several members of the group know how to journey, designate somewhere in the otherworlds where you can meet up or, if you cannot all be there at the same time, leave messages and notes for each other. Vanessa and I once did this when we were apart in wildly different time zones, and it was wonderful for me to journey each evening and see what she had left for me. There were no telephones where I was (and therefore no chance of speaking) so this was a perfect way of staying in touch.

Sometimes, you may feel you have done all you can for a member of your group and have exhausted every means of trying to help. Many people might withdraw at this point but, often, this is the very worst thing you can do. Being a witness to the suffering of another may seem pointless, even voyeuristic, but it can be incredibly powerful. To tell someone, "What you are going through is truly awful and I can do nothing to help; but I will be here for you throughout the ordeal and we will bear it together," can sometimes mean everything to someone. Do not wait for them to ask: always make sure you know what is happening to your group.

## Rites of Passage

Events in your tribe of family should always be marked and celebrated, and it is wonderful to attend weddings and christenings when they involve people with whom we are close. Less pleasurable, but still important, are funerals, which give you your chance to say goodbye to one of your members. These are all rites of passage; that is, rituals to mark your transfer from one state into another: into life, into marriage, and into death. Although marriages have become far more personal in recent years, with couples even writing their own vows, other celebrations can often feel a little standardised. Helen, for example, upon returning from a funeral, commented to me that: "I felt so detached during the service, as if it was just the same thing for every person. I was deeply moved by this death, but also cut off from what I was hearing. Funerals are about a return to the earth and should be in tune with nature, using our own words to express our own feelings." I agree entirely and perhaps you should, therefore, find your own ways of celebrating important events within the intimacy of your tribe, in addition to attending the more public and standardised service.

Moreover, if you start to develop your own rituals for the rites of passage through life, you can add occasions that are not traditionally marked. Divorce or redundancy, for example, are unpleasant but may be quite necessary stages to your life. Chapter 9 stressed that if you do not deal adequately with painful events, they can linger and cause illness or even soul loss. By marking these more sombre events with an appropriate ritual and by accepting both the *rite* and the *right* of passage through the experience, you can ensure that any lasting harm is minimised.

Another rite of passage Iron Age people recognised related to the life stages of women: from youth, through motherhood, to elder; and there are many carved statues of three women together.[3] Whilst the lifestyles of women today are very different to those of the Iron Age, our ancestors remind us that all stages of life should be honoured and celebrated, including the period of old age. A particularly modern phenomenon is that the elderly are dismissed and ignored rather than revered for the experience and knowledge they hold.

The transition to adulthood is also marginalized today. Whilst we may celebrate a person's "coming of age" at eighteen, or even twenty-one, it is perhaps a little too late. We expect our young people to take on the responsibility of adulthood much earlier, but without giving them the trappings that go with it, whereas many young people would rather have the trappings, but without the responsibility. In traditional societies, young people reaching puberty are often put through gruelling and sometimes violent initiations that mark the death of the child and the birth of the adult.[4] Whilst many of these ceremonies are too extreme to use in our society, perhaps we can capture something of the sentiment behind them by teaching our young people how to journey to the otherworlds, as part of their initiation into adulthood. Moreover, by showing your young people that many of the things they experienced in childhood—such as talking animals and make-believe worlds—have a value and a place in their lives as adults, they may not have to relearn many of the things that they once accepted instinctively.

## The Tribe of Community

By the Stone Age, people had begun to develop group identities that stretched beyond the family and incorporated people living in a much wider vicinity: their tribe of community. In particular, the pottery that people made was marked with abstract symbols and designs distinctive for each group.[5] Making a pot and firing it in a kiln was probably considered a magical and even sacred act (in much the same way that metalwork was viewed in later periods); these cherished artefacts would have seemed ideally suited to defining the identity of the group. Everyone within this larger tribe probably would not have known everyone else within it, and therefore these symbols of membership would have become extremely important.

Today, your tribe of community may be the neighbourhood in which you live, the people with whom you work, or even an Internet-based group. You probably do not know everyone in this tribe as intimately as you know your tribe of family, and so the symbol you use to represent it may be a little more defined. The symbol may be a resident's parking permit you carry on your car, a uniform you wear for work, or a computer password known only to members of the group. You may feel more disconnected from your tribe of community, but you still belong to it and must look after it in the same way as before.

---

### Exercise: The Tribe of Community

*As you did in the last journey, take some time to think of your own tribe of community, the things you share and the ways that you display this to the world. Then, journey to meet this tribe in the middle-world, setting your intention as: I am journeying to meet my tribe of community and observe how the energy flows among us. When you arrive in the middleworld, it is less likely that you will see everyone who belongs to this tribe, but you may see a symbol of its identity, such as a village, a place of work, or even a number of interconnected computers. Whatever it is, observe the energy of your tribe of community and whether it seems to flow unhindered or whether there are areas where it seems to be stagnating. You may even find pockets of negative energy that require particular attention. Whilst it may be difficult to intervene on a one-to-one basis as you did with your first tribe, ask your power animal if there is anything you can do to help restore the energy within your tribe of community (there are also some ideas below). Again, assume the role of its spiritual healer, its shaman, even though this role may have to remain a secret one.*

---

## Healing the Group

You can extract negative energy from a group in the same way that you extracted it from your home, although the entire process may need to be done in the middleworld. Nevertheless, go through exactly the same stages of identifying where the negative energy resides, gathering it up, and depositing it into a place in the middleworld where it will dissipate. As with all the extractions, ensure that you are completely full of energy before you begin, even if your work is conducted solely in the middleworld.

Chapter 4 explained how groups often have spirits of their own, and in that chapter Jane met and attempted to heal the spirit of the company for which she worked. Jane had her own very effective means of healing but she could have also tried soul retrieval. Retrieving the soul part of a company (or any other organisation or group) is no different to any other soul retrieval you have done: you just look for it in the otherworlds, gather it up, and bring it back. Since there is often nothing physical that exists to blow the soul part back into, restore it to the spirit of the company *before* you return from the otherworlds. Ask your power animal to fetch the relevant spirit of the organisation (if it is not already with you) and either hand your power animal the soul part to restore to the spirit of the organisation or follow the instructions they give you. Always make sure that the soul part finds its way home. Offer healing to follow soul retrieval, as you did with your human patients. Francine was given a wonderful suggestion by her power animal of how to do this for the firm in which she worked: "He told me to go into the office early one morning and speak directly to the spirit of [my firm]. I needed to show that I respected and honoured it and that I would take care to be a positive presence whilst working there."

Your workplace is also where you may come across difficult people and, despite these individuals being part of your tribe of community, you may feel like you would just like to be rid of them. Whilst it may be true that the faults you see in others are often those you carry yourself, this is not always the reality you want to be faced with when you encounter someone who seems to be deliberately out to provoke you. It would be nice to be able to offer help and healing whenever you meet a person who, through their unreasonable behaviour towards you, is clearly in need of it, and perhaps this is something you might be able to do later. At the time, however, there is nothing wrong with standing up for yourself and even calling your power animal to lend its assistance (and chapter 10 provided other ways of protecting your boundaries). Even if you manage to resolve the difficulty, however, there is a good chance that the encounter will have troubled you and perhaps even left you feeling upset afterwards. You know how damaging these lingering feelings can be and you must act quickly to contain them. Whilst you may want to blame the other person for upsetting you, this is not really the case. You have every *right* to be upset but that is all it is: a right, not a requirement. Never give your power away by blaming someone else for how you feel. You are upset because you *need* to be upset in order to rid yourself of the unpleasant effects of what has happened; it is our body's way of emotional purging. Treat yourself with compassion until the emotion has done its work and you feel better as a result.

If you ever consider your difficulties with another person (or, indeed, any other problem) to be insurmountable, a good technique to help overcome it is to find something really solid and immovable and push against it. Envisage the object as embodying the difficulty you are experiencing: completely unyielding and impossible to force your way through. Then, back away, pause for a moment, and think if there is another way of getting past the object (this could be as obvious as just walking around it, but still spend time *thinking* about it). This may also be a good time to journey and ask your power animal for help. When you have worked out what to do, go past the object as confidently as you can and then pause once again. What has this experience taught you about the real obstacle you are facing. Is there a way around it that you have yet to consider? As you have found before, sometimes acting things out can bring solutions that you would never have considered otherwise.

After you have recovered your composure, there is always the option of offering healing and help to difficult people. If you know them well, offer this directly, but if you are unable to do this, offer healing in the otherworlds. Never force the healing onto someone, however, regardless of how much you think they might need it. If you do not have permission to heal (or to do anything else) to someone in this world, then you should not do it in the otherworlds either. Instead, make whatever you want to offer *available* to them and leave it up to them as to whether they accept it or not. What I find effective is to ask my power animal to give the healing to the other person's power animal; since their power animal always knows what is best for them, it can decide what to do. Another occasion when similar dilemmas may arise is when you try to heal someone who is clearly dying. What should you do: heal them or let them pass to the afterlife? Both might be correct in different circumstances and you must be careful to listen to what your power animal (and other trusted spirits) tell you and not rely on your own inclinations. Whenever I journey for someone who is dying, I always ensure that I do what is right for them and not what might seem right to me.

## The Tribe of Nations

By the end of the Iron Age, Europe had divided into a number of tribes that occupied very large areas.[6] Some of these tribes are still familiar today as they gave their names to cities and, sometimes, even entire countries. The Parissi tribe, for example, gave their name to Paris, the Belgae tribe gave their name to Belgium, and the old name for Scotland, Caledonia, is named after the Caledones tribe. Many of these tribes of nations also issued their own coins, often marked with the name of the tribe and, sometimes, even with the pictures of their rulers.[7]

Many people today know which national tribe they belong to and they carry such identity with pride. For others, however, it can be a more nuanced belonging, and a person's national tribe may have more to do with their religious faith, racial grouping, or even the position they hold in a now-global society. Whichever national tribe you feel you belong to, many symbols probably mark its presence. All countries, for example, have a flag and many are also represented by a (power) animal, such as the Welsh dragon, the American eagle, and the Russian bear. You cannot know everyone in this tribe, and perhaps this is one of the reasons you can sometimes feel least attached to it; but, as before, you are still one of its members and should, therefore, care for its well-being.

---

### Exercise: The Tribe of Nations

*As you did in the previous two journeys, take some time to think of your own national tribe, how large and widespread it is, and also some of the symbols that represent it. Then, journey to meet this tribe in the middleworld, setting your intention as: I am journeying to meet my national tribe and observe how the energy flows among us. When you arrive in the middleworld, you might see a symbol of your tribe rather than all of its individual members, but you should still work with it in the usual way. Observe the energy of your national tribe, whether it is positive and flowing freely, or whether it has a tendency to stagnation and negativity. It is striking how events can sometimes alter the psyche of entire nations, such as the death of Princess Diana in Britain, or September 11 in America. Although you may feel overwhelmed by the scale of the work, try to help restore any imbalance that you find or even offer healing if you sense it is needed. Acting alone, you may feel that you will not achieve much, but if everyone worked towards putting their national tribe back into balance, just think what we could do. With this type of work, you start local and end global and, if we all work together, we can make a difference.*

---

When you work with your national tribe, you may start to reflect on the enormous number of people in the world and just how insignificant one individual can be. This is understandable; after all, what is one person compared to the billions of others? However, a short exercise might make us think differently: *Take a piece of bread and start to eat it. As you do so, think about all the people who worked to bring you that bread: the farmer who tended the land and sowed the wheat; the people who built the combine harvester used to harvest the wheat; the people who collected the wheat and who built the truck that carried it; the miller; the mixer; the baker; the packager; the shopworkers where you bought it (and all the people who built the machinery that each needed to do their jobs) and, finally, yourself, as you eat and enjoy the fruit of their labour.* Through the simple act of eating bread, you are joined to hundreds, possibly even thousands of people. In a way, there is no such thing as a single individual; we are all joined to each other in relationships that are so intricate and tightly bound that we would be nothing without them. It is a fundamental truth that we are all connected, physically, emotionally, and spiritually. For all of us, perhaps the tribe of humans is our most important tribe of all.

## The Tribe of Ancestors

There is one final tribe we all belong to and, for many of us, we sit at its head. This is the tribe of our ancestors, all those people from whom you are a direct descendent. Not even your ancestors, however, are unique to you. The further back in time you go, the more likely your ancestors will have hundreds, if not thousands of descendents, reminding us again of our connection to people we do not, and probably will never, know.

Although all prehistoric people held their ancestors in high regard, it is likely that the women of the group kept and maintained the lineage. Some of the very earliest objects known from the Ice Age are models of women, often identified as representations of the Mother Goddess.[8] Similar models, however, are found throughout the Stone Age and into the Bronze Age, sometimes, in very large numbers.[9] Whilst they were often left in shrines and other sacred places, they could also be found in the home, especially around the hearth. Rather than Goddesses, these model women might have been representations of the ancestral spirits and particularly those associated with the lineage of the group. Some of the models from Bulgaria even have concentric circles and other imagery carved upon them, signs perhaps of their otherworldly connections.[10] In the Bronze Age, women seemed to have held the wealth of the group and there are several examples of an individual being buried with fabulously valuable jewellery.[11] Perhaps these were the women whose lineage had ended through death or disease, and there was nobody left to inherit the jewellery.

Although Samhain is a good time to honour our ancestors (as well as Remembrance Sunday, a few days later), prehistoric people would have honoured their ancestors every day of the year, and you can do the same. Every morning, for example, I like to start my day by honouring all those who came before me, recognising their part in who I am, and also reaffirming that I belong to their group: the tribe of my ancestors. I also include my power animals in this tribe and my upperworld guides; it is a tribe of the spirits and the only sign of my membership is the pouch that I wear around my neck.

Caring for all of our tribes is an extremely important task for those who walk a shamanic path; a person can never truly be a shaman without serving his or her community. You need to ask yourself, however, just how far you would go in helping other people. Would you be prepared to die for your community? Probably (and quite justifiably) not, but shamans in the past were quite willing to offer their lives to their calling, sacrificing themselves to help those whom they served.

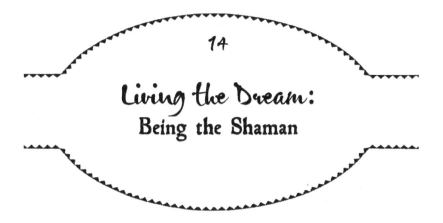

# 14

# Living the Dream:
## Being the Shaman

*Y*ou gather silently with the rest of the community to watch as the woman steps out of her hut and into the night. She is dressed only in a skin cape, beneath it, her body is naked, and her hair has been roughly shorn from her head. She walks unsteadily, as if she has been drugged, although you also notice that her spine twists awkwardly, as if her bones have grown crooked. Without once acknowledging the witnesses to her journey, she walks past the huddled community and out to the marsh, a light mist enshrouding her route. You follow discreetly, as do many others. At the marsh, two figures await her, a woman and a man. She stands upright before them and shouts some words into the night. Apart from her voice, there is no other sound. With her words still hanging in the mist, she shrugs off her cape so that she stands naked before her community. Her body gleams in the torchlight and you can see designs on her skin pricked out in blue. The man to her left takes a thin cord and passes it around her neck. The woman assists his task by bending her head slightly, allowing the knot to be pulled tight against her flesh. Without a word, the man pulls sharply on the cord and the woman's body convulses. Her back arches in an agonising spasm and phlegm sputters from her lips. Just as you think she must die from this treatment, the woman to her right *draws a blade. It flashes in the dancing torchlight and many gasp at its beauty. She moves it to the woman's throat and slashes at her flesh. The blood erupts immediately and pumps in a terrifying rhythm, covering the marsh with its gore. The woman herself does nothing to prevent these terrible injuries. Her body jerks in its death throes but it is as if she welcomes the release. As the woman's convulsions fade, she falls and the man catches her limp body. He lays it in the marsh almost with tenderness, using the discarded cape to cushion her head. There is still no sound: no cries, no keening, and no exclamation. People only bow their heads in honour of what the woman has done for them.*

## Dying for the People

Preserved bodies have been found in the raised peat bogs from across northern Europe, the majority dating to the Iron Age and early Roman periods.[1] Almost all met their deaths in a violent and brutal frenzy that seemed designed to be as dramatic as possible.[2] Moreover, the victims themselves seemed to be quite willing to die, and there is never any sign of struggle or resistance to what was done to them. Perhaps, in their minds, they were not really going to die at all. These were the shamans of the tribe and they were used to the sensation of leaving their bodies and journeying to the otherworlds, except that, this time, there would be no return. Perhaps people knew that the bodies they placed in the bogs would be preserved (the peat would have stopped the development of micro-organisms that would otherwise rot the body), and they thought that the shamans would therefore remain to look after the community forever.[3] All around them, the invading Roman army was destroying everything connected with the spirituality of the indigenous people; this was a way of ensuring that their most sacred figureheads—their shamans—would survive and not be discovered.

The raised bog itself would have been considered a portal to the otherworlds and a perfect place in which to bury the remains of the shamans. A number of other characteristic of the bog bodies also mirror what we know about historical shamans from northern Europe and parts of Siberia.[4] Many of the bodies, for example, were naked when they were buried, others had their hair sheared roughly from their head, some were marked with tattoos, a few had taken hallucinogenic drugs, one wore an animal skin armband and had an extra thumb, others were noticeably disabled, whereas all were well nourished and looked after. These are all aspects that are mirrored by historical shamans and show that the characteristics that mark someone out as being a shaman have changed little over the millennia.

## Living Between the Worlds

Shamans seem to be different from other people. They regularly cross the portal connecting this world to the otherworlds and, in a sense, live on the boundary between the two. Today, mainstream society shuns those who do not fit in and marginalises their existence and yet, in shamanic communities, these are exactly the people who are recognised and celebrated for the gifts they have been given.

Until very recently, for example, having a different sexuality to the mainstream was considered scandalous, even unnatural, and people either kept their feelings secret or suffered the consequences of a disapproving society. This, however, is not the case in shamanic communities where crossing sexual and gender boundaries is often taken as a sign of shamanic calling.[5] We cannot know the sexuality of individuals in the prehistoric past, since it leaves behind no physical trace, but two male bog bodies were found in the Netherlands who seem to have been buried whilst embracing.[6] Moreover, a Roman historian commented that the punishment for homosexuality was drowning in a bog.[7] Since this Roman historian had never witnessed anyone going to their deaths in a bog (he wrote at a much later time), he may have thought that they were being punished for something (to an outsider, why else would they be killed?). Since the only other fact he apparently knew about them was that they were homosexual, he linked the two; inadvertently revealing, perhaps, that shamans in the past did cross sexual and gender boundaries as many still do today.

The famous Greek historian, Herodotus, notes that, when the spirits call a Scythian warrior to become a shaman, he immediately gets a sickness that completely debilitates him.[8] Only by answering the call and becoming a shaman will the sickness lift. In order to acknowledge his decision publicly, however, he will spend the rest of his life in the clothes and following the lifestyle of a woman. Many shamanic societies today have similar traditions, which all recognise the special position of the shaman as a walker between all worlds.

Chapter 11 mentioned wooden figures that also seem to exist on the boundary of the sexes.[9] Whilst some are clearly male or female according to the sexual organs portrayed, others are hermaphrodite or have a pubic hole that could be a vulva, making the figure female, or that could be for the addition of a phallus, making the figure male. Or perhaps the figure could be either sex at different times. When you shapeshift, you may have merged with a power animal of a different sex and experienced blurring and even crossing this boundary. Even the God Odin, mentioned in chapter 11 as being a shaman himself, was renowned for crossing the strict gender roles that existed at the time.[10]

Another group of people in modern society who are often marginalised are the disabled. Some of the bog bodies were disabled and one woman found in the Netherlands (known as Yde girl) had a badly curved spine; another (known as Zweeloo woman) had shortened limbs.[11] Both disabilities would have been immediately noticeable. For the Iron Age people, however, rather than seeing the women as useless or as *in-valids* (as our society might), they considered them to have been "touched by the Gods" and called to work with the spirits. These were incredibly special people and the very fact that we still know of them today, some two thousand years after they died, seems to prove the point.

## Suffering as Initiation

It was not just disabled people who were recognised as having been touched by the Gods, but also people who suffered from debilitating illness. Scythian warriors, when they first received the call to work with the spirits, fell into a severe sickness, which can only be cured through answering that call and becoming a shaman. In virtually all shamanic societies today, people believe the same: that a call to work with the spirits begins with a period of suffering. For this reason, a shaman is often known as the wounded healer.[12]

Suffering is considered key to shamanic work, for without having experienced suffering yourself, you cannot generate the compassion required to heal it in others. From suffering flows compassion, and from compassion flows the power of the shaman. Whilst you may not have suffered in the same way as the Scythian shamans, with their debilitating sickness, you probably have experienced a degree of suffering in your life. A friend of mine, Pauline, is apt to say that we all carry our measure of suffering, a depth of sadness that is ours to hold through life. From this suffering your personal shamanic power can flow.

---

Exercise: Suffering as Initiation

*Think back on a time of suffering in your life (and we have all suffered to some degree). Consider what caused it and how it made you feel. With your power animal, journey to your suffering; feel what it was like to go through it and then, just for a moment, embody all those emotions you felt at the time. Next, step away from your suffering; see it from the outside and try to discern its spiritual essence. Now, imagine this essence entering into a member of your tribe of family. Think how they will suffer as you have. How does this make you feel? Does it inspire you to help? This is compassion, the desire to understand and alleviate suffering, wherever and in whomever it lies. Now, think*

*of the essence of your suffering entering into a member of your tribe*
*of community and, finally, your national tribe. Is there anyone you*
*would not want to help be healed from it?*

---

## Compassion

What exactly is compassion—is it love? I am sometimes asked this, and I always answer, "No, compassion is different from love." Love can be blind; it is the bond of parent and child, husband and wife, brother and sister: love ignores everything but the bond. Moreover, love is rarely motivated by suffering. Compassion is different. To feel compassion, you must first notice the other person and the circumstances of his or her suffering. This is not to judge, or pass comment, but merely to acknowledge and to accept them exactly as they are. Whatever the circumstances surrounding the individual, this is still a person who hurts. Next, you must take on that suffering yourself. This does not mean that you sympathise with the person and imagine what it must be like for them to suffer, nor does it mean that you empathise with them and imagine how you would feel in their place. It means that you accept that, through your shamanic way of viewing reality, everyone is bound and connected to each other. In a sense, this is not another person who is suffering but is yourself. You must take on the suffering as you took on the negative energy when you extracted it from your patients: you must hold and understand it and then do your best to take it away.

You must never judge a person who suffers; that judgment will cloud your shamanic work and you will be unable to do what is required. This also extends to yourself. If you feel that the one person whom you find it hard to feel compassion for is yourself, then try the previous exercise in reverse. Start with the suffering of others and then take on that suffering yourself: can you generate the same compassion to heal suffering even if it is only you who is affected?

Your shamanic power stems from your compassion; unless you feel it, you will never be able to help others to the best of your potential. This feeling of compassion originates from your experience of suffering. As my friend Pauline puts it, we no longer protect our wounds but open them up to let the power flow out from them. The bog people went to their deaths naked; they shed virtually every trapping of the world and met the spirits with only what was inside them. You must do the same when you journey and leave everything superfluous behind. For many of us, this means letting our egos fall away and becoming as hollow as the bone that we use to carry the souls of our patients.

Contrary to a lot that is written, your ego is not your enemy, or a dragon to be defeated; your ego is actually your best friend. Your ego is your face to the world: it protects and cares for you and enables you to interact with everything around you. Your ego makes you who you are; it gives you your reason, your humour, your feelings, and your ability to love. Your ego makes you the individual that you are and you should always respect and cherish it. When you journey to the otherworlds, however, you have little need of your ego. Your power animal will always protect you and the spirits can see straight through any mask you attempt to wear. When you journey to the otherworlds, therefore, strip away everything except your compassion: your innate desire to help (even if the only person whom you seek to help is yourself and the ego left behind). If you are to open up in this way and leave yourself so utterly vulnerable, you need to have complete trust in your power animal and other spiritual allies; without such trust, you could not work. Through your trust, you allow yourself to become a conduit for the spirits to work through: a hollow bone, who feels nothing but compassion, the all-consuming desire to help.

Although you may draw your power from the periods in your life when you have suffered in the past, you probably will suffer again in the future. In spite of your shamanic knowledge and the protection of your power animal, people who work shamanically can all too often be pulled down by the tears of the world: the intensity of the suffering around us. Whenever you feel a strong emotion, either positive or negative, accept it for what it is; never try to fight how you feel. We are all human and *to feel* is a human trait. You must be non-judgmental about yourself and just quietly acknowledge how you feel, perhaps by repeating gently whatever emotion it is. Embody your feelings completely and fully, always acknowledging that it is your ego that suffers at these times and offering it the same level of compassion as you would for another. Once you have experienced the emotion to its very depth, let it go and shed it in the same way that you shed your other emotions when you begin to journey. You should not seek to over-analyse how you feel but just accept it for what it is: a cloud that, although dark and dense, will always pass. Although modern society seems to emphasise the need for analysis until there is no corner un-explored, this is to miss one of the fundamental aspects about being human. Just as you can never step into the same river twice (since the water you touch will always be different), so you also change from minute to minute, hour to hour, and day to day. In one sense, you can never know yourself, only who you once were. Shamanism is not about over-analysing the past but about fulfilling your potential *now*, in this moment. Through expressing your compassion, for yourself as well as for those you help, you do not fight the world but just accept it for what it is. You always will have periods of darkness; it is how you walk through them that counts.

## Dismemberment

In addition to the violence used to kill the people who were found in the bogs, many of these people also suffered dismemberment after they were killed. Some had their arms and legs hacked off, whilst others were decapitated.[13] Moreover, this was not the only time during the Iron Age that such a grisly practice occurred. Býči Skála (meaning "Bull Rock Cave") in the Czech Republic is a cavern that contained the dismembered bodies of forty individuals, mostly women, who had their heads, hands, and feet severed, along with two horses chopped into four pieces, and a bronze cauldron.[14] To shed light on this grue-some scene, we have to move forward in time by almost 2,000 years and consider what an old Siberian shaman shared with a young Hun-garian researcher called Vilmos Diószegi.[15] The shaman told Diószegi that, when the spirits first called him, he journeyed through the other-worlds until he reached a cave. At its centre was a cauldron. The spir-its, who were waiting within the cave, took hold of the shaman and sliced him into many pieces, eventually tearing his flesh from bone, and throwing the remains into the cauldron. The bones were then heated and boiled until all the flesh was gone. The spirits removed what was left and reassembled the shaman's body, adding new organs and flesh as it was needed. After the experience, the shaman knew that he had been born again; his imperfections, at least in the otherworlds, had been taken away and he was made anew. The similarities are too close to be coincidental; this is what was happening in the Iron Age cave: the dismembered shamans were being remade. Even the horses make sense, because we have already seen how these animals regularly moved between this world and the otherworlds.

For the Siberian shaman Diószegi interviewed, death and dismem-berment occurred in the otherworlds, whilst he was in trance, and it could have no effect on his physical body. In contrast, for the shamans in the cave at Býči Skála, and for those whose remains lie in the bogs of northern Europe, death and dismemberment occurred in this world and, for them, there was no coming back. Although the shamans from the Iron Age were probably quite aware that they would die (in this world, at least), there seems little reason why their deaths had to be quite so dramatic. Unless, the idea was to show people exactly what it meant to be a shaman and to journey to the spirits. The way that the shamans prepared for their deaths, and the dramatic way in which they were killed and dismembered, all serve to demonstrate the se-riousness of their undertaking. The event was likely scored into the memories of the people who witnessed it for the rest of their lives.[16] The shamans could not die whilst their names were remembered.

In places where there were no bogs or caves through which the shamans could enter the otherworlds, such as the chalk grasslands of southern England, people found a different portal through which to pass. In the huge hillforts that people built across the landscape, the seed grain for sowing the following year was kept through the winter in vast pits.[17] The grain was packed tightly to force out the air and, as a consequence, only the outer layers would rot. Stories probably were told of the death and rebirth of the grain (and such stories still survive today, such as the tale of John Barleycorn, traditionally told at Lughnasadh), and perhaps the pits themselves were seen as some sort of regeneration chamber. That may be why, after they were emptied, they were used for the final resting places of the shamans of these tribes: buried for eternity under the earth.[18] Since only the bones have survived the acidic conditions of the soil, we cannot tell as much about these people as we could about the bodies in the bog. However, they probably also met their deaths naked (cloth would have disintegrated, but the fastenings would not, and none have been found), most had been beheaded or dismembered,[19] some showed signs of similar disabilities to the bodies in the bogs,[20] and, perhaps most tellingly, many had been branded on the left side of their face by a red-hot sword.[21] The wooden figures mentioned in chapter 11 also were damaged on the left side of their face, often in the eye. The bodies in the pits suffered the same disfigurement. Whilst it is impossible to understand completely the symbolism contained in such an act, in Renaissance art, obscuring the left eye, while leaving the right eye unblemished, was a sign of intense spirituality.[22] Could this be a more recent echo of a tradition started by our ancestors so long ago?

Dismemberment, when it occurs in the otherworld, can be a powerful, albeit quite frightening, experience. When you feel it is time to undergo such an experience and be reborn anew, journey to your power animal and ask if it will arrange the dismemberment. Little instruction is given for this journey, as your power animal decides what is to happen and how it should be carried out. Trust in the spirits and be guided by them.

---

### Exercise: Dismemberment

*If (and only if) you feel ready to experience dismemberment, journey to the upperworld or lowerworld and, calling in your power animal, explain what it is you want. If your power animal is agreeable, then follow its instructions carefully. There is no set pattern for dismemberment, you might be hacked to pieces, boiled, burnt, or even vaporised. However, you will feel no pain and you will be put back together again straight afterwards, a different person certainly, and, perhaps, a more powerful being.*

---

The journey of dismemberment is not one to repeat often. In fact, I have never asked for dismemberment; when it has happened, it has always been spontaneous and unexpected. The first time I experienced dismemberment, I was in a part of the upperworld that I call the barren land. As I walked, a volcano exploded in a hail of molten rock. The lava surrounded me and I began to melt. I could feel my skin blister and my flesh singe. My internal organs boiled away until only my bones were left. These separated and were blown apart by the force of the lava. I could now only observe what was happening as a disembodied form. As I watched, the spirits hurried around collecting my remains. They cleaned and polished my bones and gave each in turn to an old man. He laid out the bones on the ground and arranged them into their rough order. The volcano spat more lava, which passed over the bones. As it flowed away, it left a ball of glowing fire in the place of my heart. The spirits fashioned internal organs out of clay. Before inserting them, they touched the clay to the fireball and each instantly became real. After the organs were in place, the spirits fashioned my muscle, flesh, and skin. The old man himself made my face and I began to recognise myself again. Eventually, the body was complete and the old man looked directly at where my disembodied form was watching and beckoned me forward. All the other spirits departed, but the old man told me to lie over my body. I did so and immediately merged with it. I could now feel my new body and moved each limb to stretch it. I sat up and thanked the old man, except now, I could see that he was a great and powerful shaman.

## Death and Rebirth

The controlled violence of the otherworlds is an ancient phenomenon and was even painted upon the cave walls by those who lived during the Ice Age. The artists very rarely included people in their paintings but, when they did, the figures were shown wounded in some way, usually through having been speared.[23] This same imagery is found in the far later carvings of the Inuit of Greenland, where it is the shamans who are shown speared with harpoons.[24] Shamanism has always been associated with death and rebirth: you die to this world to be reborn in the otherworld, and you suffer dismemberment and death at the hands of the spirits, only to be reborn whole again. Those watching the shamans going about their work might have thought that the shamans died and came back to life again. Death and rebirth flow from the very core of shamanism.

The bodies in the bog, however, died for their communities in barbaric and gruesome executions that must have truly shocked those who witnessed them. At the same time, people probably were awed at what the shamans had done for them and the enormity of the task they had taken on. If you are to follow in their footsteps, ask yourself how far you would go in your service for others, just how much you would be prepared to sacrifice.

A little time ago, for example, I was asked to help Ruth, a woman suffering dreadfully from breast cancer. The cancer had got so bad, and her blood count was so low, that the hospital had cancelled all further treatment; her body just could not take it. I did not know Ruth personally but a mutual friend asked me if I could help. I journeyed to the otherworld with the intention of finding an animal power to help Ruth in any way it could. I met up with my power animal who helps me at these times and she said: "I will go." At first, I thought she meant that she would find an animal power to help Ruth, but I was wrong. My power animal was telling me that she should leave me and go to Ruth herself. I had been working with that particular power animal for ten years and so I hesitated. My mind raced with alternatives: Would another animal do instead? Could I find the same type of animal as mine and send that? Could I just say "No"? At the centre of my racing mind was the still and silent realisation that I could do none of these things; my power animal must go. She left with my blessing. The next day, I was told that Ruth had rallied quite miraculously. The doctors were flabbergasted and her blood count had improved so much that not only was she able to continue with her treatment but its intensity could even be increased. Giving up my power animal was a hard sacrifice to make but it was so clearly the right thing to do. Although Ruth will probably never know about the animal that now cares for her, I am pleased to say that the cancer has now disappeared completely.

## Service

As you have found, shamanism can be an extremely rewarding but also a very hard path to walk. In traditional shamanic societies, becoming a shaman was rarely something that people took on willingly, and the spirits had to fight to obtain the recruit they wanted. You have seen how those who resist the call from the spirits are often struck down with a debilitating illness, finding salvation only if they agree to become a shaman. One way or another, the spirits claim the lives of those whom they desire. Even when someone becomes a shaman, life remains hard; the rewards are scant and the dangers are many. Unable to support themselves, shamans rely on the generosity of their communities to maintain them: the shaman supports the community and the community supports the shaman. Often, however, a community both reveres and shuns their shamans: they revere them because of the power that they hold, and they shun them because what they do is rarely understood. There is also the risk that the spirits will abandon the shaman and his or her power will disappear. This is especially common where the shaman gets delusions of grandeur and starts to think that the power they wield comes from them alone, rather than being solely the gift of the spirits.

Shamanism is a hard path and very few people in traditional societies willingly walk it. When these shamans hear that people in the West want to become shamans themselves, they can scarcely believe it: why would someone want such a thing? Perhaps because, in our society, the pendulum has swung too far the other way. The idea of the sacred has all but left our communities and the spirits are largely forgotten. Our modern world desperately needs shamans; it is how we were meant to live and, at an instinctual level, people are beginning to recognise this. People today are drawn to shamanism because it is a way of redressing the balance in our lives. Very few people in the West, however, would ever actually call themselves a shaman.

There are many theories as to the origin of the word *shaman*, but most agree that it came from a Siberian language.[25] Different traditional societies, who had people performing similar functions (as we know, the ability to practice shamanism is wired into the brains of everyone), called their spiritual practitioners many different things. In the West and especially in academic circles the term *shaman* was applied to them all. *Shaman* has therefore become a word that can mean many things to many people. At base, though, calling someone a shaman (or any other word with similar connotations) is an honorary title; the community bestows the name upon those who give their lives to serve that community. The nearest equivalent might be *hero*. Whilst this book can show you the techniques of shamanism, its words cannot make you a shaman, any more than it can make you a hero. Only the spirits and your community can do that.

Being a shaman is a hard path that begins by empowering yourself but quickly leads to the service of others. Where is your limit? What are you seeking from the power it gives you? Although very few people might call themselves shamans in modern-day society, many quietly work with the spirits for the good of others, largely unseen, and hardly ever celebrated. These people sacrifice their lives for the benefit of their communities. Touching the spirits is a powerful thing; it changes you, makes you a better person, and, ultimately, helps to make a better world.

The shamans found in the raised bogs of northern Europe gave what was perhaps the ultimate sacrifice to their communities: they died horrible and gruesome deaths so that their people might live. Just why did they do it? We have already seen how shamans heal and care for members of their community; ultimately, their empowerment was not to further their own desires but to serve others. The Iron Age shamans would have cared for the well-being of their communities every day of their lives. History, however, tells us what happened at the end of the Iron Age: the coming of the Romans and the destruction of indigenous beliefs. Eventually, this culminated in the massacre of the Druid priesthood and the burning of the sacred groves. To the shamans who had cared for their communities all their lives, what could they do? The answer seems to have been to enter the otherworlds permanently, to undergo a dismemberment, a purification, so dramatic that it ended their lives. This was self-empowerment on a stupendous scale, and the results still haunt us today.

Did the shamans succeed in their aims? Was the ancient wisdom saved from destruction at the hands of the Romans? Perhaps, but only just. You have almost come to the end of your initiation onto the path of the shaman and it now falls to you to take up the ancient wisdom of your ancestors and apply it to the world today. The Iron Age shamans may have died for their communities, but they also died for us: you and me.

# Conclusion:
# Leading the Way

You stand in the midst of an enormous warband on the shore of the sacred isle: Ynys Môn, Anglesey. Across the narrow strait, dividing the island from the mountains of the mainland, are the massed ranks representing the might of Rome, more than 8,000 battle-hardened men. But they are fearful; you can feel it in the breeze. The warband assails the enemy with a din to make even the Gods tremble, the warriors banging swords on shields and roaring their battle cries. The carynx booms its notes of death and the women scream and tear at their clothes and hair, entreating all who hear to fight and to kill. The Druids, standing on the rise just behind you, raise their arms to the sky and invoke all the spirits they know, beseeching the might of the otherworlds to crush the Roman foe. The Romans have every reason to fear and yet, even at this distance, you can tell they are resolved to fight. You did not notice the signal for their ballistae to be unleashed but flaming jars of tar smash into your ranks, each engulfing more than a dozen in a convulsive dance of death. Bolts of iron spear flesh, pinioning warrior to warrior in a fatal embrace. It is as if the thunder God himself fights against you. At last, the Romans advance. Some cross the water in boats; others swim. The cavalry remain on their beasts. You surge forward to meet them and, yet, the Romans manage to regroup on the shore, forming a cruel line *of shield and spike. You smash into the foe again and again, the weight of the front lines driven on by those who are behind. The Romans expect such charges and absorb their power, gaining only a firmer foothold against you. Then, the killing begins. The Romans smash your ranks with their shields and kill with their swords. Bone shatters and flesh rips. It is a slow advance, as there are many to butcher. The thud of flesh on wood and the screams of the dying crush the resolve of the warband until some turn to flee. Now the Roman cavalry charges. The battle is lost. Only the Druids remain. Rounded up, the Romans take them inside the forest, forcing them to enter their sacred groves. Pyres are swiftly assembled and lit, the damp wood providing a slow burn. The Druids are bound but not gagged, and some still shriek their invocations to the spirits. It is too late. They, like the sacred groves of the tribe, will burn before the Romans. Will everything be destroyed this day?*

## The Fall of the Shamans

The battle of Anglesey, off the coast of north Wales, was the day the Romans burnt the groves and massacred the Druids, along with their people. A Roman historian recorded the events of the day and wrote his account many years later.[1] The battle coincided with the uprising of Boudica and her Iceni tribe, and came at a time when the Romans realised that the spiritual traditions of the Iron Age people, and particularly the Druid priesthood, were providing a rallying point for resistance to Rome. This is not surprising. For people who had been journeying to the otherworlds and calling upon the help of the spirits all their lives, it was only natural that they should do so now. You saw in the last chapter how some shamans underwent horrific executions and entered permanently into the otherworlds in order to protect their people. Elsewhere, the Druid priesthood protected the sacred groves of Anglesey, which Caesar says were the centre of Druid learning in Europe, until they too fell before the Roman onslaught.[2]

The Druid priesthood was the final flowering of shamanic wisdom in ancient Europe. The Druids and the shamans may have been the same individuals or the priesthood may have developed independently out of the earlier shamanic traditions. The Druids, who took on the role of spiritual leaders for their communities, were complemented by the Ovates, who foretold the future, and by the Bards, who kept the myths and stories of the people alive. These were all roles that, previously, would have fallen to the shaman and, perhaps, at a time when nations were forming and tribes were assimilated into larger and larger groups, having an organised priesthood was a better means of meeting the spiritual needs of the people. The role of the community shaman had developed into an organised Celtic religion. That is, until the Romans arrived.

Was everything lost after the battle of Anglesey? A cursory glance might make you think so. Villages arose with a single large house surrounded by others of far lesser size;[3] Roman writers suggest that these were the domains of feudal lords, living in comfort whilst lesser-ranked individuals worked their land.[4] Fences were built around these settlements and, unlike the ditches in the past, which were dug and then immediately backfilled, these boundaries were permanent. Feasting continued but, instead of it taking place in the natural world, with the remains buried for the spirits, it now centred on the large houses and the remains were left where they fell.[5] Instead of swords being placed in rivers so that their spirits could return to the otherworlds, they were now kept by those who once wielded them, accompanying their owners into their graves.[6] Furthermore, in another attempt to usurp what had once been the preserve of the spirits, phosphenes were engraved upon coins, along with the heads of the kings.[7] Did these monarchs now consider themselves as rulers of the otherworlds? Is this what the Romans had brought to the people? A slavish desire for the so-called civilisation Rome brought, whilst turning their backs on everything they once held dear? Another Roman summed up these events when he wrote that the Iron Age people: "Spoke about such novelties as 'civilisation', when really they were a feature of their enslavement."[8] The proliferation of shackles and chains at this time serves only to underline the point.[9]

The impression of a completely broken people is false, however. In some areas, people still revered the spirits and remembered the Gods and Goddesses of old. Some of the shamans met brutal deaths at the hands of their communities and now lay in their watery graves; they would not easily have been forgotten. Even at the heart of Roman religion, in the shrines built to worship their Gods, some contained a tree at their centre, a reminder of how people once journeyed to the otherworlds.[10] This accommodation of the old with the new may have continued but, over time, a new religion entered Europe and this one would tolerate no rivals: Christianity. Moreover, the Christian Church had an insidious way of fighting the battle. Whilst establishing its hold, it made the lowerworld into hell, the spirits into demons, and told the people that the soul was not theirs to heal but for the church to own. The natural world withered as a wasteland to be tamed and the Master of the Animals, standing proud in his antlers, was turned into the devil.

## Leading the Way

Some of the ancient wisdom survived even this onslaught, stored away as folklore and custom. The church could never stamp out everything, and even with the persecution of heretics and the execution of the witches, people still maintained something of the ancestral beliefs. Even after the Enlightenment and the rise of modern science, society still retains a kernel of the old ways. We speak of soulless institutions without realising that their soul can be retrieved; we ask our friends "what has got into you?" without knowing that it is actually a spirit intrusion; and we still look to power animals to symbolise the spirit of our countries. Scratch the surface of our world and shamanism will be revealed underneath.

Today, people yearn for meaning and some direction to their lives that none of the new religions seems able to satisfy. This lack of a sacred focus has left a gaping hole at the very heart of our society. Now, more than ever, we need to reconnect with the spirits of the otherworlds. People are crying out for it but they have only broken threads to follow. Some, often the most desperate for meaning in their lives, try to reach the otherworlds by abusing drugs; they might get some way there but their lack of control bars any meaningful interaction. Others seek the dismemberment of shamanic initiation through mindless violence and aggression, with no real knowledge of the power they are forsaking. Then, there are those who have lost contact with their tribe and enter into meaningless relationships for the brief high of physical contact rather than the profound empowerment of reconnection. Shamanism could change their lives if only there were those who could lead the way.

This book has shown that *you* can lead the way. You have incredible potential and a source of unlimited power. Integrate all that you have learnt from this book and then leave it behind: fly far with the wings you have grown. It is now up to you to remake the world as you want it to be; dream it well. Across the thousands of years since people first painted the sacred caves, their wisdom has been retained. This is the true gift of our ancestors: the gift of the shaman.

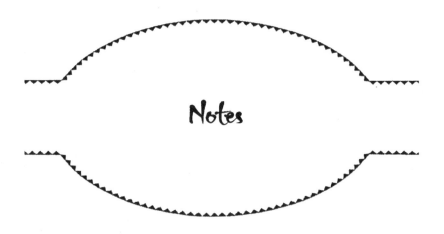

# Notes

## Introduction

1. For a more detailed explanation of all the prehistoric evidence referred to in this book and its relationship to shamanism, see Williams, forthcoming.

## Chapter 1

1. Clottes 2008 is the best introduction to cave art.
2. Lewis-Williams and Dowson 1989 analyse the art of the Bushmen and demonstrate its shamanic origins.
3. Richards 1971 outlines the distortions to vision caused by migraines.
4. Lewis-Williams and Dowson 1988 is the seminal paper linking Stone Age rock art to shamanic trance.
5. Lewis-Williams 2002, 216–20.
6. Dowson 1998, 73.
7. Bourguignon 1974.
8. Nunez and Srinivasan 2006: 215–43.
9. Oster 1970; and Walker 1981 analyse the forms of the phosphenes seen in trance.

10. Kellog, Knoll, and Kugler 1965 compare the phosphenes of trance to children's doodles.
11. Graziano, Andersen, and Snowden 1994.
12. Siegel and Jarvik 1975, 111 and 139.
13. Kosslyn 1983 shows how the brain generates and interprets images.
14. Tooby and Cosmides 1992: 94–108 and Boyer 2000 consider how people think about things using chunks of information
15. Jung 1959; Campbell 1949.
16. Dobkin de Rios 1996: 131–2; Halifax 1982, 23–4 and 86–7; Lewis-Williams 1997, 813–7; Pearson 2002, 118–9.
17. Lewis-Williams and Dowson 1990, 10.
18. Mithen 1994: 120–1.
19. Capelle 1995a.
20. Gamble 1999 is the best introduction to the people who lived through the Ice Age.
21. Gazzaniga 1998 analyses the division of the brain into right and left hemispheres.
22. D'Aquili and Newberg 1999, 161–2; Winkelman 2002; and Rossano 2007 all show how trance states enhance brain function.
23. Eliade 1964 is the classic work on shamanism and is subtitled *Archaic Techniques of Ecstasy*.
24. Pomponious Mela De Situ Orbis 3.2.18–19 (Translations of most of the classical works referred to can be found in Koch 2005).

## Chapter 2

1. Albrethsen and Brinch Peterson 1976, 8–9.
2. Harding 2000, 322.
3. Piggott 1983, 109–16 and 120–2; and Pare 1992, 28–30 have examples of vessels with water birds around them.
4. Hedges 1990 studies the tomb and its eagles.
5. Siegel 1978, 311.

6. Mithen 2003, 168.

7. Brunaux 1988 is the best introduction to these, so-called, sanctuary sites.

8. Ingold 1986, 247–73.

9. Kruta 2004, 224–9.

10. Dowson and Porr 2001 study these models and relate them to shamanism.

11. Gamble 1999, 329.

12. Ingold 1986, 247–73.

13. Kaul 1998, 16–19.

14. Bosinski and Fischer 1980 is a corpus of the animal images discovered.

15. Clarke 1954 is the excavation report for the site and Conneller 2004 analyses the dance of the deer and relates it to shapeshifting.

16. Dowson and Porr 2001, 169.

17. Phillips 1965, 37–8.

18. Radovanovi 1996 is a comprehensive analysis of the site and its sculptures and Radovanovi 1997, 88–9 analyses the sculptures and relates them to shapeshifting.

19. Giovanni Della Porta *Natural Magic*, 8.2.

## Chapter 3

1. Sveen 1996 is the best introduction to the site.

2. Helskog 1999 considers the position of the carvings and relates it to the interface between the worlds.

3. Helskog 1987 compares the images on the rocks to those on the Sámi drums.

4. Randsborg 1993 is the excavation report for the site and the engraved slabs.

5. Haeberlin 1918, 252.

6. Hingley 1996, 188.

7. Armit 1999 analyses the underground chambers in Scotland and Clark 1961 does the same for Cornwall.

8. Thomas 1999, 113–20.

9. Waterman 1997 is the excavation report for the site.

10. Lynn 1992 and Newman 1996 both analyse the labryrinth.

11. Brennand and Taylor 2003 is the excavation report for the site.

12. Anisimov 1963, 87–9.

13. Vorren 1985, 75–6.

14. Horowitz 1975 analyses hallucinations and their origins.

15. Sherratt 1991, 58–9.

16. Watson and Keating 1999 first documented the effect.

17. Barfield and Hodder 1987 suggest that the sites may have been saunas.

18. Balázs 1996, 40–4.

19. Kaul 1998 is a corpus of every razor found.

20. Kaplan 1975 shows that the items in the boats are mushrooms.

21. For example, Lambrick and Robinson 1979, 83; Cunliffe and Poole 2000, 152.

22. Rätsch 1987.

23. Sherratt 1991, 52–6.

24. Herodotus *The Histories* 4.74.

25. van der Sanden 1996, 118.

26. Wasson, Ruck, and Hoffman 1978 give a detailed analysis of the ceremonies and their origins in drug-induced trances.

27. Schultes, Hoffman, and Rätsch 1980 is the best introduction to entheogens around the world.

## Chapter 4

1. Gamble 1999, 387–414.

2. Soffer, Vandiver, Klíma, and Svoboda 1993, 268–9.

3. Ingold 1986, 247–73.

4. Harvey 2005 provides a good introduction to animism.

5. Ralph Lewis 2001, 59–63.

6. Lucan *Pharsalia* 1.422–65; and analysis in Green 1997a, 78.

7. Hill 1995, 105–8.

8. Green 1986 and Green 1995 are good introductions to the Gods and Goddesses of the Celts..

9. Rolle 1980 is the best introduction to the Scythians and has copious illustrations of their art.

10. Phillips 1965, 62–3.

# Chapter 5

1. Rasmussen 1908, 111–2.

2. Spindler 1994, is a good introduction to the Ice Man and pages 87–91 analyse his axe.

3. Nerlich et al. 2003 analyses the wound on Ötzi's hand; and Pernter et al. 2007 shows that he was killed by an arrow.

4. Binant 1991: 127–31.

5. Sherratt 1994a, 174.

6. Mercer 1981 is the excavation report for the site.

7. Bradley 1998a, 86.

8. Collett 1993 and Reid and MacLean 1995 analyse traditional iron working in Africa.

9. Bradley 1998a, xix.

10. O'Sullivan 1997, 119–20.

11. Kaul 1985 is the excavation report for the site.

12. Robins 1953 looks at the history of the smith and the traditions that have adhered to the craft.

13. Budd and Taylor 1995; Hingley 1997; and Giles 2007 all consider the magical process of metalworking in prehistory.

14. Needham 1981, 37–40 examines an axe that is prolific in south Wales, despite there being no corresponding moulds to go with it.

15. Collett 1993; Reid and MacLean 1995.

16. Gamble 1999, 319.

17. Woodward 2002 shows how Bronze Age people kept items from earlier periods.
18. Thomas 1999, 179.
19. Bradley 1998a, 99–109.
20. Pryor 2001, 421–9.
21. Nebelsick 2000 analyses such ritualistic violence inflicted on weapons in the Bronze Age.
22. Bradley and Gordon 1988 studies the Thames; and ter Schegget 1999 studies the Meuse.
23. Bradley 1998a, 109–29.
24. Rohl and Needham 1998 use lead-isotope analysis to show the central European origin of the metal used in southern Britain.
25. Rowlands 1980, 39; Needham and Burgess 1980, 442.
26. Barrett and Needham 1988, 137.
27. Levinsen 1989, 452.
28. Cunliffe 2005 gives a comprehensive introduction to Iron Age life in Britain.

## Chapter 6

1. Bradley 1998b, Chapter 4.
2. Metcalf and Huntington 1991, 79–130 give examples of the transition of death and how the stages are marked in traditional communities.
3. Harding 2000, 318–9.
4. Taylor 1994, 401.
5. Parker Pearson, Chamberlain, Craig et al. 2005 analyse the mummies in detail.
6. Morse and Perry 1990, 11.
7. Siculus *Histories* 5.28; Pomponious Mela *De Situ Orbis* 3.2.18–19 and discussed in Green 1997a, 51.

# Chapter 7

1. Hingley and Unwin 2006 is a good introduction to Boudica; and Waite 2007 examines her revolt and defeat.
2. Dio *Roman History* 63.6.1–4.
3. Cunliffe 1997, 190.
4. Green 1997a, 88.
5. Diodorus Siculus *Histories* V, 31; and Tacitus *Annals* XIV, 30 both provide evidence for this gruesome event.
6. Arnold 1995, 154–5.
7. Creighton 2000, 49–50.
8. Lewis-Williams 2002, 216–20.
9. Waterbolk and van Zeist 1961 is the excavation report for the site.
10. Tick 2001 examines the ancient Asklepieia and also more recent attempts to revive the tradition.
11. Pace 2000 is a detailed guide to the site, which is well worth visiting.
12. Nicander of Colophon *De Anima* 57.10.

# Chapter 8

1. Arnott, Finger, and Smith 2003 is a good introduction to the history of trepanation.
2. Martin 1965 analyses these models.
3. Peintner, Poder, and Pümpel 1998 examines Ötzi's fungus and it medicinal uses, including as a laxative and also for staunching wounds, such as the cut to his hand.
4. Koot and Vermeeren 1993, 103.
5. Pliny the Elder *Natural History* 16.24 relates how much the Celts revered the plant as well as the highly unlikely way they harvested it.
6. Green 1997a, 118–9.

# Chapter 9

1. Kruta 2004, 224–9.
2. Branwen, Daughter of Llyr, from the *Mabinogion* (there are various editions available but Davies 2007, 22–34 is a recent translation).
3. Bancroft Hunt 2003, 87.
4. Fitch 2006, 196–7.
5. Ingerman 1991, 43. The book is also the best introduction to soul retrieval.

# Chapter 10

1. Armit 2003 is a good introduction to brochs.
2. Giles and Parker Pearson 1999, 224.
3. SSaladin d'Anglure 1992, 164.
4. Oswald 1997 analyses the orientations of the roundhouse doorways from Britain.
5. Williams 2003, 234–6.
6. Yates 2007, 134–8.
7. Sherratt 1994b, 172–3.
8. Parker Pearson 1996, 119–21.
9. Yates 1989 is a detailed examination of the symbolic arrangement of the Sámi kåhte.
10. Brück 1995 analyses the bones found on Bronze Age sites, which are mostly skulls.
11. Examples include Rams Hill in Bradley and Ellison 1975, 34; Crab Farm in Papworth 1992, 54; and South Lodge in Pitt Rivers 1898: 240 where a large urn was preserved unbroken in the ditch due to the rapidly accumulating silt.
12. Herodotus *Histories* 4.71.
13. Chauvet, Deschamps, and Hillaire 1996, 50.

# Chapter 11

1. Darvill 2006, 134–41.
2. Darvill 2007 outlines these ideas.
3. Ingold 1986 is a detailed look at what the author calls "the appropriation of nature".
4. Bradley 1993 charts the development of monuments during the Stone Age.
5. Bradley 1998b, 116–146.
6. Ruggles 2001 is a good introduction to the astronomy of prehistoric monuments.
7. Harding 2003 explores henges in Britain.
8. Bradley 2000 examines the sacredness of natural places in prehistory.
9. Bradley 2002, 19–28.
10. Bradley 2001, 53.
11. Cunliffe 1997, 106.
12. Caesar *The Conquest of Gaul* 6.13; Lucan *Pharsalia* 3.372–417.
13. Coles 1990 considers the figurines from Britain and Ireland; and Capelle 1995b covers those from continental Europe.
14. Coles 1998 examines the wood species used for the figurines.
15. Lucan *Pharsalia* 3.400–25.
16. Simek 1993, 240–1.
17. Capelle 1995b, 16–18.
18. Glob 1969, 180–5.
19. Raftery 1996, 285–7.
20. Loveday 2006 is a good introduction to cursus monuments.
21. Barrett, Bradley, and Green 1991, 49–50.
22. Burl 1993 examines the occurrence of stone rows in Britain, Ireland, and Brittany.
23. David 2002 is a good introduction to the Dreamtime and its archaeological evidence.
24. Mithen 2005 explores the origins of music and song.

25. Lame Deer and Erdoes 1972, 1–7 is a first-hand account of a vision quest.
26. Lewis-Williams 2002, 224.

# Chapter 12

1. Stout 2002 is a good introduction to Newgrange and the surrounding monuments.
2. Brennand and Taylor 2003 is the excavation report for the site.
3. Mukerjee 2003 outlines the astronomic alignments for the site.
4. Darvill 2006, 119–24.
5. Patton, Nash, Finch, and Rodwell 2002 is the excavation report for the site.
6. Pina 1976 is the excavation report for the site.
7. Gosden 1994 is a study of how people formulate time when they have no mechanical means of measuring it.
8. Giles and Parker Pearson 1999, 227.
9. Kaul 1998, 32.
10. Ibid., 262.
11. Wihlborg 1977–8 is the excavation report for the site.
12. Le Contel and Verdier 1997 examines the calendar in detail.
13. Ross 1995, 433.
14. Caesar *The Conquest of Gaul* 6.18.
15. Fitzpatrick 1996 analyses each sword that carries a design of the moon on its surface.
16. Pliny the Elder *The Natural History* 17.95.
17. Romer 2007 is a good introduction to the Great Pyramid.
18. Pásztor and Roslund 2007 analyses the designs on the Nebra disc.

# Chapter 13

1. Gamble 1999 is a comprehensive study of groups and communities in the Ice Age, how they formed and what kept them together.

2. Lewis-Williams 2002, 92–4.

3. Cunliffe 1997, 187.

4. van Gennep 1960 is the standard work for rights of passage in traditional societies.

5. Thomas 1991, 96–8.

6. Cunliffe 2008, 371–84.

7. de Jersey 2006 is a good introduction to the latest research on Celtic coins.

8. Gimbutas 1974 introduces the idea of a Mother Goddess for Stone Age Europe.

9. Bailey 2005 is a comprehensive introduction to figurines.

10. Whittle 1996, 94.

11. Harding 2000, 82, and 92 gives examples of wealthy female graves; and Kristiansen 1998, 394–9 analyses why these might have occurred.

# Chapter 14

1. van der Sanden 1996 is the best introduction to bog bodies.

2. Williams 2002, 103–73.

3. Painter 1995 is a study of how bodies are preserved in peat.

4. Williams 2002, 101–3.

5. Bleibtrau-Ehrenberg 1970; and Vitebsky 2001, 93 both explore the associations between shamanism and different sexuality.

6. van der Sanden 1996, 101.

7. Tacitus *Germania* 12.

8. Herodotus *The Histories* 1.105; 4.67; Hippocrates *Airs, Waters, Places* 22; and analysis in Taylor 1994, 396–8.

9. Green 1997b, 902.

10. Solli 1999 explores the ambiguity relating to Odin's gender.

11. van der Sanden 1996: 138 and 141.

12. Eliade 1958, 88; Lewis 1989, 61.

13. van der Sanden 1996, 162–3 examines injuries sustained by the bog bodies.

14. Green 2001, 87.
15. Diószegi 1960, 62–4.
16. Williams 2002, 103–73.
17. Cunliffe 1995, 49.
18. Cunliffe 1993 explores the use of these pits for human burials.
19. Green 2001, 132–5.
20. Ibid., 159–60.
21. Cunliffe 1991, 429–31.
22. Hall 2008 is a comprehensive study of this phenomenon in Renaissance art.
23. Lewis-Williams 2002, 277–84.
24. Halifax 1982, 4.
25. Hutton 2001, vii–ix.

## Conclusion

1. Tacitus *Annals* 14.29–30.
2. Caesar *The Conquest of Gaul* 7.13.
3. Jensen 1982, 209–10; Hedeager 1992, 244–5.
4. Polybius *The Histories* 2.17; Diodorus Siculus 5.27; Strabo *Geography* 4.4.2.
5. Hvass 1985, 175.
6. Parker Pearson 1993, 208.
7. Williams and Creighton 2006, 53–7.
8. Tacitus *Agricola* 21.
9. Thompson 1993 explores the occurrence of such items in the Iron Age and Roman period.
10. Green 1997a, 108–9.

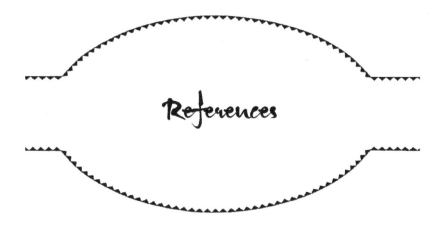

# References

Those books that are starred are particularly recommended for further reading.

Albrethsen, S., and E. Brinch Petersen. 1976. Excavation of a Mesolithic Cemetery at Vedbæk, Denmark. *Acta Archaeologica* 47: 1–28.

Anisimov, A. 1963. The shaman's tent of the Evenks and the origin of the shamanistic rite. In *Studies in Siberian Shamanism*, ed. H. Michael. Toronto: Arctic Institute of North America, Anthropology of the North: Translations from Russian Sources 4: 84–123.

Armit, I. 1999. The Abandonment of Souterrains: Evolution, Catastrophe, or Dislocation. *Proceedings of the Society of Antiquaries of Scotland* 129: 577–96.

———. 2003. *Towers in the North: The Brochs of Scotland*. Stroud: Tempus.

Arnold, B. 1995. "Honorary Males" or Women of Substance? Gender, Status, and Power in Iron-Age Europe. *Journal of European Archaeology* 3: 153–68.

Arnott, R., S. Finger, and C. Smith. 2003. *Trepanation: History, Discovery, Theory*. London: Psychology Press.

Bailey, D. 2005. *Prehistoric Figurines: Representation and Corporeality in the Neolithic*. London: Routledge.

Balázs, J. 1996. The Hungarian shaman's technique of trance induction. In *Folk Beliefs and Shamanic Traditions in Siberia*, V. Diószegi, and M. Hoppál, eds. Budapest: Akadémiai Kiadó: 26–48.

Bancroft Hunt, N. 2003. *Shamanism in North America*. New York: Firefly.

Barfield, L. and M. Hodder. 1987. Burnt Mounds as Saunas, and the Prehistory of Bathing. *Antiquity* 61: 370–9.

Barrett, J., and S. Needham. 1988. Production, circulation and exchange: Problems in the interpretation of Bronze Age bronzework. In *The Archaeology of Context in the Neolithic and Bronze Age: Recent Trends*, J. Barrett and I. Kinnes, eds. Sheffield: J. R. Collis: 127–40.

Barrett, J., R. Bradley and M. Green. 1991. *Landscape, Monuments, and Society: The Prehistory of Cranborne Chase*. Cambridge: Cambridge University Press.

Binant, P. 1991. *Les Préhistoire de la Mort: les Premières Sépultures en Europe*. Paris: Editions Errance.

Bleibtrau-Ehrenberg, G. 1970. Homosexualität und Transvestition im Schamanismus. *Anthropos* 65: 189–228.

Bosinski, G., and G. Fischer. 1980. *Mammut und Pferdedarstellungen von Gonnersdorf*. Weisbaden: Franz Steiner.

Bourguignon, E. 1974. Cross-cultural perspectives on the religious uses of altered states of consciousness. In *Religious Movements in Contemporary America*, I. Zaretsky, and M. Leone, eds. Princeton: Princeton University Press: 228–43.

Boyer, P. 2000. Functional Origins of Religious Concepts: Ontological and Strategic Selection in Evolved Minds. *Journal of the Royal Anthropological Institute* 6: 195–214.

Bradley, R. 1993. *Altering the Earth*. Edinburgh: Society of Antiquaries of Scotland.

———. 1998a. *The Passage of Arms: An Archaeological Analysis of Prehistoric Hoards and Votive Deposits*. 2nd ed. Oxford: Oxbow.

*———. 1998b. *The Significance of Monuments: On the Shaping of Human Experience in Neolithic and Bronze Age Europe*. London: Routledge.

——. 2000. *An Archaeology of Natural Places*. London: Routledge.

——. 2001. Orientations and origins: A symbolic dimension to the long house in Neolithic Europe. *Antiquity* 75: 50–6.

——. 2002. *The Past in Prehistoric Societies*. London: Routledge.

Bradley, R., and A. Ellison. 1975. *Rams Hill: A Bronze Age Defended Enclosure and its Landscape*. Oxford: British Archaeological Reports (British Series) 19.

Bradley, R., and K. Gordon. 1988. Human Skulls from the River Thames: Their Dating and Significance. *Antiquity* 62: 503–9.

Brennand, M., and M. Taylor. 2003. The Survey and Excavation of a Bronze Age Timber Circle at Holme-next-the-Sea, Norfolk, 1998–9. *Proceedings of the Prehistoric Society* 69: 1–84.

Brück, J. 1995. A Place for the Dead: The Role of Human Remains in Late Bronze Age Britain. *Proceedings of the Prehistoric Society* 61: 245–77.

Brunaux, Jean-Louis. 1988. *The Celtic Gauls: Gods, Rites, and Sanctuaries*. London: Seaby.

Budd, P., and T. Taylor. 1995. The Faerie Smith Meets the Bronze Industry: Magic Versus Science in the Interpretation of Prehistoric Metalworking. *World Archaeology* 27: 133–143.

Burl, A. 1993. *From Carnac to Callenish: Prehistoric Stone Rows of Britain, Ireland, and Brittany*. New Haven, CT: Yale University Press.

Campbell, J. 1949. *The Hero with a Thousand Faces*. London: Pantheon Books.

Capelle, T. 1995a. Bronze Age stone ships. In *The Ship as Symbol in Prehistoric and Medieval Scandinavia*, O. Crumlin-Pedersen, and B. Munch Thye, eds. Copenhagen: Publications from the National Museum,Studies in Archaeology and History, Volume I: 71–5.

——. 1995b. *Anthropomorphe Holzidole in Mittel- und Nordeuropa*. Lund: Scripta Minora: Regiae Societatis Humanorum Litterarum Lundensis 1.

Chauvet, Jean-Marie, É. Deschamps, and C. Hillaire. 1996. *Dawn of Art: The Chauvet Cave. The Oldest paintings in the World.* New York: Abrams.

Clark, E. 1961. *Cornish Fogous.* London: Methuen and Co.

Clark, J. 1954. *Excavations at Star Carr.* Cambridge: Cambridge University Press.

*Clottes, J. 2008. *Cave Art.* London: Phaidon Press.

Coles, B. 1990. Anthropomorphic Wooden Figures from Britain and Ireland. *Proceedings of the Prehistoric Society* 56: 315–33.

———. 1998. Wood species for wooden figures: a glimpse of a pattern. In *Prehistoric Ritual and Religion: Essays in Honour of Aubrey Burl,* A. Gibson and D. Simpson, eds. Stroud: Sutton.

Collett, D. 1993. Metaphors and representations associated with precolonial iron-smelting in Eastern and Southern Africa. In *The Archaeology of Africa: Food, Metals, and Towns,* T. Shaw, P. Sinclair, B. Andah, and A. Okpoko, eds. London: Routledge: 499–511.

Conneller, C. 2004. Becoming Deer. Corporeal Transformations at Star Carr. *Archaeological Dialogues* 11: 37–56.

Creighton, J. 2000. *Coins and Power in Late Iron Age Britain.* Cambridge: Cambridge University Press.

Cunliffe, B. 1993. *Fertility, Propitiation, and the Gods in the British Iron Age.* Amsterdam: Universiteit van Amsterdam.

———. 1995. *Danebury: An Iron Age Hillfort in Hampshire. Volume 6: A Hillfort Community in Perspective.* York: Council for British Archaeology Research Report No. 102.

———. 1997. *The Ancient Celts.* Oxford: Oxford University Press.

*———. 2005. *Iron Age Communities in Britain.* 4th ed. London: Routledge.

*———. 2008. *Europe between the Oceans. Themes and Variations 9000 BC–AD 1000.* New Haven: Yale University Press.

Cunliffe, B., and C. Poole. 2000. *The Danebury Environs Programme: Volume 2 – Part 6: Houghton Down, Stockbridge, Hants, 1994.* Oxford Committee for Archaeology Monograph No. 49.

D'Aquili, E., and A. Newberg. 1999. *The Mystical Mind: Probing the Biology of Religious Experience.* Minneapolis: Fortress Press.

Darvill, T. 2006. *Stonehenge: The Biography of a Landscape.* Stroud: Tempus.

————. 2007. Message in the Stones. *Current Archaeology* 212: 12–9.

David, B. 2002. *Landscapes, Rock-Art, and the Dreaming.* London: Leicester University Press.

Davies, S. 2007. *The Mabinogion.* Oxford: Oxford University Press.

de Jersey, P., ed. 2006. Celtic Coinage: New Discoveries, New Discussion. BAR Oxford: British Archaeological Reports (International Series) 1532.

Diószegi, V. 1960. *Tracing Shamans in Siberia: The Story of an Ethnographical Research Expedition.* Oosterhout: Anthropological Publications.

Dobkin de Rios, M. 1996. *Hallucinogens: Cross-Cultural Perspectives.* Prospect Heights: Waveland Press.

Dowson, T. 1998. Rock art: Handmaiden to studies of cognitive evolution. In *Cognition and Material Culture: The Archaeology of Symbolic Storage,* C. Renfrew and C. Scarre, eds. Cambridge: McDonald Institute for Archaeological Research: 67–76.

Dowson, T., and M. Porr. 2001. Special objects—Shamanistic imagery and the Aurignacian art of south-west Germany. In *The Archaeology of Shamanism,* N. Price, ed. London: Routledge.

Eliade, M. 1958. *Rites and Symbols of Initiation: The Mysteries of Birth and Rebirth.* New York: Harper Torchbooks.

*————. 1964. *Shamanism: Archaic Techniques of Ecstasy.* London: Pantheon.

Fitch, W. T. 2006. The Biology and Evolution of Music: A Comparative Perspective. *Cognition* 100: 173–215.

Fitzpatrick, A. 1996. Night and Day: The Symbolism of Astral Signs on Later Iron Age Anthropomorphic Short Swords. *Proceedings of the Prehistoric Society* 62: 373–98.

*Gamble, C. 1999. *The Palaeolithic Societies of Europe*. Cambridge: Cambridge University Press.

Gazzaniga, M. 1998. The Split Brain Revisited. *Scientific American* 279: 34–9.

Giles, M. 2007. Making Metal and Forging Relations: Ironworking in the British Iron Age. *Oxford Journal of Archaeology* 395–413.

Giles, M., and M. Parker Pearson. 1999. Learning to live in the Iron Age: Dwelling and praxis. In *Northern Exposure: The Iron Age in Northern Britain*, B. Bevan, ed. Leicester: Leicester Archaeology Monographs No. 4: 217–31.

Gimbutas, M. 1974. *The Gods and Goddesses of Old Europe*. London: Thames and Hudson.

Glob, P. 1969. *The Bog People: Iron Age Man Preserved*. London: Faber and Faber.

Gosden, C. 1994. *Social Being and Time*. Oxford: Blackwell.

Graziano, M., R. Andersen and R. Snowden. 1994. Tuning of MST Neurons to Spiral Motions. *The Journal of Neuroscience* 14: 54–67.

Green, M. 1986. *The Gods of the Celts*. Stroud: Sutton.

———. 1995. *Celtic Goddesses: Warriors, Virgins and Mothers*. British Museum.

*———. 1997a. *Exploring the World of the Druids*. London: Thames and Hudson.

———. 1997b. Images in Opposition: Polarity, Ambivalence and Liminality in Cult Representation. *Antiquity* 71: 898–911.

———. 2001. *Dying for the Gods: Human Sacrifice in Iron Age and Roman Europe*. Tempus.

Haeberlin, H. 1918. SBeTeTDA'Q, A Shamanic Performance of the Coast Salish. *American Anthropologist* 20: 249–57.

Halifax, J. 1982. *Shaman: The Wounded Healer*. London: Thames and Hudson.

Hall, J. 2008. *The Sinister Side: How Left-Right Symbolism Shaped Western Art*. Oxford: Oxford University Press.

*Harding, A. 2000. *European Societies in the Bronze Age*. Cambridge: Cambridge University Press.

Harding, J. 2003. *Henge Monuments of the British Isles*. Stroud: Tempus.

Hedeager, L. 1992. *Iron-Age Societies: From Tribe to State in Northern Europe, 500 BC to AD 700*. Oxford: Blackwell.

Hedges, J. 1990. *Tomb of the Eagles: Life and Death in a Stone Age Tribe*. London: New Amsterdam Books.

Helskog, K. 1987. Selective depictions. A study of 3,500 years of rock carvings from Arctic Norway and their relationship to the Sami drums. In *Archaeology as Long Term History*, I. Hodder, ed. Cambridge: Cambridge University Press: 17–30.

———. 1999. The Shore Connection. Cognitive Landscape and Communication with Rock Carvings in Northernmost Europe. *Norwegian Archaeological Review* 32: 73–94.

Hill, J. D. 1995. *Ritual and Rubbish in the Iron Age of Wessex: A Study on the Formation of a Specific Archaeological Record*. Oxford: British Archaeological Reports (British Series) 242.

Hingley, R. 1996. Ancestors and Identity in the Later Prehistory of Atlantic Scotland: The Reuse and Reinvention of Neolithic Monuments and Material Culture. *World Archaeology* 28: 231–43.

———. 1997. Iron working and regeneration: A study of the symbolic meaning of metalworking in Iron Age Britain. In *Reconstructing Iron Age Societies: New Approaches to the British Iron Age*, A. Gwilt and C. Haselgrove, eds. Oxford: Oxbow Monograph 71: 9–18.

Hingley, R., and C. Unwin. 2006. *Boudica: Iron Age Warrior Queen*. London: Hambledon and London.

Horowitz, M. 1975. Hallucinations: An information-processing approach. In *Hallucinations: Behaviour, Experience, and Theory*, R. Siegel and L. West, eds. New York: Wiley: 163–95.

Hutton, R. 2001. *Shamans: Siberian Spirituality and the Western Imagination*. London: Hambledon and London.

Hvass, S. 1985. *Hodde. Et vestjysk landsbysamfund fra ældre jernalder*. Copenhagen: University of Copenhagen Archaeological Studies Volume VII.

*Ingerman, S. 1991. *Soul Retrieval: Mending the Fragmented Self*. New York: Harper Collins.

Ingold, T. 1986. *The Appropriation of Nature: Essays on Human Ecology and Social Relations*. Manchester: Manchester University Press.

Jensen, J. 1982. *The Prehistory of Denmark*. London: Methuen.

Jung, C. 1959. *The Collected Works. Volume 9, Part I: The Archetypes and the Collective Unconsciousness*. London: Routledge and Kegan Paul.

Kaplan, R. 1975. The Sacred Mushroom in Scandinavia. *Man* 10: 72–9.

Kaul, F. 1985. Sandagergård. A Late Bronze Age Cultic Building with Rock Engravings and Menhirs from Northern Zealand, Denmark. *Acta Archaeologica* 56: 31–54.

———. 1998. *Ships on Bronzes: A Study in Bronze Age Religion and Iconography*. Copenhagen: Publications from the National Museum Studies in Archaeology and History. Vol. 3.

Kellog, R., M. Knoll and J. Kugler. 1965. Form-Similarity between Phosphenes and Preschool Children's Scribblings. *Nature* 208: 1129–30.

Koch, J. 2005. *The Celtic Heroic Age: Literary Sources for Ancient Celtic Europe and Early Ireland and Wales*. 4th ed. Aberystwyth: Celtic Studies Publications.

Koot, C., and C. Vermeeren. 1993. Natural Wood Resources and Human Demand: Use of Wood in Iron Age Houses in the Wetlands of Midden-Delfland. *Analecta Praehistoria Leidensia* 26: 99–110.

Kosslyn, S. 1983. *Ghosts in the Mind's Machine: Creating and Using Images in the Brain*. New York: W. W. Norton.

Kristiansen, K. 1998. *Europe Before History*. Cambridge: Cambridge University Press.

Kruta, V. 2004. *Celts: History and Civilisation*. London: Hachette.

Lambrick, G., and M. Robinson. 1979. *Iron Age and Roman Riverside Settlements at Farmoor, Oxfordshire*. London: Council for British Archaeology Research Report No. 32.

Lame Deer, J., and R. Erdoes. 1972. *Lame Deer: Seeker of Visions*. New York: Washington Square Press.

Lawlor, R. 1992. *Voices of the First Day: Awakening in the Aboriginal Dreamtime*. Rochester, VT: Inner Traditions.

Le Contel, J. M., and P. Verdier. 1997. *Un Calendrier Celtique: Le Calendrier Gaulois de Coligny*. Paris: Éditions Errance.

Levinsen, K. 1989. The introduction of iron in Denmark. In *The Bronze Age – Iron Age Transition in Europe: Aspects of Continuity and Change in European Societies, c. 1200 to 500 BC*, M. L. S. Sørensen, and R. Thomas, eds. Oxford: British Archaeological Reports (International Series) 483: 440–56.

Lewis, I. 1989. *Ecstatic Religion: A Study of Shamanism and Spirit Possession*. 2nd ed. London: Routledge.

Lewis-Williams, J. D. 1997. Agency, Art and Altered Consciousness: A Motif in French (Quercy) Upper Palaeolithic Parietal Art. *Antiquity* 71: 810–30.

*————. 2002. *The Mind in the Cave: Consciousness and the Origins of Art*. London: Thames and Hudson.

Lewis-Williams, J. D., and T. Dowson. 1988. The Signs of All Times: Entoptic Phenomena in Upper Palaeolithic Art. *Current Anthropology* 29: 201–45.

————. 1989. *Images of Power: Understanding Bushman Rock Art*. Johannesburg: Southern Book Publishers.

————. 1990. Through the Veil: San Rock Paintings and the Rock Face. *South African Archaeological Bulletin* 45: 5–16.

Loveday, R. 2006. *Inscribed Across the Landscape: The Cursus Enigma*. Stroud: Tempus.

Lynn, C. 1992. The Iron Age mound in Navan Fort: a physical realisation of Celtic religious beliefs? *Emania* 10: 33–57.

Martin, R. 1965. Wooden Figures from the Source of the Seine. *Antiquity* 34: 247–52.

Mercer, R. 1981. *Grimes Graves, Norfolk: Excavations 1971–2*. London: DoE Archaeological Report No. 11.

Metcalf, P., and R. Huntington. 1991. *Celebrations of Death: The Anthropology of Mortuary Ritual*. 2nd ed. Cambridge: Cambridge University Press.

Mithen, S. 1994. The Mesolithic age. In *The Oxford Illustrated History of Prehistoric Europe*, B. Cunliffe, ed. Oxford: Oxford University Press: 79–135.

*———. 2003. *After the Ice: A Global Human History 20,000–5000 BC*. London: Weidenfeld and Nicolson.

———. 2005. *The Singing Neanderthals: The Origins of Music, Language, Mind and Body*. London: Orion.

Morse, M., and P. Perry. 1990. *Closer to the Light: Learning From Children's Near-Death Experiences*. London: Souvenir Press.

Mukerjee, M. 2003. Circles for Space: German "Stonehenge" Marks Oldest Observatory. *Scientific American* (online).

Nebelsick, L. 2000. Rent asunder: Ritual violence in Late Bronze Age hoards. In *Metals Make the World Go Round: The Supply and Circulation of Metals in Bronze Age Europe*, C. Pare, ed. Oxford: Oxbow: 160–75.

Needham, S. 1981. *The Bulford-Helsbury Manufacturing Tradition. The Production of Stogursey Socketed Axes During the Later Bronze Age in Southern Britain*. London: British Museum Occasional Paper 13.

Needham, S., and C. Burgess. 1980. The Later Bronze Age in the Lower Thames Valley: The metalwork evidence. In *Settlement and Society in the British Later Bronze Age*, J. Barrett and R. Bradley, eds. British Archaelogical Reports (British Series) 83: 437–69.

Nerlich, A., B. Bachmeier, A. Zink et al. 2003. Ötzi had a Wound on his Right Hand. *The Lancet* 362: 334.

Newman, C. 1996. Woods, Metamorphosis and Mazes: The Otherness of Timber Circles. *Archaeology Ireland* 10: 34–7.

Nunez, P., and R. Srinivasan. 2006. *Electric Fields of the Brain: The Neuophysics of EEG*. 2nd ed. Oxford: Oxford University Press.

O'Sullivan, A. 1997. Interpreting the Archaeology of Late Bronze Age Lake Settlements. *The Journal of Irish Archaeology* 8: 115–21.

Oster, G. 1970. Phosphenes. *Scientific American* 222: 83–7.

Oswald, A. 1997. A doorway on the past: Practical and mystic concerns in the orientation of roundhouse doorways. In *Reconstructing Iron Age Societies: New Approaches to the British Iron Age*, A. Gwilt and C. Haselgrove, eds. Oxford: Oxbow: 87–95.

Pace, A. 2000. *The al Saflieni Hypogeum 4000 BC – 2000 AD*. Malta: National Museum of Archaeology.

Painter, T. 1995. Chemical and microbiological aspects of the preservation process in *Sphagnum* peat. In *Bog Bodies: New Discoveries and New Perspectives*, R. Turner and R. Scaife, eds. London: Trustees of British Museum Press: 88–99.

Papworth, M. 1992. Excavation and Survey of Bronze Age Sites in the Badbury Area, Kingston Lacy Estate. *Proceedings of the Dorset Natural History and Archaeological Society* 114: 47–76.

Pare, C. 1992. *Wagons and Wagon Graves from the Early Iron Age in Central Europe*. Oxford: Oxford University Committee for Archaeology.

Parker Pearson, M. 1993. The Powerful Dead: Archaeological Relationships Between the Living and the Dead. *Cambridge Archaeological Journal* 3: 203–29.

———. 1996. Food, fertility and front doors in the First Millennium BC. In *The Iron Age in Britain and Ireland: Recent Trends*, T. Champion and J. Collis, eds. Sheffield: J. R. Collis Publications: 117–32.

Parker Pearson, M., A. Chamberlain, O. Craig et al. 2005. Evidence for Mummification in Bronze Age Britain. *Antiquity* 79: 529–46.

Pásztor, E., and C. Roslund. 2007. An Interpretation of the Nebra Disc. *Antiquity* 81: 267–78.

Patton, M. G. Nash, O. Finch, and W. Rodwell. 2002. *La Houge Bie.* La Société Jersaise.

Pearson, J. 2002. *Shamanism and the Ancient Mind: A Cognitive Approach to Archaeology.* London: AltaMira Press.

Peintner, U., R. Poder and T. Pümpel. 1998. The Iceman's Fungi. *Mycological Research* 102: 1153–62.

Pernter, P., P. Gostner, E. Egarter Vigl, and F. Rühli. 2007. Radiologic Proof for the Iceman's Cause of Death (ca. 5300 BP). *Journal of Archaeological Science* 34: 1784–6.

Phillips, E. 1965. *The Royal Hordes: Nomad Peoples of the Steppes.* London: Thames and Hudson.

Piggott, S. 1983. *The Earliest Wheeled Transport: From the Atlantic Coast to the Caspian Sea.* London: Thames and Hudson.

Pina, H. 1976. Cromlechs and Menhire bei Evora in Portugal. *Madrider Mitteilungen* 17: 9–20.

Pitt Rivers, A. 1898. *Excavations in Cranborne Chase, near Rushmore on the Borders of Dorset and Wiltshire 1893–1896. Vol. IV.* Printed Privately.

Pryor, F. 2001. *The Flag Fen basin: Archaeology and Environment of a Fenland Landscape.* London: English Heritage.

Radovanovie, I. 1997. The Lepenski Vir culture: a contribution to its ideological aspects. In *Antidoron Dragoslavo Srejovici: Completis LXV Annis ab Amicis Collegis Discipulis Oblatum.* Belgrade: University of Belgrade: 85–93.

Raftery, B. 1996. *Trackway Excavations in the Mountdillon Bogs, Co. Longford, 1985–1991.* Dublin: Crannog Publications.

Ralph Lewis, B. 2001. *Ritual Sacrifice: A Concise History.* Stroud: Sutton.

Randsborg, K. 1993. Kivik, Archaeology and Iconography. *Acta Archaeologica* 64: 1–147.

Rasmussen, K. 1908. *The People of the Polar North: A Record* (Compiled from the Danish Originals and Edited by G. Herring). London: Kegan, Paul, Trench, Trübner, and Co.

Rätsch, C. 1987. Der Rauch von Delphi. Eine Ethnopharmakologische Annäherung. *Curare* 10: 215–28.

Reid, A., and R. MacLean. 1995. Symbolism and Social Contexts of Iron Production in Karagwe. *World Archaeology* 27: 144–61.

Richards, W. 1971. The Fortification Illusions of Migraines. *Scientific American* 224: 89–94.

Robins, F. 1953. *The Smith: The Traditions and Lore of an Ancient Craft.* Ethnopharmakologische Rider and Company.

Rohl, B., and S. Needham. 1998. *The Circulation of Metal in the British Bronze Age: The Application of Lead Isotope Analysis.* Ethnopharmakologische British Museum Occasional Paper Number 102.

*Rolle, R. 1980. *The World of the Scythians.* Oxford: Batsford.

Romer, J. 2007. *The Great Pyramid: Ancient Egypt Revisited.* Cambridge Cambridge University Press.

Ross, A. 1995. Ritual and the Druids. In *The Celtic World*, M. Green, ed. London: Routledge: 423–44.

Rossano, M. 2007. Did Meditating Make Us Human? *Cambridge Archaeological Journal* 17: 47–58.

Rowlands, M. 1980. Kinship, alliance and exchange in the European Bronze Age. In *Settlement and Society in the British Later Bronze Age*, J. Barrett and R. Bradley, eds. Oxford: British Archaeological Reports (British Series) 83: 15–55.

Ruggles, C. 2001. *Astrology, Cosmology and Landscape.* Oxford: Oxbow Books.

Saladin d'Anglure, B. 1992. Rethinking Inuit shamanism through the concept of 'third gender.' In *Northern Religions and Shamanism: The Regional Conference of the International Association of the History of Religions: Selected Papers*, M. Hoppál, and J. Pentikäinen, eds. Budapest: Akadémiai Kiadó: 146–50.

Schultes, R. E., A. Hoffman, and C. Rätsch. 1980. *Plants of the Gods: Their Sacred Healing and Hallucinogenic Powers.* London: Hutchinson.

Sherratt, A. 1991. Sacred and profane substances: The ritual use of narcotics in later Neolithic Europe. In *Sacred and Profane*, P. Garwood, D. Jennings, R. Skeats, and J. Toms, eds. Oxford: Oxford University Committee for Archaeology Monograph No. 32: 50–64.

———. 1994a. The emergence of elites: Earlier Bronze Age Europe. In *The Oxford Illustrated History of Prehistoric Europe*, B. Cunliffe, ed. Oxford: Oxford University Press: 244–276.

———. 1994b. The transformation of early agrarian Europe: The later Neolithic and Copper Ages 4500–2500 BC. In *The Oxford Illustrated History of Prehistoric Europe*, B. Cunliffe, ed. Oxford: Oxford University Press: 167–201.

Siegel, R. 1978. Cocaine Hallucinations. *American Journal of Psychiatry* 135: 309–14.

Siegel, R., and M. Jarvik. 1975. Drug-induced hallucinations in animals and man. In *Hallucinations: Behaviour, Experience and Theory*, R. Siegel and L. West, eds. New York: John Wiley: 81–161.

Simek, R. 1993. *Dictionary of Northern Mythology*. London: Brewer.

Soffer, O., P. Vandiver, B. Klíma and J. Svoboda. 1993. The pyrotechnology of performance art: Moravian Venuses and wolverines. In *Before Lascaux: The Complete Record of the Early Upper Palaeolithic*, H. Knecht, A. Pike-Tay, and R. White, eds. Boca Raton: CRC Press: 259–75.

Solli, B. 1999. Odin the queer? On ergi and shamanism in Norse mythology. In *Glyfer och Arkeologiska Rum – en Vänbok till Jarl Nordbladh*, A. Gustafsson and H. Karlsson, eds. Göteborg: Gotarc Series A: 341–9.

*Spindler, C. 1994. *The Man in the Ice: The Amazing Inside Story of the 5000-Year-Old Body Found Trapped in a Glacier in the Alps*. London: Weidenfeld and Nicolson.

Stout, G. 2002. *Newgrange and the bend of the Boyne*. Cardiff University Press.

Sveen, A. 1996. *Rock Carvings, Jieprialuokta Hjemmeluft, Alta*. Alta: Trykkforum Finnmark.

Taylor, T. 1994. Thracians, Scythians, and Dacians, 800 BC–AD 300. In *The Oxford Illustrated History of Prehistoric Europe*, B. Cunliffe, ed. Oxford: Oxford University Press: 373–410.

ter Schegget, M. 1999. Late Iron Age human skeletal remains from the River Meuse at Kessel: A river cult place? In *Land and Ancestors: Cultural Dynamics in the Urnfield Period and the Middle Ages in Southern Netherlands*, F. Theuws and N. Roymans, eds. Amsterdam: Amsterdam University Press: 199–240.

*Thomas, J. 1999. *Understanding the Neolithic*. Cambridge: Cambridge University Press.

Thompson, H. 1993. Iron Age and Roman Slave-Shackles. *Archaeological Journal* 150: 57–168.

Tick, E. 2001. *The Practice of Dream Healing: Bringing Ancient Greek Mysteries into Modern Medicine*. Wheaton: Quest Books.

Tooby, J., and L. Cosmides. 1992. The psychological foundations of culture. In *The Adapted Mind: Evolutionary Psychology and the Generation of Culture*, J. Barkow, L. Cosmides, and J. Tooby, eds. Oxford: Oxford University Press: 19–136.

*van der Sanden, W. 1996. *Through Nature to Eternity: The Bog Bodies of Northwest Europe*. Amsterdam: Batavian Lion International.

van Gennep, A. 1960. *The Rites of Passage*. London: Routledge and Keegan Paul.

*Vitebsky, P. 2001. *The Shaman*. London: Duncan Baird Publishers.

Vorren, Ø. 1985. Circular sacrificial sites and their function. In *Saami Pre-Christian Religion: Studies on the Oldest Traces of Religion Among the Saamis*, L. Bäckman and Å. Hultkrantz, eds. Stockholm: Almqvist and Wiksell: 69–81.

Waite, J. 2007. *Boudica's Last Stand: Britain's Revolt Against Rome AD 60–61*. Stroud: Tempus.

Walker, J. 1981. About Phosphenes: Luminous Patterns that Appear When the Eyes are Closed. *Scientific American* 244: 142–52.

Wasson, G. R., C. Ruck and A. Hoffman. 1978. *The Road to Eleusius: Unveiling the Secret of the Mysteries*. London: Harcourt, Brace, Jovanovich.

Waterbolk, H., and W. van Zeist. 1961. A Bronze Age Sanctuary in the Raised Bog at Bargeroosterveld (Dr.). *Helinium* 1: 5–19.

Waterman, D. 1997. *Excavations at Navan Fort 1961–71, County Armagh*. Belfast: The Stationery Office.

Watson, A., and D. Keating. 1999. Architecture and Sound: An Acoustic Analysis of Megalithic Monuments in Prehistoric Britain. *Antiquity* 73: 325–36.

*Whittle, A. 1996. *Europe in the Neolithic: The Creation of New Worlds*. Cambridge: Cambridge University Press.

Wihlborg, A. 1977–78. Sagaholm. A Bronze Age Barrow with Rock-Carvings. *Meddelanden från Lunds Universitets Historiska Museum* 2: 111–28.

Williams, M. 2002. Tales from the dead: Remembering the bog bodies in the Iron Age of north-western Europe. In *Archaeologies of Remembrance: Death and Memory in Past Societies*, H. Williams, ed. London: Kulwer.

———. 2003. Growing Metaphors: The Agricultural Cycle as Metaphor in the Later Prehistoric Period of Britain and North-Western Europe. *Journal of Social Archaeology* 3: 223–55.

*———. Forthcoming. *Prehistoric Belief: Shamans, Trance, and the Afterlife*. Stroud: The History Press.

Williams, M., and J. Creighton. 2006. Shamanic practices and trance imagery in the Iron Age. In *Celtic Coinage: New Discoveries, New Discussion*, P. de Jersey, ed. Oxford: British Archaeological Reports (International Series) 1532.

Winkelman, M. 2002. Shamanism and Cognitive Evolution. Cambridge: *Cambridge Archaeological Journal* 12: 71–101.

Woodward, A. 2002. Beads and Beakers: Heirlooms and Relics in the British Early Bronze Age. *Antiquity* 76: 1040–7.

Yates, D. 2007. *Land, Power and Prestige: Bronze Age Field Systems in Southern England*. Oxford: Oxbow.

Yates, T. 1989. Habitus and social space: Some suggestions about meaning in the Saami (Lapp) tent ca. 1700–1900. In *The Meaning of Things: Material Culture and Symbolic Expression*, I. Hodder, ed. London: Unwin Hyman: 249–62.

## To Write to the Author

If you wish to contact the author or would like more information about this book, please write to the author in care of Llewellyn Worldwide and we will forward your request. Both the author and publisher appreciate hearing from you and learning of your enjoyment of this book and how it has helped you. Llewellyn Worldwide cannot guarantee that every letter written to the author can be answered, but all will be forwarded. Please write to:

Mike Williams, Ph.D.
% Llewellyn Worldwide
2143 Wooddale Drive
Woodbury, Minnesota 55125-2989
Please enclose a self-addressed stamped envelope for reply,
or $1.00 to cover costs. If outside U.S.A., enclose
international postal reply coupon.

Many of Llewellyn's authors have websites with additional information and resources. For more information, please visit our website at http://www.llewellyn.com.